MELVILLE

From the portrait by Joseph O. Eaton

HERMAN MELVILLE

MELVILLE

By
GEOFFREY STONE

OCTAGON BOOKS

A DIVISION OF FARRAR, STRAUS AND GIROUX

New York   1976

Reprinted 1976
by special arrangement with Sheed & Ward, Inc.

OCTAGON BOOKS
A DIVISION OF FARRAR, STRAUS & GIROUX, INC.
19 Union Square West
New York, N.Y. 10003

Library of Congress Cataloging in Publication Data

Stone, Geoffrey.
    Melville.

    Reprint of the ed. published by Sheed & Ward, New York, which
was issued as no. 4 of Great writers of the world.

    Bibliography: p.
    Includes index.
    1. Melville, Herman, 1819-1891.   I. Title.   II. Series: Great
writers of the world; [4].
PS2386.S8   1976   813'.3   [B]   76-18221
ISBN 0-374-97632-5

Manufactured by Braun-Brumfield, Inc.
Ann Arbor, Michigan
Printed in the United States of America

PREFACE

SINCE THIS BOOK IS ADDRESSED TO THE GENERAL READER, I have dispensed with scholarly impedimenta: my footnote references are intended only as a courtesy to those whose opinions I quote. Melville scholars, if they look into it, will recognize how much the book is indebted to their labors and, more learned in their subject than I can ever hope to be, will instantly have in mind chapter and verse, from Melville's text or their own, supporting or refuting anything I have said. The general reader will have to accept my statements on faith. I think it more polite to ask this of him than to cite a vast number of books and periodicals in the presumption that he will have the time, strength, cash, and patience to search them out.

For personal kindnesses that made the writing of the book much easier, I owe a great deal to Dr. and Mrs. Frederick W. Pratt of New York and to Fr. Thomas Stack of Bloomfield, Conn. My thanks are also owing to various members of my family, whose anonymity here is a symbol of their selfless generosity.

GEOFFREY STONE

March 4, 1949
Fiesole

For the expectation of the creature waiteth for the revelation of the sons of God. For the creature was made subject to vanity: not willingly, but by reason of him that made it subject, in hope. Because the creature also itself shall be delivered from the servitude of corruption, into the liberty of the glory of the children of God. For we know that every creature groaneth and travaileth in pain, even till now.

ROMANS, VIII, 19–22

CONTENTS

MELVILLE

THE PROBLEM

THE BEGINNINGS OF LITERATURE IN AMERICA AS A SELF-justified pursuit were coeval with the establishment of the Romantic tradition. What is usually accounted the first American novel, *The Power of Sympathy*, is an exercise in Romanticism of the sentimental variety and an account of sexual misbehavior and physical violence that is, except for 18th-century politeness and garrulity, much like the work of John Steinbeck. The first American to become a professional novelist, Charles Brockden Brown, enjoyed the approval of his and Shelley's master, William Godwin, and the best of his novels deals with fornication, madness, uxoricide, infanticide, and suicide, all brought about by spirit voices contrived by a ventriloquist. American fiction from the first has been touched by the Romantic vision and given to the Romantic attitude. The essence of Romanticism is revolt; it asserts the superiority of the individual's impulses over all that is established, organized, and rationally articulated. Every false theory eventually works out to its own negation, because falsehood is of its nature contradictory; and the absolute freedom sought by the first Romantics has resulted in our time in tyrannies, whether of practice or theory, as thoroughgoing as any the world has ever seen. The same course of development is plain in the lives of the chief figures of Romanticism.

The European Romantics fundamentally were in revolt against the fact or the memory of the self-imposed, but externally determined, discipline that the Catholic Church teaches to be necessary to man's individual salvation, and they were incidentally in revolt against most of the human wisdom that over the centuries has accumulated as a corollary to what is central in the Church. The revolt was not, of course, in all cases immediately directed against the Church: it often turned against what remained of Catholicism in the various Protestant religions, or it was a logical outcome of certain dogmas peculiarly developed, some to the point of being humanly intolerable, by these religions. Romanticism protests against order, and not so much against order as it is established by the state or society, more or less arbitrarily with respect to the individual, as against the order that the individual must painfully win and constantly re-establish amongst his own divergent promptings. External order of this other sort the Romantic often finds attractive; the perfectly "organized" state or society meets his taste for the monstrous, and the most degrading thing in the circumstances of the slave—that he is required to make no victory over himself—gives him the inner life of the Romantic hero, who exalts and follows his natural bent.

American Romanticism has an ambiguous affinity with Puritanism. Men who revolt against an insufficient creed usually make their new one by a kind of Hegelian dialectic, synthesizing the old and the new and bearing out the fact that by taking thought a silk purse is not to be made of a sow's ear. But no general theory of ideas is needed to point up the fact that American Romanticism was modified by the thing it opposed. So far as there was any established order in the intellectual realm of America at the opening of the 19th century, it was one derived, in varying degrees of immediacy, from the attempts of the great Puritan theologians to construct a picture of a rationally coherent universe. Jonathan Edwards, one of the last of these gifted men, had nearly succeeded in that effort; by relying on his great powers of argument and on his reading of the Bible and by abandoning common sense and the facts of daily experience, he had managed, to his own satisfaction and the disquietude of those whom his teaching reached, to take from man the gift of free will: he had maintained that free will was a gift God could not afford to make and, seeking to add to it, had in fact diminished God's glory. When Romanticism appeared, it likewise made man's will a mere illusion necessary to action, for since the autonomous will was not to be guided by the intellect its ability for choice was really canceled out: if a man is driven by the mysterious promptings of his own will, and owes no other allegiance, what freedom has he? He is a victim of circumstance, even though the circumstance is himself.

Any reading of Romantic literature that is at all critical will uncover this contradiction: the Romantic insistence on absolute freedom resulted, in the case of every writer of sufficient caliber to push the tenet to its full conclusion, in the conviction that human existence was a trap. The one escape from this trap was suicide or some spiritual equivalent of it—materialism, racialism, Marxism, or any other system in which the uniqueness of the individual disappears. Though, in the necessity of things, the suicide who would go on living must attempt to erase his human distinctness, the actual suicide, as G. K. Chesterton once pointed out, seeks to destroy the universe rather than himself, and the multitude of Romantic heroes who took their own lives, in the day-to-day world as well as in novels and poems, were intent on extinguishing the whole vast creation that opposed the absolute sovereignty of their own wills. Romantic heroes, from Tristran to André Malraux's social revolutionaries with their locomotive fire-boxes and long black Cadillacs, have been thoroughly in love with easeful death, because for them the act that to ordinary mankind represents the ultimate human failure has been the last possible assertion of their independence.

Oddly enough, right here Romanticism and Puritanism have their closest point of identity: they both foster a mind that comes to reject creation as evil. The reason for the Manichaean strain in Calvinism is established by too subtle a theological argument to go into here, even were I competent to deal with it, but the Calvinist distrust of the world and the flesh stands as evidence of the Manichaean bent in all provinces of Calvinist thought and activity, and a dualism often exaggerated to a pathological extreme may be assumed to characterize the Calvinist mind. The same distrust—though with different emphases because of the rejection of Christian morality—is found in the Romantic mind, which at almost every point in creation encountered obstacles to the unlimited expression of self in which lay its highest good. Both Romanticism and Puritanism had an idealistic tendency of thought; they inclined to view all personal experience as the particular, and so of its nature imperfect, expression of values that existed anterior and superior to the human realm. The Calvinist notion of election is a species of idealism, for the fact of the individual's election exists quite apart from anything he is or does in his present avatar; and the Romantic worship of beauty is certainly one of an ideal that the individual realizes only in the most transient fashion, if he ever does realize it.

In traditional Christian thinking, man's temporal condition is short of the potential fullness of his being, but in no sense is there a fundamental opposition of what he is to what he may be (hence the resurrection of the body), and one state is the reasonable preliminary of the other. For the Puritan heretic and his Romantic heir, the traditional order is, so to speak, reversed: the Calvinist saint is saved before he is born and the Romantic hero, good by nature, is a far better man than circumstances can ever allow him to be. The ideal, obviously, never *can* be fully realized, and the real—the whole material and spiritual complex of man's earthly existence—is natively imperfect and evil to the degree of its imperfection. This conclusion was only in a few cases logically arrived at, but the rest of creation is just as rational as the human mind, and the consequences of a false assumption are no less inevitable than those of a true one.

A concern with metaphysical and religious problems of this sort is a necessary accompaniment to any thorough under-standing of Herman Melville, and it is a mark of the man's greatness that no merely "literary" explanation will account for his stature. The full extent of his stature is, admittedly, found in a single book—*Moby-Dick*; but that book is not only the greatest novel written by an American (if we stretch the word novel to include a prose epic unique of its kind) but also the one work written in 19th-century America to be compared with-out disadvantage to any European imaginative work of the same period. No other thing that Melville wrote approaches this height, and some of his writings are very far from it in-deed. ". . . It is because Melville was throughout so uneven and undisciplined in his artistry, so chaotic in his miscellaneous exuberance," Mr. Weaver has said, "that most of his really attentive readers have been primarily interested in him as a tormented and cryptic personality." [1] The artistic failures and the personal difficulties, as I shall try to show, had the one source—which was Melville's partly Calvinist, partly Roman-tic attitude of mind. But the same attitude of mind provided the subject-matter of *Moby-Dick*. Though it is self-evident that, other things being equal, any artist is better off for having a valid philosophy and the one valid religion, I do not see that any infallible correlation can be made between right thinking

[1] *Herman Melville: Journal up the Straits, October 11, 1856–May 5, 1857* edited with an introduction by Raymond Weaver (New York, 1935: The Colophon).

and artistic ability: to have a work of art, we must first have an artist. We do not know we have the first (in order of time) until we have examined the second, and the existence of both is therefore determined by objective criteria, but it none the less remains true that the formula explaining the individual artist is still undiscovered.

In literature, not to try to speak for too large a field, there is a sense in which each work of art is unique and unique in terms of the artist's personality. If a work of art is taken to be a kind of problem, the substance of that problem is derived from or through the artist's personality, and there is neither material for him to work nor possible ways of working it except as each is given to him within the limits and peculiarities of his personality. A great variety of factors (the most important of which is religion) will help to develop his personality, thus further opening the realm outside of it, but, to begin with, the personality is something "given" and what is given must in some degree set the complexion of everything it subsumes.

So much as this must be allowed fully to appreciate *Moby-Dick*, and as idle a dogma as any in the literature which has grown up around Melville is the one that Melville himself was not involved in the dilemma which is the central problem of his masterpiece. However, if the problem is unique in being Melville's, it is also unique in the way it is set forth in his book, where the imponderable elements of his genius have given it a body that may be contemplated both for our instruction and our delight (for the intellect delights not in what is "pleasing" but in what is true). Melville—as a life testifies that was more steadily given to writing than the legend of his "long seclusion" allows—could not solve his problem solely in the exercise of his artistic genius, but on two occasions, in *Moby-Dick* and in *Billy Budd*, he was able to state the problem with an entire objectivity—all its dimensions given and each seen in its proper

6

perspective—and to state it in a language that carried the subtleties of feeling which are as much a part of reality from the standpoint of the experiencing agent as anything the disinterested intellect can discover. Nor need the particular fashion in which his work was unique or personal or even American obscure the fact that he dealt with a problem which is recurrently presented to the human heart in its errancy. "I stand for the heart," he said. We can see the flaws in that single loyalty, but it is the tormented Melville who reveals them to us.

THE AMIABLE CHILD

HERMAN MELVILLE WAS BORN AT 6 PEARL STREET IN NEW
York City, August 1st, 1819, the third child and second son
of Allan and Maria Gansevoort Melville. His father was a
second-generation Bostonian of Scottish ancestry, who—at the
time of the birth of the son who was to prove this rather ordinary man's only claim to the attention of posterity—appeared
to be prospering as a dry-goods merchant. To have an extraordinary son should be no mark against an unexceptional man; it
should instead seem a token that, in the total scheme of things,
he is favored of Heaven; but few of Herman Melville's com-
mentators have been very kind to Allan, and most seem to suggest that Allan's stiff-jointed respectability somehow engendered Herman's "quenchless feud" with things as they are.
That Allan always wrote the name of God, to Whom in his
correspondence he referred frequently, with three capital letters, while his son was to ask Nathaniel Hawthorne if there
was not a "dash of flunkeyism" in using the capital for pro-
nouns referring to the Deity, indicates the formal courtesy of
one and the desperate revolt of the other, which could extend
itself even to common English usage; but that Allan Melville
felt politeness was owing to God with some more lavish gesture
than, say, to President Monroe does not mean he was insuf-
ferably narrow-minded.

Those letters that survive of the elder Melville to his wife
and to his relatives give us no glimpse directly into the interior
man. Perhaps, indeed, there was no such creature that Allan
Melville was aware of; for there are persons—"perfectly ad-

justed" is a modern term for them—who find the maxims of
the copybooks entirely adequate to their own experience and
the criterion of whose satisfaction is its correspondence with
the satisfactions of others. The man who appears in these
papers subscribes to the sovereign power of God and is at the
same time keenly aware of the delegated power of money ("the
only solid substratum on which man can safely build in this
world"); he always addresses his father, his wife, and his
prosperous relatives in respectful terms; he is much concerned
with the health of his children and their progress in learning
and piety. This picture is of a kind familiar enough: it is that
of the person in whom the first ardor of Calvinism no longer
stirs but in whom its world picture and its pattern of behavior
are still strong; the facts of election and the perseverance of
saints can as well manifest themselves in an expanding dry-
goods business as in anything where the profit and loss are less
easily reckoned; God's wisdom must have foreseen all the
forms and formalities of society, so it is hardly the righteous
man who questions them. From the hero in sanctity to the
good-natured wastrel, there are certainly more attractive
human types, but human kindness is various enough to show
itself even amongst systems that do not notably allow for it,
and we have no reason to think that Allan Melville was deficient in this respect. Where he is mentioned in his son's books,
it is at least with the ordinary measure of regard, and even if the
lapse of the elder Glendinning in *Pierre* could be shown to
have its model in an early love affair of Allan Melville's (of
which there is no convincing evidence), there hardly follows
from this that he must have been a harsh father toward his
legitimate children.

There is no doubt that Herman in time came to revolt
against most of what his father stood for, by implication as
well as explicitly, but it is only a present-day superstition to

suppose that every such difference between parent and child is of necessity a personal conflict and that the genesis of *Moby-Dick* must be found in obscure and infant resentments. Yet at least part of the genesis of that book is in Melville's Calvinist heritage. This legacy Allan Melville passed on more nearly intact than he did his share in the estate of his father, Major Thomas Melville (against which he had borrowed, by the time of his death, more than $20,000 for his business ventures). Allan must have been well grounded in his religion by the Major, who had been an aspirant to the ministry and had studied divinity at Princeton, probably inspired by the example of *his* grandfather, a minister of the Scottish Church for almost fifty years. Precisely in his adherence to the faith of his forebears, Allan Melville was doubtless less than he otherwise might have been, and there is a judgment on his nature implicit in the fact that the inadequacies of his creed did not gall him; but that judgment is suggested only because his son, developing what was potential in the Calvinist attitude and protesting against it, came in his thirtieth year to a depth of tragic vision that, for the century, was to have no equal in his country and few anywhere else. The general nature of this vision we can trace out, as well as the historical antecedents which made it especially what it was, but why the same elements should have come to such very different issues in father and son nothing in the way of biographical facts, each with its footnote, will explain. Following any man's life closely, and puzzling to know why amongst all the legions of his kind he should have been what he was, we must either allow that something has intervened there which we can only recognize in its effects or that to explain him we must ignore what first inspires our effort. "Divine imaginings, like gods, come down to the groves of our Thessalies, and there, in the embrace of wild, dryad reminiscences, beget the beings that astonish the world."

The Amiable Child

When Herman was twelve years old, his father died, bankrupt and delirious, though certainly not the raving madman that has now and then been suggested.[1] What the effect of this death was on his young mind we do not know, for the only death resembling it in his writings is the death of the father in *Pierre*, and all that is said about this is subordinated to a plot which, despite the autobiographical spirit of the book, is only distantly related to the literal facts of its author's youth. Although the deaths of those near to him were frequent in Herman Melville's life, we know curiously little of just how these touched him, and his one reflection on death not meant for public view concerns a man to whom he may never even have spoken—a sailor on a ship on which Melville sailed as a passenger in his forty-second year. The inquirer into his life meets everywhere something of this kind—there are only the scantiest documents to show the personal opinions of the man whose books were mainly spun out of his personal problems—and it is perhaps the triumph of the artist that what we wish to know about the man must be learned from what he addressed to us as fiction, as it is his failure, on the other hand, that we often insist on asking more. Anyway, whatever his father's death meant to the boy (and, in the endless resiliency of childhood, it may have had very little meaning except for the financial

---

[1] On January 15th, 1832, Herman's Uncle Thomas wrote concerning his brother Allan to Lemuel Shaw (Herman's future father-in-law): "I found him *very sick*—induced by a variety of causes—under great mental excitement—at times fierce, even *maniacal.*—in short, my dear sir, Hope, is no longer permitted of his recovery, in the opinion of the attending Physician. . . ." This, plus the likelihood that twenty-five years later Herman came under the psychiatric attention of Dr. Oliver Wendell Holmes, has been used to support the thesis that there was a strain of hereditary insanity in the family. Jean Simon, in *Herman Melville: Marin, Métaphysicien, et Poète* (Paris, 1939: Boivin & Cie), records the opinion of Dr. Henry A. Murray—a practising psychiatrist and long a student of Melville—that Allan's delirium was something normal in the course of his disease. In Herman's case, I would hazard that not every man with an unresolved metaphysical problem has an organic mental defect.

effects that followed from it), to his mother it meant that she must assume the captaincy of the family, which by that first month of 1832 included eight children.

For this post Maria Gansevoort Melville seems to have been well fitted, though it is not to be supposed that she was her husband's equal in all things. Had Allan Melville lived, there might have been rather more "culture" in the Melville household, not only because there are some things that go under that name which only money can buy, but also because he was a man who had been about the world in his time, crossing the Atlantic frequently in his business pursuits, living two years in Paris in his young manhood, acquainted with England and Scotland, and keeping on his shelves, if he did no more with them, volumes of *The Spectator*, D'Alembert, and Fénelon. Maria's horizons did not extend greatly beyond her native Albany, from which, so far as I know, she never traveled much farther than New York in one direction and Boston in another. She was born in Albany in 1791—so that just a century would intervene between her birth and the death of her second son— of a family that, in the subtle gradations of a society in which there is no openly acknowledged hierarchy, stood above her husband's.

The first Allan Melville [2] (the grandfather of Herman's father) came to Boston at the turn of the 18th century, a man in whose lineage his grandson was later to uncover a noble branch extending back to the reign of Edward I but who did not distinguish himself much beyond making a modest fortune and marrying well. His son Thomas, as has been said, studied at Princeton, visited England and Scotland, married a Scollay,

[2] Both the Gansevoorts and the Melvilles repeated given names, masculine and feminine, with a regularity maddening to their chroniclers and the latters' readers. Of Herman's four children, all had names borne by relatives, and his younger son's name commemorated both a cousin and a place famous in the Gansevoort annals. Melville himself was named after an uncle, his mother's brother.

joined in the Boston Tea Party—more than seventy-five years
later, his daughter brought out in a bottle, for the instruction
of one of Herman's literary friends, the tea leaves that Thomas
had brought home in his Indian costume that memorable
December night—and achieved the rank of Major serving in
the Revolutionary War. In 1779 he became Fire Warden of
Boston (a post Herman's father-in-law would later hold) and
in the incendiary year 1789 he became Naval Officer of the
Port of Boston, in which position he remained for thirty-five
years, one of the sights of the town because he went about his
official duties in the costume of his more heroic days—knee
breeches and cocked hat. Though any relation of cause and
effect is doubtful, it may be remarked that Herman was to have
a similar, but lesser, job in New York for nineteen years. However, Maria's family, the Gansevoorts, could look to a hundred
years' precedence over the Melvilles in America, and their
background was land-owning rather than mercantile, though
there had been a Gansevoort brewery at their nameplace, a
town about thirty-five miles north of Albany.

All through his life Melville was to take considerable pride
in his Gansevoort ancestry. Some of this pride could have been
of the sort that almost anyone takes in his better-placed relatives: if his kin's worldly eminence reflects adversely on a man's
own achievements, still there remains the identity of blood, so
that what his kin have made manifest only circumstance conceals
in him. Of course, the failure of the world to recognize this
blood-deep equality often causes bitterness in the person so
placed, and Melville, who spent more time than any man
should gazing like Narcissus at "the tormenting, mild image
he saw in the fountain", was hardly free of this bitterness; but
his high estimation of his own forebears was, it seems, something "given" in Maria Melville's household. She must have
held in particular reverence the name of her father, General

Peter Gansevoort, who had served under General Richard Montgomery in the unsuccessful assault on Québec, and had, the next year, commanded at Fort Stanwix (after which his descendants, with Herman's approval, were to name a hotel and Herman was to name his second son) in such a manner as to prevent the juncture of the troops of St. Leger and Burgoyne and to contribute materially to the failure of the latter's campaign. Besides filial pride, there may have been something in Mrs. Melville's regard for her father of what her son called "the dreary heart-vacancies of the conventional life". Yet this American concern with genealogy is not always a form of senseless snobbery; in a country where class is not openly avowed though class distinction is real enough, and where the passage from class to class is a constant process, with some going down for all who go up, the genealogical table provides the solid assurance of history against the fluid uncertainties of the future. When, after her husband's death, Maria Melville had to take in needlework and two of her sons ran a cap store, the figure of General Peter Gansevoort was an assurance that this sort of thing need not be permanent, and the figure therefore deserved homage.

A few months after her husband's death, Mrs. Melville joined the Dutch Reformed Church of Albany, making a public profession of faith, and the evidence is that she was no less devoted than Allan in the religious instruction of her children. How thoroughgoing in a doctrinal way was the Calvinism which Melville imbibed in his childhood and adolescence there appears to be no way of telling, but the habit of mind and general attitude of a particular creed will often outlast even its central dogmas, so that, though there is no reason to suppose that any Puritanical gloom was endemic in the Melville household, the manner in which the human lot was envisaged there cannot have been entirely optimistic. This fundamental pessimism we should be wrong in thinking of as a species of emotional contagion, something that attacks the marrow in a curtained and varnished "Sunday parlor". In Mrs. Melville's home "the Sabbath was strictly kept. All frivolous books, sewing, knitting, or any other handiwork, were put away and religious tracts took their place. They had a cold dinner and attended church twice." [3] Here is a measure of austerity, and of a kind dictated by Judaic literalness; but a cold dinner and twice to church on Sunday are not more than flesh can bear or the young spirit can willingly submit to.

Melville's earlier books and a good part of his correspondence indicate that he had enough of what Karl Bühler has called "joy of right function", and what his age called animal spirits, to throw off the contagion, current once a week, of hushed tones and an atmosphere generally crepuscular. (Of course, neither of these in itself need depress anybody, since those who have lost the faculty of awe have also lost that of happiness.) A clue to why Melville gave no very convincing expression to optimism in any but his last work is indicated by those "frivolous books"—not, of course, by the books themselves, whose smug moralizing probably had neither the effect intended nor its opposite, but by the way they were regarded. Those books, though morally acceptable, were all right for weekdays but not for the Sabbath; and the cleavage on which this judgment was based was fundamental to the Calvinist and Puritan point of view. There was a department of things and human affairs with which Providence was only negatively concerned; the moral law might operate there, but in essence as no more than a "nay", since a large part of creation was divinely planned for destruc-

[3] Mrs. Eleanor Metcalf, Melville's granddaughter, in a letter of January 10th, 1933, to William Braswell, quoted by him in *Melville's Religious Thought* (Durham, N. C., 1943: Duke University Press).

tion, so that, however good its source, it itself was full of evil; and in moving toward the goal for which he was made, man was in daily contact with things made for another end. Jonathan Edwards's uncle-by-marriage Hawley, when his brilliant nephew's preaching carried to him the full implications of this appraisal of the universe, cut his throat; Maria Melville it merely confirmed in her rather imperious habits; but her second son it moved to a protest so furious that all he said in the next forty years of his life, though he still pondered the same problem he was never to solve, lacked the full eloquence for which his genius was fitted.

A revised edition of Diedrich Knickerbocker's *History of New York* appeared, ten years after its original issue, in the year that Herman Melville was born. Irving's book was as much concerned with making fun of contemporary matters as of earlier ones, but its affectation of antiquity seems not to have been a joke at the expense of a city that, like an adolescent, claimed a maturity everything about it denied. Around six generations had appeared since Peter Minuit purchased New Amsterdam's site (well after its founding) and New York was, in 1819, eighty years older than Melbourne is today, and its population, while of fairly recent growth, was only a little short of the present white population of Capetown. The city in which most of Melville's life was passed, and where his main attachments lay, was not, even when he first opened his eyes there, a provincial town in the sense of being untutored and rude. It was not, certainly, Megalopolis—which, even so late as this, had only two full-fledged exemplars, London and Paris. These were still the great rival cities, in which alone the highest energies and ambitions of their respective countries could find expression, because they were the capitals of the first of the great national states. Toward both of these cities New York looked for its cultural nutriment, but a city need not have an entirely autocthonous culture to escape intellectual dullness; indeed, the insistence on what is native and peculiar to the place, largely negative in character, will stifle thought as much as anything else. The New York of the first quarter of the 19th century may have been a little "retarded", with something in its intellectual atmosphere recognizably belonging to the 18th—the pages of Irving, Cooper, and even J. K. Paulding still have that effluvium. But the 18th century was, above all, international in the references of its thought, and a New Yorker of 1760 need have felt that he lived on the periphery of his world only in a geographical sense.

In Melville's first years, "your insular city of the Manhattoes" was more obviously the seaport than it is today, when this one of its functions is much overshadowed by both its growth in size and its central position in the two distinctive activities of capitalism—the retailing of luxuries and bookkeeping. A hundred years and more ago, the tang of salt must have been evident almost everywhere in the city's air, and one did not have to walk far to be reminded that in the beginning the town had been, as it were, carried ashore from ships. "There now is your insular city of the Manhattoes," said Melville in 1850, writing *Moby-Dick* and perhaps thinking back some ten years, "belted round by wharves as Indian isles by coral reefs—commerce surrounds it with her surf. Right and left, the streets take you waterward. Its extreme down-town is the battery, where that noble mole is washed by waves, and cooled by breezes, which a few hours previous were out of sight of land." And a year earlier, speaking of himself as Wellingborough Redburn, a boy of seventeen, Melville had written of Coenties Slip

somewhere near ranges of grim-looking warehouses, with rusty iron doors and shutters, and tiled roofs; and old anchors and chain-cable piled on the walk. Old-fashioned coffee-houses, also, much abound in that neighborhood, with sunburnt sea-captains going in and out, smoking cigars, and talking about Havana, London, and Calcutta.

All these my imaginations were wonderfully assisted by certain shadowy reminiscences of wharves, and warehouses, and shipping, with which a residence in a seaport during early childhood had supplied me.

Particularly, I remembered standing with my father on the wharf when a large ship was getting under way, and rounding the head of the pier. I remembered the *yo heave ho!* of the sailors, as they just showed their woolen caps above the high bulwarks. I remembered how I thought of their crossing the great ocean; and that that very ship, and those very sailors, so near to me then, would after a time be actually in Europe.

These thoughts, here given with some literary embellishment, may even have been entertained by the little Herman whom, when he was approaching seven, his father described as "backward in speech and somewhat slow in comprehension" though, so far as his comprehension went, "both solid and profound and of a docile and amiable disposition". This was in the summer of 1826; the Melvilles were now living in suburban Bleecker Street; and Allan described Herman thus in a letter that preceded the child's visit to his mother's people in Albany. Herman would also go to visit his grandfather in Boston and his Uncle Thomas Melville at Pittsfield in Massachusetts. When Herman was nearly eleven and attending the New-York Male High School, with his shirt collar "turned over, and tied with a black ribbon", he seems not to have changed too much from the child of six, for in May of 1830 his father wrote to Grandfather Thomas that "Herman I think is making more progress than formerly, & without being a bright Scholar, he retains a respectable standing, & would proceed farther, if he could be induced to study more—being a most amiable & innocent child, I cannot find in my heart to coerce him, especially as he seems to have chosen Commerce as a favorite pursuit, whose practical activity can well dispense with much book knowledge". Forty-two years later, Herman's wife would estimate his talents as quite the opposite: "Herman from his studious habits and tastes being unfitted for practical matters, all the *financial* management falls upon me."

Of the two Major Thomas Melvilles, grandfather and uncle, Herman was more influenced by the younger (the elder died in the same year as Herman's father). The younger had lived a long time in France, where he married a French wife who bore him six children, and he had gained his rank of major when, after returning to America, he served in the War of 1812. Going to Pittsfield in 1816, he settled in the handsomest house in town, Broadhall, and took to farming. In after years, Melville recalled his uncle's antique French manners and his habit of pausing, while he was out in the fields raking hay into windrows, to take a pinch of snuff from his elegant snuffbox. This combination of polished ways and simplicity was always to fascinate Melville and, towards the end of his life, apparently writing only for his own amusement, he would sketch out a group of characters of the "Burgundy Club", all of whom probably owed something to Major Thomas Melville the younger, although they exceeded even that old gentleman in polish and in the powers of reminiscence.

From Bleecker Street, the Melvilles moved to 675 Broadway and a more spacious home; but within two years Allan's business affairs had taken so much of a turn for the worse that he was forced to retreat to Albany, from which eleven years before he had set out so hopefully for the "great universal mart of trade". Enough money remained to send Herman to the Albany Academy, where what little formal education he ever received was completed and where his teachers remarked his truthfulness and his incompetence in mathematics. This last may explain the briefness of the period he spent in 1834, after his father's death, working in the New York State Bank, where the good offices of his Uncle Peter, who was an official of the establishment, had secured him a job as clerk. Though Allan's death had placed the Melvilles in one of the most humiliating of positions—that of poor relations—there is no evidence that the Gansevoorts ever failed in kindness toward them. Peter Gansevoort, a most substantial kind of citizen, had a life-long record of kindnesses toward his nephew Herman, and in this his daughter Catherine succeeded him. But it is always more difficult to receive than to give, and if the adolescent Redburn was also the adolescent Melville, the latter cannot have been the most graceful recipient of favors. The "son-of-a-gentleman", he was no doubt nice enough in his manner and prompt enough in his thanks, but the son of a gentleman and the grandson of two Revolutionary heroes might well have felt that it was not properly in the nature of things that he should have to accept any favors.

Redburn, shipping aboard the *Highlander* as the least of ordinary seamen, once he is well out to sea puts on his threadbare best to pay a social call upon the captain, and we can't be too far wrong in imagining that his original, in the fresh-water atmosphere of Albany in the days before his first voyage, was guilty of similar examples of lese majesty—perhaps certain artless assumptions of equality from behind the counters of the New York State Bank and of his brother Gansevoort's cap and fur store, in the last of which he was a clerk in 1835. It does not seem unjust to assume that the boy who was working one year in his uncle's bank, the next in his brother's shop, and the third on another uncle's farm at Pittsfield had a little more than the usual allotment of stiff adolescent pride and was what his seniors would now call "difficult": he had moved out of the vale of childhood, where even the arbitrary is none the less certain, and into that region where the adolescent makes the recurrently heartbreaking discovery that most values are to be established only in his own experience. All this would be borne in on the young Melville not only by the faint burgeonings of his own maturity but also by the circumstances of his life. However "aristocratic" his background might be, here he was in a strange present in which he found himself clothed in a many-pocketed shooting-jacket with skirts that came to his knees. A proper heredity could not yet make all things plain to this blue-eyed, brown-haired boy who had not finished school, where his grades had not been exceptional.

When Melville left home to go to sea in May or June of 1837, it probably was, as he later said was the case with Wellingborough Redburn, because "sad disappointments in several plans which I had sketched for my future life, the necessity of doing something for myself, united to a naturally roving disposition, had now conspired within me, to send me to sea as a sailor". However, his "everlasting itch for things remote" may also have been stimulated by the conversation of two of his cousins. One was the son of the uncle after whom Herman had been named, Leonard Herman Gansevoort. This young man, Guert Gansevoort, seven years Herman's senior, had sailed the Mediterranean and the Pacific off South America, and the romance that surrounded him might well have seemed to Herman something made actual of what was potential in himself. The other cousin, Pierre François Henry Thomas Wilson Melville, the son of the uncle at Pittsfield, must surely have recounted some time during the greater part of the year 1836 that Herman spent at Broadhall his adventures in 1829 and 1830 when, as a midshipman aboard the U. S. S. *Vincennes*, he toured the South Seas and spent two weeks at Nukaheva, the scene of what ten years later was to be Herman's first book and the most popular during his lifetime. Added to this preliminary inspiration, an immediate deciding factor may have been the fact that Uncle Thomas sold Broadhall in 1837 and emigrated to Galena, Illinois. Once this good gentleman, with his meditative snuff-box and "faded brocade of old French breeding", had gone West with the vulgar hopeful of the time, what remained for a boy whose father had traveled "by water 48,460 miles" except to put to sea? At any rate, "on a raw, cold, damp morning toward the end of spring" with, as he said, the mildew on his young soul Melville set out from his mother's house to take the Hudson River boat for New York, carrying in his pocket only half the necessary fare—or in his young mind the embarrassment of which this was to be the later symbol. And this actual sea on which he was about to launch himself would provide him with a symbol that he should embody into more cause for pride than the boy in the ample-skirted and bone-buttoned coat could yet know.

BRICKS FROM HOLLAND
AND BOOBLE ALLEYS

". . . I HOPE I SHALL NEVER WRITE SUCH A BOOK AGAIN," SAID Melville in a letter from London in December of 1849, shortly after the publication of *Redburn: His First Voyage,* to the chief of his literary friends in New York, Evert Duyckinck, "—tho' when a poor devil writes with duns all around him, & looking over the back of his chair—& perching on his pen & diving in his inkstand—like the devils about St: Anthony—what can you expect of that poor devil?—What but a beggarly 'Redburn!' " This was the fourth of Melville's books and the third to draw more or less directly on his adventures as a seaman for its substance. It seems not improbable that the devils in his inkwell contrived to put things into *Redburn* that might be more to the public taste than anything that had actually occurred in the first voyage of a sailor boy, but we can safely assume that the boy who appears in the book tells us a good deal about his creator when he was in the same circumstances. There are few important characters in any of Melville's books that are not, in one way or another, identifiable with himself—even Ahab seems a mask through which he speaks rather than the exponent of a point of view the author assumes only for the purposes of drama—and in a book written hurriedly for money there is not likely to be a great deal of invention.

Wellingborough Redburn—named after his great-uncle, "Senator Wellingborough, who had died a member of Congress in the days of the old Constitution"—set out for New York from "a pleasant village on the Hudson River, where we

lived in a small house, in a quiet way", with a determination
not to "think of those delightful days, before my father became
a bankrupt, and died, and we removed from the city". The
mood of Redburn's departure was a mixed one: he thought
"how fine it would be to be able to talk about remote and
barbarous countries; with what reverence and wonder people
would regard me, if I had just returned from the coast of Africa
or New Zealand; how dark and romantic my sunburnt cheeks
would look; how I would bring home with me foreign clothes
of a rich fabric and princely make, and how grocers' boys would
turn back their heads to look at me as I went by"; and at the
same time, he said, "I had learned to think much and bitterly
before my time; all my young mounting dreams of glory had
left me; and at that early age I was as unambitious as a man
of sixty". These contradictory attitudes Melville doubtless
heightened a little in retelling, for, as Willard Thorp has observed, he "was seeking to create an atmosphere of pathos
mingled with romance",[1] and perhaps he invented the incident
which he described as taking place on the Hudson River boat,
where, because the passengers were looking at him since he had
been able to pay only half his fare, he took the fowling piece
his brother had given him to sell in New York and presented it
at one of them "point-blank, full in the left eye". Apocryphal
or not, the gesture is representative of what the man was to do,
leveling his talent against a universe which he felt showed a
hostile curiosity towards him and seeking to carry by "fierce
escalade" the heights to be won only by less direct ways.

From New York, Redburn shipped aboard the *Highlander*,
a vessel irregularly sailing between New York and Liverpool.
Introduced for the job as a wealthy merchant's son who wished
to go abroad as a sailor rather than to make the Grand Tour

[1] *Herman Melville: Representative Selections, with Introduction, Bibliography, and Notes* by Willard Thorp (New York, 1938: American Book Company).

with a tutor, Redburn was hired by Captain Riga of the *Highlander* at wages of three dollars a month and was refused the advance on his salary he needed to buy the clothes necessary for the voyage. So Redburn took his place in the fo'c'sle, dressed in his hunting jacket, a red shirt bought with the money got from pawning the fowling piece, pantaloons, with "a slit on the outside of each leg, at the foot, to button up with a row of six brass bell-buttons", that had been copied from those of a cousin "who was a young man of fortune and drove a tilbury", and tall boots whose "edges were mounted with red morocco". In 1837 the society in the fo'c'sle was, it seems, even less polite than it is today and, like all groups of men gathered together under a harsh discipline, it subjected the newcomer to a cruel initiation. That initiation was more cruel in Redburn's case not only because he was a landlubber, ignorant of the esoteric ways and language of ships, but also because of his fantastically arrayed gentility and a certain delicacy of speech which he maintained even in that inappropriate place. He was alien to his shipmates in class as well as in other things, and, meeting them on their level, he had no protection against their resentments.

In time the sailors came to accept Wellingborough Redburn, not because they understood and forgave his slightly priggish seriousness or because he made any pretense of conversion to their manners and mores, but because he proved himself apt in seamanship and quick even in the lowest of the tasks assigned to him. In the four months he served aboard the *Highlander*, Redburn made no friendships amongst the crew and received few kindnesses from them. They had rebuffed, it is true, what overtures he made, but perhaps he was as intent as they on observing his difference and used whatever mastery of seamanship he gained to show them that their craft was no distinction from which they could claim superiority to him. Melville always carried himself aloof, and after his death a friend observed that "in spite of all later influences it [his home training] made him for all his later life an inbred gentleman in manners, in thought and in soul. No influence, before the mast or elsewhere, could change that." He probably had the mixed sense of superiority and fear of betraying it that the apparently frigid person often has, but he always retained a general sympathy with his inferior associates, following from his conviction of man's "innate dignity . . . buried among the holiest privacies of the soul", and, in his writings, expressed it vigorously enough to mislead some of his modern critics into thinking him a prophet of latter-day democracy.

Life aboard the *Highlander* was a rough and sudden introduction to the world that lies beyond childhood. In Albany and Lansingburgh, this introduction might have presented less obvious contrasts, since adult life there cannot have departed too widely from the standards of respectability in which the child was brought up, so that all the affairs of the world would have seemed to be run according to an at least apparently rational set of rules. There is no reason to suppose that Melville would not have seen through "respectability" as a self-sufficient way of life had he not seen a very different way of life at sea in his early years, but it does not seem unlikely that his immature experience of crudity and violence made him question that much sooner the universal pretensions of the morals of Lansingburgh. Like most of the figures of his time, he did not ever question the Christian ethic in its broad outlines—that questioning was to become general some time later with doubts of the rationality of chastity and to end, in our own time, with the establishment of Buchenwald and the Soviet camps in the Arctic and the bombing of Hiroshima—though he was always doubtful of the belief on which the Christian ethic rests, that the universe is created for a benevolent purpose, and the debauched and miserable lives of the *Highlander's* crew would, on first examination, have appeared to serve no benevolent intention.

Melville, in the fullness of his Protestant temperament, had an oppressive awareness of evil, but for him evil was a quality that permeated things as they were rather than something exemplified in the lives of men. In only two of his works do we find characters in whom evil is dominant, and one of these is in *Redburn*, which deals with the earliest period of his life given in any of his books (excepting some passages in *Pierre* of doubtful verisimilitude), and the other in the story which occupied the last three years of his life. It is significant of his progress in the forty-two years intervening between the two works that in *Redburn* Jackson merely gives off the effluvium of his corruption, while in *Billy Budd* Claggart[2] *embodies evil* by acting it out.

Yet Jackson is one of Melville's most memorable portraits, especially impressive because, approaching the end of his life, he is set in contrast to Redburn, whose real life is beginning. There is in young Wellingborough the promise all youth holds and the native purity which, because we think of it as merely a negative quality, we too often forget may be the thing in which youth's fulfillment lies, while Jackson is the same creature come, through whatever circumstances, to a conclusion in which that purity, so far as the natural man goes, is hopelessly lost. Syphilitic and tuberculous, Jackson dominated the crew out of his contempt and hatred for them, much as did James Waite in *The Nigger of the Narcissus*. Made the physical inferior of all of them by his illness, he "sogered" on every job except the one calling for skill and daring in the rigging, where his contempt

[2] Claggart is anticipated in *White-Jacket* (1850), Melville's fifth book, by the sergeant-at-arms. Bland, however, though perhaps closer to his and Claggart's original, is merely a scoundrel without metaphysical dimensions, despite some speculations Melville makes on the origin of his ill-will.

for everything was extended to danger and where he came to his death in the expression of his bitter pride.

He was as yellow as gamboge, had no more whisker on his cheek than I have on my elbows. His hair had fallen out, and left him very bald, except in the nape of his neck, and just behind the ears, where it was stuck over with short little tufts, and looked like a worn-out shoebrush. His nose had broken down in the middle, and he squinted with one eye, and did not look very straight out of the other. He dressed a good deal like a Bowery boy; for he despised the ordinary sailor-rig, wearing a pair of great over-all blue trowsers, fastened with suspenders, and three red woollen shirts, one over the other . . . and he had a large white wool hat, with a broad rolling brim.

. . . He was a great bully, and being the best seaman on board, and very overbearing every way, all the men were afraid of him, and durst not contradict him, or cross his path in anything. And what made this more wonderful was that he was the weakest man, bodily, of the whole crew. . . . But he had such an overawing way with him, such a deal of brass and impudence, such an unflinching face, and withal was such a hideous-looking mortal, that Satan himself would have run from him. And besides all this, it was quite plain that he was by nature a marvelously clever, cunning man, though without education; and understood human nature to a kink, and well knew whom he had to deal with; and then, one glance of his squinting eye was as good as a knock-down. . . . I would defy any oculist to turn out a glass eye half so cold, and snaky, and deadly.

Nothing was left of this Jackson but the foul lees and dregs of a man; he was thin as a shadow; nothing but skin and bones; and sometimes used to complain that it hurt him to sit on the hard chests. And I sometimes fancied it was the consciousness of his miserable, broken-down condition, and the prospect of soon dying like a dog, in consequence of his sins, that made this poor wretch always eye me with such malevolence as he did. For I was young and handsome . . . whereas *he* was being consumed by an incurable malady, that was eating up his vitals. . . .

He seemed to be full of hatred and gall against everything and everybody in the world; as if all the world was one person, and had done him some dreadful harm, that was rankling and festering in his heart.

". . . Don't talk of heaven to me [howled Jackson through a cough]—it's a lie—I know it—and they are all fools that believe in it. Do you think, you Greek, that there's any heaven for *you?* Will they let *you* in there, with that tarry hand, and that oily head of hair? Avast! when some shark gulps you down his hatchway one of these days, you'll find, that by dying, you'll only go on from one gale of wind to another; mind that, you Irish Cockney! Yes, you'll be bolted down like one of your own pills: and I should like to see the whole ship swallowed down in the Norway maelstrom, like a box on 'em. That would be a dose of salts for ye!" And so saying, he went off, holding his hands to his chest, and coughing as if his last hour was come.

Every day this Jackson seemed to grow worse and worse, both in body and mind. He seldom spoke, but to contradict, deride or curse; and all the time, though his face grew thinner and thinner, his eyes seemed to kindle more and more, as if he were going to die out at last, and leave them burning like tapers before a corpse.

Though he had never attended churches, and knew nothing about Christianity; no more than a Malay pirate; and though he could not read a word, yet he was spontaneously an atheist and an infidel; and during the long night-watches, would enter into arguments, to prove that there was nothing to be believed; nothing to be loved, and nothing worth living for; but everything to be hated, in the wide world. He was a horrid desperado; and like a wild Indian, whom he resembled in his tawny skin and high cheek-bones, he seemed to run amuck at heaven and earth. He was a Cain afloat; branded on his yellow brow with some inscrutable curse; and going about corrupting and searing every heart that beat near him.

But there seemed even more woe than wickedness about the man;

and his wickedness seemed to spring from his woe; and for all his hideousness there was that in his eye at times that was ineffably pitiable and touching; and though there were moments when I almost hated this Jackson, yet I have pitied no man as I have pitied him.

The strain of Titanism that had already appeared in *Mardi* (Melville's third book) and was to re-appear in later works of Melville's is not contradicted by the following reflections on Jackson's evilness. Melville's defiance of the heavens, as it is spoken by Ahab and Pierre, is made from an outraged moral sense, a feeling that fate is malignant, and is no desperate espousal of evil because good seems unobtainable or the attractions of evil equal to those of good. In his long torment over the problem of evil, Melville always felt that "that which shall not be still *ought* to be", and though in the exasperation of his pride he approached a kind of diabolism, it was in the conviction that he was serving what was right. Oddly enough, in the light of his remarks on Milton's Satan in the following passage, Melville would in later years mark, apparently with approval, Shelley's reference to the moral superiority of the same personage. But no man grows inevitably in wisdom, and our lost selves are often wiser than we know.

I can never think of him, even now, reclining in his bunk, and with short breaths panting out his maledictions, but I am reminded of that misanthrope upon the throne of the world—the diabolical Tiberius at Capreae; who even in his self-exile, embittered by bodily pangs, and unspeakable mental terrors known only to the damned on earth, yet did not give over his blasphemies, but endeavored to drag down with him to his own perdition all who came within the evil spell of his power. And though Tiberius came in the succession of the Caesars, and though unmatchable Tacitus has embalmed his carrion, yet do I account this Yankee Jackson full as dignified a personage as he, and as well meriting his lofty gallows in history;

even though he was a nameless vagabond without an epitaph, and none, but I, narrate what he was. For there is no dignity in wickedness, whether in purple or rags; and hell is a democracy of devils, where all are equals. There, Nero howls side by side with his own malefactors. If Napoleon were truly but a martial murderer, I pay him no more homage than I would a felon. Though Milton's Satan dilutes our abhorrence with admiration, it is only because he is not a genuine being, but something altered from a genuine original. We gather not from the four gospels alone any high-raised fancies concerning this Satan; we only know him from thence as the personification of the essence of evil, which, who but pickpockets and burglars will admire? But this takes not from the merit of our high priest of poetry; it only enhances it, that with such unmitigated evil for his material, he should build up his most goodly structure.

But in historically canonizing on earth the condemned below, and lifting up and lauding the illustrious damned, we do but make ensamples of wickedness; and call upon ambition to do some great iniquity, and be sure of fame.

These are, of course, the prose rhythms of Sir Thomas Browne, with which Melville had already experimented in *Mardi* and which he was to absorb more successfully in *Moby-Dick*, but there are few other instances of them (an exaltation of cooks above doctors, for example, and praise of America's "universal paternity") in *Redburn*. At the time of the book's appearance, Evert Duyckinck wrote to his brother George that it was "Defoe at sea" and John Freeman, in his excellent little study in the English Men of Letters series, has noted that *Redburn* "has the single eye of Defoe, the straightness of perfect narrative unembarrassed by foreign interests".[3] Aside from the two instances noted, any Gothic embellishments are of incidents, not style, and the cool, rather matter-of-fact prose gives a poignancy to Redburn's adolescent experiences that a more elaborate

[3] *Herman Melville* by John Freeman (New York, 1926: The Macmillan Company).

way of writing might have made merely cloying. While it is true that here Melville is not attempting the depth and scope he essayed elsewhere, it may be asked whether he did not have in the prose of *Redburn* an instrument capable of further extension than he realized, with a discipline implicit in its form sufficiently strict to keep him from the failures of over-ornamentation into which he occasionally fell in other places. Even in the loftiest flights of his rhetoric, Melville starts from, or utilizes, concrete observation, and it is the multiple extensions he makes of this observation that give his prose a poetical quality in the best sense. If the great prose of *Moby-Dick* is thus poetic in its use of the image, the simpler prose of *Redburn* also has its poetry, though it gains it as much from its material as from its method—its sober and unadorned procedure sets forth the subject-matter with a coolness and detachment that make the general nostalgia more acceptable, an experience sufficiently contained for the reader to participate in it willingly: this is certainly emotion recollected in tranquility.

". . . During my early life, most of my thoughts of the sea were connected with the land; but with fine old lands, full of mossy cathedrals and churches, and long, narrow, crooked streets without sidewalks, and lined with strange houses." Redburn dreamed on these prospects as he lay in his bunk on shipboard, and the Liverpool towards which the *Highlander* made her slow way became for him an object of delight and the goal of a pilgrimage, for his father's business as a merchant had taken him there and the boy thought to retrace his father's steps, experiencing in his own person all that he had heard about "of winter evenings in New York, by the well-remembered sea-coal fire in old Greenwich Street". This seemed a sufficient compensation for the hardships of seafaring—attending to the pigs that were penned in the longboat; the dreadful moment when he was first sent aloft at dead of night to loose the mainskysail that "from the forecastle looked no bigger than a cambric pocket-handkerchief"; the meals, foul stuff for eating which he had neither dish nor spoon; the broken sleep; the swabbing down of the decks in coldest weather (which had so annoyed Dana, too); and the helplessly lost and alien feeling that came from being in a world of strange objects, all with stranger names. He reflects on these last:

I wonder whether mankind could not get along without all these names, which keep increasing every day, and hour, and moment; till at last the very air will be full of them; and even in a great plain men will be breathing each other's breath, owing to the vast multitude of words they use that consume all the air, just as lamp-burners do gas. But people seem to have a great love for names; for to know a great many names seems to look like knowing a good many things; though I should not be surprised if there were a great many more names than things in the world.

But it was not so very long before the sea became something more than a "wide blank" between two worlds of "cities and towns and villages and green fields and hedges and farmyards and orchards". After his first seasickness had been cured with rum—despite his qualms of conscience as a member of the Juvenile Total Abstinence Society—he was fascinated by "a certain wonderful rising and falling of the sea; I do not mean the waves themselves, but a sort of wide heaving and swelling and sinking all over the ocean. . . . I felt as if in a dream all the time; and when I could shut the ship out, almost thought I was in some new, fairy world, and expected to hear myself called to out of the clear blue air, or from the depths of the deep blue sea." While they were passing through a fog on the Newfoundland Banks and he was tolling the bell, "the most strange and unheard-of noises came out of the fog at times; a vast sound of sighing and sobbing. What could it be? This would be followed

33

by a spout, and a gush, and a cascading commotion, as if some
fountain had suddenly jetted out of the ocean." These sounds
came from whales, which did not appear "the hills and valleys
of flesh" that the story of Jonah had led Redburn to expect.
From that day, whales fell greatly in Redburn's estimation—
one point on which he is surely not to be identified with his
author. On the Grand Banks, they also passed the dismasted
wreck of a New Brunswick lumberman, on which "lashed, and
leaning over sideways against the taffrail, were three dark,
green, grassy objects, that slowly swayed with every roll, but
otherwise were motionless"—the corpses of sailors. This episode, well written though it is, seems an interpolation of one of
the devils in the inkwell, for it is improbable that any sailor
would leave himself lashed to the taffrail and famish there.

At last the *Highlander* made the mouth of the Mersey and
the next day sailed into Liverpool, the first sight of which
"seemed very deficient in the elements of the marvelous; and
bore a most unexpected resemblance to the warehouses along
South Street in New York". However, Redburn's entire disillusionment was not immediate. To be sure, dockside Liverpool, its
sailors' boarding houses and taverns, its booble alleys and other
mean places were all a vast slum and whatever antiquity they
may have had, relative to America, was hidden under an unro-
mantic grime. Even that antiquity was doubtful, for Redburn
remembered that the bricks for a "gable-pointed mansion" belonging to his grandfather had been brought from Holland in
the days of Dutch rule in America. Like so many American
visitors to England in the early 19th century, he was appalled
by the widespread poverty and beggary, and in a brief account
of a young Chartist [4] addressing a crowd in St. George's Square

---

[4] Melville writes: "I was not long within hearing of him before I became
aware that this youth was a Chartist." The term "Chartist", however, seems
not to have come into currency until a year after this first visit of his to
Liverpool.

on a Sunday afternoon he neatly contrived to set forth the contrast between England's commercial-imperial might (then in the first quarter of the brief century of its apogee) and the "want and woe [that] staggered arm in arm along these miserable streets":

Presently the crowd increased, and some commotion was raised, when I noticed the police officers augmenting in numbers; and by and by they began to glide through the crowd, politely hinting at the propriety of dispersing. The first persons thus accosted were the soldiers, who accordingly sauntered off, switching their rattans, and admiring their high-polished boots. It was plain that the Charter did not hang very heavy round their hearts. For the rest, they also gradually broke up; and at last I saw the speaker himself depart.

And there is the celebrated chapter, "What Redburn Saw in Launcelott's-Hey", where again Melville's simple and unadorned style allows his subject-matter to speak with its own eloquence. Passing along a street called Launcelott's-Hey, he "heard a feeble wail, which seemed to come out of the earth".

At last I advanced to an opening which communicated downward with deep tiers of cellars beneath a crumbling old warehouse; and there, some fifteen feet below the walk, crouching in nameless squalor, with her head bowed over, was the figure of what had been a woman. Her blue arms folded to her livid bosom two shrunken things like children, that leaned toward her, one on each side. At first, I knew not whether they were alive or dead. They made no sign; they did not move or stir; but from the vault came that soul-sickening wail.

He sought aid for these people, but the various police said the matter was not in their province and others were equally indifferent. He went to the boarding house where the crew of the *Highlander* were fed during its six-weeks stay in Liverpool and from there, because he was penniless, he took some bread to Launcelott's-Hey, as well as carrying water in his tarpaulin hat.

While the girls were breaking and eating the bread, I tried to lift the woman's head; but, feeble as she was, she seemed bent upon holding it down. Observing her arms still clasped upon her bosom, and that something seemed hidden under the rags there, a thought crossed my mind, which impelled me forcibly to withdraw her hands for a moment; when I caught a glimpse of a meager little babe, the lower part of its body thrust into an old bonnet. Its face was dazzlingly white, even in its squalor; but the closed eyes looked like balls of indigo. It must have been dead some hours.

For two days he passed the vault, dropping bread to its in-mates; and on the third day the smell that came from the vault made plain what had happened, and he went to the police again. Later on the same day, "in place of the woman and chil-dren, a heap of quicklime was glistening".

The early history of modern industrialism and the growth of cities is famously unpretty. Whether or not Melville related an actual historical incident there is no way of telling—*Redburn* contains a story, also told with a moral purpose, of a corpse that spontaneously burst into flame—but at least art comes here to bring its peculiar immediacy and conviction to a thing as to whose general kind there is documentation enough. The sketch might be said to be the demonstration of what Melville was able imaginatively to experience, even if the substance of the sketch was, in a different sense, "imaginative". It is certain that Melville's first acquaintance with the fullest squalor of poverty in Liverpool deeply touched him, for in many of his later works where poverty is dealt with it has an English reference. The hero of *Israel Potter* (1854), which contains Melville's best account of poverty, spends many years of hardship in London. In a number of short stories or sketches of the same period, there is a kind of international contrast. "Paradise of Bachelors and Tartarus of Maids" compares the lot of women workers in one of the dark satanic mills, a paper factory appropriately set in a region of Tartarean cold in the Berkshires, with the comforts enjoyed by bachelors in their quarters in the Temple. "Poor Man's Pudding and Rich Men's Crumbs" gives two pictures of poverty—one in rural America and the other in London. In "The Two Temples" a poor man is refused admittance to a New York church (Grace Church apparently, since the piece was refused by *Putnam's* for fear of offending that congregation) but is received with kindness in a London theater. Of sixteen shorter pieces written before 1856, poverty is an important theme in seven, and it is nowhere treated as what Melville called "povertiresque"; it is for those who suffer it always a cold and comfortless humiliation of the kind Redburn experienced in his own penniless state.

Redburn's disillusionment in Liverpool was less effected by the want he saw than by what happened to him when he tried to follow a certain itinerary for his pilgrimage. This itinerary had been planned during the voyage—"pleasant afternoon rambles through the town; down St. James Street and up Great George's, stopping at various points of interest and attraction" —and it was drawn from an old guidebook to Liverpool that had belonged to Redburn's father, the much-traveled merchant. In the guidebook his father had marked his various trips about Liverpool by "a number of dotted lines, radiating in all directions from the foot of Lord Street, where stands marked '*Riddough's Hotel*', the house my father stopped at". "By these marks I perceive that my father forgot not his religion in a foreign land; but attended St. John's Church near the Haymarket, and other places of public worship; I see that he visited the News Room in Duke Street, the Lyceum in Bold Street, and the Theatre Royal; and that he called to pay his respects to the eminent Mr. Roscoe,[5] the historian, poet, and banker." But Redburn, dressed "three parts sportsman, and two soldier, to one of the sailor", is turned away from a reading room and thrown out of the Lyceum, and in church the usher seats him behind a pillar, while Riddough's Hotel he cannot find and learns, at last, that it has been pulled down more than a generation before. Nor can he find "the venerable Abbey of Birkenhead" and "the mansion once occupied by the old earls of Derby" and when "in the land of Thomas à Becket and stout John of Gaunt" he at last comes upon something which seems familiar to his reveries, "it is the spot where the Manchester railroad enters the outskirts of the town", which he has seen illustrated in *The Penny Magazine*, though at the time he does not recall this.

William Ellery Sedgwick—who reads in Melville's thought a more consistent development than I think the text warrants, but who seems correct enough in his statement of its general direction—finds in this disappointment of Redburn's in his guidebook the most significant episode of the story. Melville writes:

Here, now, oh Wellingborough, thought I, learn a lesson, and never forget it. This world, my boy, is a moving world; its Riddough's Hotels are forever being pulled down; it never stands still; and its sands are forever shifting. This very harbor of Liverpool is gradually filling up, they say; and who knows what your son (if you ever have one) may behold, when he comes to visit Liverpool, as long after you as you came after his grandfather. And, Wellingborough, as your father's guide-book is no guide for you, neither would yours (could you afford to buy a modern one today) be a

---

[5] William Roscoe (1753–1831) was a Liverpool lawyer of Liberal political leanings and a most various literary production. He knew Washington Irving, who mentioned him in his *Sketch Book*. Roscoe's son married Sarah Walker of Hazlitt's *Liber Amoris*.

true guide to those who come after you. Guide-books, Welling-borough, are the least reliable books in all literature; and nearly all literature, in one sense, is made up of guide-books. Old ones tell us the way our fathers went, through the thoroughfares and courts of old; but how few of those former places can their posterity trace, amid avenues of modern erections; to how few is the old guide-book now a clue! Every age makes its own guide-books, and the old ones are used for wastepaper. But there is one Holy Guide-Book, Wellingborough, that will never lead you astray, if you but follow it aright; and some noble monuments that remain, though the pyramids crumble.

"Whether the episode is fiction or not," [6] says Mr. Sedgwick, "it shows that Melville had glimpsed, in his initial experience of the world, that his father's world of social privilege and economic security, of right and wrong firmly established by the sanctions and prescriptions of Presbyterian orthodoxy (or, as it had become, Presbyterian respectability), did not rest on immutable foundations. . . . The world he had to face . . . was a wider and vaguer, a more indefinite and dangerous world than his father's." [7] Growth always brings something of this kind, because if the boy does not grow out of his father's world, he at least grows out of his ideas of what his father's world is. There is an opposite growth, too, in which the boy grows into his father's world, but this can be done only within the framework of orthodoxy, whose values are greater than any single man's experience of them, and Melville's heritage was not sufficient to meet the intensity of his experience. Writing later to Hawthorne, Melville would say that all his growth dated from his twenty-fifth year, so if the episode of the guidebook is symbolic of its author's break with the world into which he had

[6] Willard Thorp, in "Redburn's Prosy Old Guidebook" (*PMLA*, December, 1938), has offered evidence that Melville did own such a guidebook.

[7] *Herman Melville: The Tragedy of Mind* by William Ellery Sedgwick (Cambridge, Mass., 1944: Harvard University Press).

been born, in the actual course of his life it probably did not have this meaning.

Reading *Redburn* with the knowledge of what Melville was later to say, we are perhaps tempted to place upon things a conscious significance that was not in them, and his comment on the guidebook may be just such a reflection on the transience of things as any man might make had he Melville's talents. Finally, this matter is not really more meaningful if we succeed in giving a personal twist to it, then generalize therefrom. Norman Douglas once remarked that the wisdom of mankind resolves to a few platitudes—which, so far as that wisdom can be reduced to simple statement, is true enough; but the wisdom of mankind has its real existence in individual experience: it is potential in the platitude and realized in the person's full grasp of the platitude in his own activity. Melville's realization was by the writer's means, writing, and in the way he wrote of it we can achieve our realization too, joining in Redburn's "sad . . . solemn, and . . . most melancholy thought" where it is embodied with that quality of the particular which makes good art enduring.

THE SCHOOLMASTER AND THE HOODED PHANTOM

AFTER A RETURN VOYAGE THAT SAW MUCH BAD WEATHER AND an epidemic amongst a company of miserably cared-for Irish immigrants, Redburn landed in New York, where Captain Riga promptly did him out of his wages. The actual Melville who arrived in New York some time in October, 1837, cannot have profited much more from the trip than did Redburn, for on the last day of December of the same year we find him writing to his Uncle Peter Gansevoort from near Pittsfield, where he was teaching school:

My scholars are about thirty in number, of all ages, sizes, ranks, characters, & education; some of them who have attained the ages of eighteen can not do a sum in addition, while others have travelled through the Arithmatic; but with so great swiftness that they can not recognize objects on the road on a second journey: & are as about ignorant of them as though they had never passed that way before.

My school is situated in a remote and secluded part of the town about five miles from the village [under Washington Mountain], and the house at which I am now boarding is a mile and half from any other tenement whatever—being located on the summit of as savage and lonely a mountain as ever I ascended. The scenery however is most splendid & unusual, embracing an extent of country in the form of an Ampitheatre sweeping around for many miles & encircling a portion of your state in its compass.

The man with whom I am now domicilated is a perfect embodiment of the traits of Yankee character,—being shrewd bold & independant, carrying himself with a genuine republican swagger, as hospitable as "mine host" himself, perfectly free in the expression of his sentiments, and would as soon call you a fool or a scoundrel, if he thought so—as, button up his waistcoat.—He has reard a family of nine boys and three girls, 5 of whom are my pupils—and they all burrow together in the woods—like so many foxes.

After acknowledging receipt of John C. Taylor's *District School*, which his uncle perhaps sent him as a Christmas gift,[1] and commenting on it with several professional turns of phrase, the young schoolmaster expresses a thought that must have occurred since to many in his calling: "Orators may declaim concerning the universally-diffused blessings of education in our Country, and Essayests may exhaust their magazine of adje[ctives] in extolling our systim of common school instruction,—but when reduced to practise, the high and sanguine hopes excited by its imposing appearance in *theory*—are a little dashed." Twelve years later he noted in his travel diary that Rousseau, when a schoolmaster, "could have killed his scholars sometimes" and that Dr. Johnson had found teaching "intolerable".

The literary flourishes in this letter may be in part a mark of respect for Uncle Peter and in part a mark of Melville's respect for his own office as a schoolteacher, but they are also the indication of a more single-minded interest in literature. In the spring of 1839, Melville was teaching school at Greenbush, near Albany, and at this time he made two contributions to *The Democratic Press and Lansingburgh Advertiser* which show that he contemplated himself—not without admiration—through the lens of his reading and formed his thoughts according to the dictates of a lush and romantic style. The immature writer

[1] The Melville branch of the family may have followed the Scottish practice of gift-giving on New Year's, adopting the pagan holiday (not, of course, the Feast of the Circumcision) in preference to seeming to endorse the Papist celebration of the Nativity, since a number of gift copies of Melville's books have his inscription dated in January.

is rarely original; he is usually the sedulous ape, attempting to reproduce in literature his own experiences with literature, and the impact on him of the world of books is so fresh and marvelous, bringing in so much that he has not met in his own life, that he avoids the few subjects on which he might write with authority. Melville's newspaper pieces are immature even for a boy of nineteen and they are a further testimony to the solid innocence of Redburn. The figure that emerges from them is, or rather is intended to be, the figure that the gauche young man always elaborates in his reveries: sharp with disdainful wit, learned beyond anyone's expectation of youth, elegant, light-heartedly irresistible to the ladies, and (that least possible.of aspirations) not at all serious about himself. This is the adolescent ideal of the Dandy which Baudelaire spent his life in cultivating with such curious results; in Melville's life, the figure makes these two early, and normal enough, appearances, then is not seen for many years until he returns in the "Burgundy Club" exercises as the Marquis de Grandvin or Major Jack Gentian, grown of course considerably thicker about the waist and more benevolent in his outlook.

The first of these early fragments is an epistle—letter is hardly the word—addressed to "My dear M—" which reports with a wealth of literary allusions and irony at the expense of self how the writer has overcome the "hang-dog modesty" for which his correspondent used to upbraid him. Now, by finding in himself "the symmetry of the Phidian Jupiter . . . the idol of the women, and the admiration of the tailor" along with a mind "stored with universal knowledge, and embellished with every polite accomplishment", he is emboldened to lead the ladies in to supper while the other young men are left "like a drove of dumb cattle, strayed into the apartment, stumbling, blushing, stammering, and alone". We are not being unkind if we suppose that, really, it was Herman who stood in the parlor and some youth who did not even know the names of "old Burton" and "our gentle Coleridge" who "stepped forward and with a profound obeisance to the ladies . . . escorted them right gallantly and merrily to the banquet". Raymond M. Weaver, in his first edition of Melville's collected works,[2] notes that on the clipping of this "Fragment from a Writing-Desk" Melville had written in long hand: "When I woke up this morning, what the devil should I see but your cane along in bed with me. I shall keep it for you when you come up here again." So "my dear M——" may not have been a necessary fiction but another young man with whom Herman walked "the Broadway of our village with a certain air", exchanging literary allusions, pretending to feel no terror at the necessity of ogling the girls, and stopping for enough up-state beer to bring about an exchange of much-flourished sticks by bedtime.

If there was such a young man, sufficiently of a mind with Herman to be his ideal audience, he had addressed to him only one more "Fragment". Gothic and oriental in its atmosphere, this piece leaves the narrator in an apartment "fitted up in a style of Eastern splendor", "gracefully sinking on one knee" before "a creature, whose loveliness was of that spiritual cast that depended on no adventitious aid" and exclaiming: "Here do I prostrate myself, thou sweet Divinity, and kneel at the shrine of thy beauty." It cannot have been in quest of any such Lallah Rookh that Melville appeared eighteen months later, just after Christmas in 1840, in New Bedford, ready to go on a whaling voyage; but he was no doubt in quest of something the houri stood for, since the erotic images of a young man's imaginings may well intend other adventures. By the time that Melville came to write about his first setting out on a whaler,

---

[2] *The Works of Herman Melville* (*Standard Edition*) edited by Raymond W. [sic] Weaver (London, 1922–1924: Constable & Company).

he was no longer writing books of the straightforward, though not always factually accurate, autobiographical pattern that he had followed in four of his first five books, so when the "I" of *Moby-Dick* says going to sea is his "substitute for pistol and ball", we have not full warrant for supposing that Melville was equally desperate toward the end of 1840. Mr. Weaver, Melville's first full-length biographer,[3] however, accepts this and believes that "his desperate transit was made in the mid-winter of his discontent" and that, indeed, this was something recurrent in his life and of the five times Melville went to sea "the first four of these, at least, were instigated in desperation".[4] Other writers have variously conjectured that a revolt of his pupils and his failure as a schoolmaster drove him to sea, that a reading of *Two Years Before the Mast* inspired his venture (he afterwards wrote Dana that he had read the book in the latter part of 1840), that "the 'Invisible Police Officer of the Fates' knew more about the reason for Melville's voyage than he himself did",[5] or that he was after the historical white whale, Mocha-Dick, an account of which had appeared in a New York magazine in the same month as his "Fragments" in the Lansingburgh paper.

Probably all these motives combined to send Ishmael to sea and he took to ship in a state of mind no more single than Redburn's. To what extent Melville was Ishmael in the winter of 1840–1841 there is no way of telling: Ishmael—the "wild

[3] Possibly Melville was his own first biographer. The account of him in the Duyckincks' *Cyclopaedia of American Literature* (1855) is much concerned with his distinguished ancestry and the MS. for it, which survives in the Duyckinck Collection of the New York Public Library, has corrections and additions in Melville's hand. "The chirographical incoherencies of his manuscripts" (a phrase Melville used of Pierre) were often copied out by his sister Augusta for the printer.

[4] See his *Herman Melville: Mariner and Mystic* (New York, 1921: George H. Doran & Company) and his introduction to *Journal up the Straits*.

[5] *Herman Melville* by Lewis Mumford (New York, 1929: Harcourt, Brace & Company).

man; his hand . . . against every man, and every man's hand against him" (Gen. 16, 12)—may have been elected because he was appropriate to the mood of the story he was to narrate or because in 1850 Melville had begun to feel that there was something which set him apart in the society of his fellows or because there had been a touch of Ishmael-like wildness in him ten years before. Or, again, all three reasons may hold, for they do not exclude each other, any more than do the number of reasons that Ishmael himself says, in the first chapter of *Moby-Dick*, moved him to make a whaling voyage. ". . . I abominate," he says, "all honorable respectable toils, trials, and tribulations of every kind whatsoever." Stepping lively to the orders of "some old hunks of a sea-captain" may go a bit hard "if you come of an old established family in the land" and have lately "been lording it as a country schoolmaster", but in this "the universal thump is passed round" and, a most important consideration for a country schoolmaster, you are *"being paid,—* what will compare with it?" Further, "the Commodore on the quarter-deck gets his atmosphere at second from the sailors on the forecastle", though why Melville should have chosen the flavorsome air of a whaler in preference to that of a merchantman he cannot say altogether. But reviewing the hidden springs and motives, now that the plan of his book lies before him, they become a little plainer:

Chief among these motives was the overwhelming idea of the great whale himself. . . . Then the wild and distant seas where he rolled his island bulk; the undeliverable, nameless perils of the whale; these, with all the attending marvels of a thousand Patagonian sights and sounds, helped to sway me to my wish. . . . I love to sail forbidden seas, and land on barbarous coasts. Not ignoring what is good, I am quick to perceive a horror, and could still be social with it—would they let me—since it is but well to be on friendly terms with all the inmates of the place one lodges in.

By reason of these things, then, the whaling voyage was welcome; the great flood-gates of the wonder-world swung open, and in the wild conceits that swayed me to my purpose, two and two there floated into my inmost soul, endless processions of the whale, and, midmost of them all, one grand hooded phantom, like a snow hill in the air.

When Melville set sail on January 3rd, 1841, from New Bedford (or, to be exact, from Fair Haven on the north side of the Acushnet River), that town was the greatest whaling port in the world, and all its "brave houses and flowery gardens . . . were harpooned and dragged up . . . from the bottom of the sea". The whaling industry did not attain its maximum expansion until rather more than fifteen years after Melville's first acquaintance with it and, though it had a history of well over a century by that time, its "romance" would have had none of the antiquary flavor that is part of *Moby-Dick's* modern appeal. "Whaling," Charles Olson points out, "was production . . . and, in capital and function, forerunner to a later America, with more relation to Socony than to clippers and the China trade." [6] Mr. Olson apparently deduces from this that Melville had a prophetic faculty or, at least, *Moby-Dick* a prophetic substance. But, I think, we can also gather something else from the status of whaling as "production"; and this is that when Melville started out as a working whaleman, for him the exoticism of his trade lay mainly in the forbidden seas and barbarous coasts where it was plied. The whale—the one brute creature whose creation Genesis specifically mentions—would, of course, be an object of romantic awe, no matter how commercially pursued or used, but its pursuit was not romantic in the sense that we now speak of the "romance" of railroads, of meat-packing, or whatever. Whaling, absorbed into the vast

[6] *Call Me Ishmael* by Charles Olson (New York, 1947: Reynal & Hitchcock).

47

poetic trope that is *Moby-Dick*, did become a Romantic symbol (in the stricter sense of the adjective) capable of the widest extension; it was, however, Melville's genius which gave it this plurality of significances.

The *Pequod* on which Ishmael sailed was a veteran of fifty years' whaling; the *Acushnet* on which Herman Melville, "Age 21/ Height 5′ 9½″/ Complexion, dark/ Hair, brown", sailed as twentieth of a crew of twenty-six under Captain Valentine Pease had been completed only four days before she started on the maiden voyage that this one of her crew members would make so celebrated. The real events of the voyage cannot be determined from Melville's account of it, since it was not his intention that we should do so nor to give a typical account of a whaling cruise. Captain Valentine Pease cannot have been such a maleficently inspired tyrant as Captain Ahab, but Melville's first book—which begins with his deserting the *Acushnet* in the Marquesas and adheres fairly closely to the facts of his personal experience—indicates that Pease, though he may have lacked Ahab's rhetorical powers, was a man whose "prompt reply to all complaints and remonstrances was—the butt-end of a hand-spike". Melville's judgment on Captain Pease was not peculiar to himself, for he enlisted a comrade in his desertion, and a memorandum he made out in later years shows that eight other members of the crew, that "parcel of dastardly and mean-spirited wretches", likewise jumped ship, one of them insuring his escape by suicide. Four others "went ashore half dead", two with a "disreputable disease" and another "spitting blood". When after more than four years of cruising, the *Acushnet* put into New Bedford, the cargo she carried meant she could not have taken much over five whales for each year at sea, and Captain Pease, who was one of her owners, apparently decided to leave the arduous business of whaling to others, retired, and went to live "in asylum at the Vinyard".

The Schoolmaster and the Hooded Phantom

Scholarly investigations of the past fifteen years have shown that Melville's books about his travels in the South Seas do not have just the kind of authenticity that his critics (contemporary hostile ones excepted) supposed. This misconception was fostered as much by Melville as by anybody else. To the doubts expressed concerning the literalness of the adventures related in his first two books, he replied in a two-sentence preface to his third, the first sentence of which was: "Not long ago, having published two narratives of voyages in the Pacific, which, in many quarters, were received with incredulity, the thought occurred to me of indeed writing a romance of Polynesian adventure, and publishing it as such; to see whether the fiction might not, possibly, be received for a verity: in some degree the reverse of my previous experience." This tart statement raises a nice moral question concerning Melville's character, for he had not only rearranged his adventures according to the convenience of his art—with, to be sure, far better results than he might have got from a scrupulously literal narrative—but he had also borrowed heavily from other authors of Pacific voyages, frequently without acknowledgement though always with improvement. He seems hardly ever to have been false to facts or events in the places he describes, and the reality of a beachcomber's life in Polynesia in the forties or a common sailor's on a square-rigged man-of-war he evoked convincingly and accurately; but in all cases he presented these matters with the pretended authority of personal experience. For us, who actually know more of his wanderings in the Pacific than did his contemporaries and for whom his literary borrowings when recognized are examples of skill, his rather arrogant protestation of what he knew was not true does not impugn the deeper veracity of his work, but it does bring up the issue of his general trustworthiness.

A man may be not entirely trustworthy in matters of fact

49

without his being morally culpable: he may be incapable of exact observation or inclined to place his emotions prior to the evidences of his reason or simply careless. Melville's case was not of this kind; he was rather the man who says something he is deeply convinced is true—as it incidentally is—then gives evidence false in circumstance but not in itself to support his truth. When John Murray accepted *Typee* for publication, he did so only after having been assured of its authenticity. This he had from Melville's elder brother Gansevoort, who, we may suppose, had it from Herman. What we may infer from this is that the criterion of truth for Melville was not external; it was the inmost man by whom the final judgment was made, and against this interior person no affirmation or denial could prevail that he did not know through his own experience. Of course, in *Typee, Omoo,* and *White-Jacket* Melville appropriated experiences that were not his own, but the seal of worth was set on them because they corroborated what was his own. This analysis of his personality would be absurdly ponderous if it were made in connection with only the three books; but, starting with them, where it is easily grasped, we can see that the egocentricity of Melville's vision developed as he went on to more difficult things. Here two influences were at work and interactive: his Protestant heritage and his feeling that he was one of the "Isolatoes". The former made "conversion" the central thing in all experience—that interior happening by which the full extent of God's omnipotence was made known to a man and, in this same knowledge, he knew his election. The latter was to a great extent the former without its theological complexion—a kind of unique certainty which no external reference could make plain to others. In such a conviction, a thoroughgoing predestinarian might rest happy if his heart did not protest against the strange withdrawal it entailed; and a madman, too, might be held in a similar prison; but Melville, though he remained bound within himself by his allegiance to his own will, still had the clarity to see that in these circumstances "appallingly vacant as vast is the soul of man!" The simple fact that the soul cannot fill itself Melville never grasped, though he was to know in a terrible way the emptiness that testifies to this.

Melville's wanderings in the realm of thought were perhaps less affected by his wanderings in the South Seas than some of his critics have thought, but in both journeys he returned to the neighborhood of his starting place. Jean Simon points out that Melville's thought, "après un long et douloureux circuit", came back to much the same Calvinism it had started from; and the young voyager, who was then sailing away from this Calvinism, landed in Boston on October 3rd, 1844, only three months short of four years after leaving New Bedford. In those years, he had rounded Cape Horn both going and coming (the *Acushnet* did not follow the *Pequod's* course around the Cape of Good Hope), seen Peru, Chile, and the Galapagos, Marquesas, Society, and Hawaiian Islands. He had deserted one whaler and been party to the mildest sort of mutiny on another. In the Marquesas, he had been a captive or a guest of the Typees, though for considerably less than the four months which the first of his books announced. He had been a beach-comber in the Society Islands and a clerk in a store in Honolulu. Finally, in the course of getting home, he had served for more than a year as a sailor on the U. S. Frigate *United States,* a ship that a generation before had been commanded by Stephen Decatur.

In his old age, Melville wrote of

> Marquesas and glenned isles that be
> Authentic Edens in a Pagan sea

and said that he had "breathed primeval balm", but the history of the individual usually sufficiently recapitulates that of the race for him to remember something of Paradise in his youth. The voyage to Liverpool had carried young Herman beyond some of what appeared to be the certainties of 19th-century America, and his sailings in the South Seas made those universal pretensions even more questionable, especially as they were displayed in the effects of Protestant missionary zeal amongst the Polynesians. Both the destruction of Polynesian culture through its contact with the white man and the form the white man's culture took in the fo'c'sle of a whaler or among the "people" of a man-of-war were *points d'appui* for Melville's criticism of his time and its beliefs. In his third book, he wrote a far-ranging satirical allegory that had a Pacific archipelago for its scene, and the last story he wrote, in which the ways of God to man are justified at least to his own satisfaction, takes place on a battleship.

Had he never been in the whale fishery, lived with the natives of Nukuheva, and served as a man-of-war's man, it hardly needs saying that Melville's books would not have been the books we know, but surely the essential core of them would have been the same. The notion of the noble savage, it can be argued, is a dialectical development from the Calvinist hopelessness about man's condition, a radical pessimism that despairs of what man can do and wishes to strip him of almost all that he has done. If Melville fell into despair—and I think he did —he did not try to make himself comfortable in it by abjuring all the demands that had led to it and saying the final wisdom was to loll under a coconut palm. He was one

> . . . who so feels the stars annoy,
> Upbraiding him—how far astray!—
> That he abjures the simple joy,
> And hurries over the briny world away.

V

A THOUSAND PATAGONIAN SIGHTS AND SOUNDS

WHILE HERMAN WAS EATING ROAST PORK AND UNCOOKED FISH with cannibals, his elder brother Gansevoort was pursuing a career better suited to the two names he bore. He chose (as did his brother Allan) the course chosen by so many ambitious young men of his time—the law. In America perhaps more dignity attaches to the practice of law than does anywhere else because the American social structure is, in a sense, coeval with the Constitution, the source of law. Law might in time become a mere instrument, subservient to the purposes of an expanding industrial capitalism, but in Gansevoort Melville's age it still appeared the preordained pattern of the just and necessary which the growth of the social body would have to follow. Gansevoort and Allan opened an office at 10 Wall Street in New York, and in 1845 Gansevoort received an appointment in which may have lain the beginnings of a political future; he was made secretary of the American Legation in London under Minister Louis McLane. When he sailed late in 1845 to take his post in London, he carried with him the manuscript of Herman's first book. The imprint of a London publisher would give the book more prestige and, with Gansevoort on the spot to care for them, the financial arrangements would be better made.

Herman doubtless came back from the South Seas with many good stories for the family circle, "verbally repeated" with "frequency", but we need not suppose that it did not occur to him, as one of his memorialists has said, to put them in writing until a member of the family suggested it. The young school-master's letter to his Uncle Peter and his contributions to the Lansingburgh newspaper already show a rather specialized interest in literary expression, and *Typee* is something more complex than sailors' yarns written out. As Melville went through his Pacific adventures, he can hardly always have had the printed page in his mind's eye; but even then he must have had some acquaintance with the literature of Pacific voyages and compared what befell him with what he had read of, so that the agreement or disparity between books and life may well have suggested another book that would confirm or deny. When Melville told Hawthorne that all his growth had been from his twenty-fifth year, his ideal of the writer had become the Romantic figure who storms the heavens and asks the ultimate questions he knows cannot be answered; it was toward this he had made his growth. The author of *Typee* was obviously less ambitious, and as he sat writing his narrative in his mother's house in Lansingburgh or his Uncle Peter's in Albany,[1] he probably was content with the thought that this was a not too disagreeable way to earn a living, especially if in the end it led to the distinction of belonging to the Knickerbocker literary set and being seen in the Astor House with N. P. Willis or Fitz-Greene Halleck.

In London Gansevoort served Herman well, though this must have been one more drain on the life of a man who was to be dead before the year was half gone. On New Year's, 1846, he wrote in his diary that he had that day been to Baring Brothers "to discount the note Mr Jno Murray gave me for Herman's Mss., having now 7 mos to run & being for £100".

---

[1] Among the papers gathered together by Mrs. Abraham Lansing (Peter Gansevoort's daughter) is a sheet of manuscript that may be a first draft of *Typee*. A letter of Melville's to his sister Catherine shows he was in New York the first month of 1845. Some of his writing may have been done there because of the availability of books he needed to consult.

Murray was to publish the book in his Colonial and Home Library, a series of "popular reading for all classes" which included works by George Borrow, Washington Irving, and Charles Darwin. When Irving, on his way home from his ministry in Spain, stopped at the Legation, Gansevoort gave him the proofs of Herman's book to read and Irving "was very much pleased—declared portions to be 'exquisite', sd the style was very 'graphic' & prophesied its success". Gansevoort also arranged for the book's American appearance through the first George Palmer Putnam, who was then living in London in order to attend to the English branch of his firm. Putnam was "delighted with the opening chapters—sd that they kept him from church—that it had all the interest of Robinson Crusoe, superadded to that of being a work of fact—He expressed his desire to publish it in N Yk in Wiley & Putnam's Library of choice reading" on a royalty basis that would "give Herman 6¼ cts on each copy sold".[2] Gansevoort distributed a few copies where they would do the most good and when the first reviews appeared sent them to Herman. *The Athenaeum* dealt with it at length in successive numbers, and *The Examiner* and *The Critic* noticed it favorably. Indeed, in a few months even *le Journal des Débats* would devote two articles to *Typee*.

In America Evert Duyckinck, the editor of Wiley & Putnam's Library of Choice Reading, was impressed with the exoticism of the book by an American author which had come to him by way of London and wrote to Nathaniel Hawthorne (who reviewed books for the Salem *Advertiser*):

Next week a Frenchy coloured picture of the Marquesan islanders will appear in the Library from the pen of a Mr Melville, who, according to his story, was graceless enough to desert from a New England whale ship, preferring the society of cannibals to the interminable casks of corned beef and impracticable bread which

[2] A generous royalty, since the retail price of the book was fifty cents.

so afflicted his imagination in the hold of that vessel. It is a lively and pleasant book, not over philosophical, perhaps—but I will send you a copy.

Hawthorne sent a clipping of his review to Duyckinck. "The book," he said in the *Advertiser*, "is lightly but vigorously written. . . . The narrative is skilfully managed, and in a literary point of view, the execution of the work is worthy of the novelty and interest of its subject." When Hawthorne later came to know him, Melville would prove anything but "not over philosophical" and instead, as Hawthorne noted, always ready to talk "about time and eternity, things of this world and of the next . . . and all possible and impossible matters . . . deep into the night".

Melville's lively and pleasant book (and by any strict literary criterion it is no more) opens with the whaler *Dolly* approaching the Marquesas Islands after "six months out of sight of land; cruising after the sperm whale beneath the scorching sun of the Line, and tossed on the billows of the wide-rolling Pacific—the sky above, the sea around, and nothing else!" Though Melville implies that the *Dolly* put into the bay at Nukuheva,[3] the largest of the islands, in April of 1842, the *Acushnet* actually drew up there toward the end of June in the same year, and Captain Pease later filed an affidavit at Lahaina that Melville deserted the ship on July 9th.[4] Hard usage aboard her and the fact that one joined up for a whaling voyage for the duration decided him on this, he says.

[3] Actually Anna Maria Bay, but I have made no effort either to correct Melville's geography or to indicate where his spelling of Polynesian words departs from our present-day usage. Melville's spelling indicates a 19th-century American flatness in his pronunciation, e. g. *Happar* for *Hapa*, an instance also noted by Robert Louis Stevenson.

[4] Melville's Pacific wanderings have been carefully traced out by Charles Roberts Anderson in *Melville in the South Seas* (New York, 1939: Columbia University Press).

Some long-haired, bare-necked youths, who, forced by the united influences of Captain Marryat and hard times, embark at Nantucket for a pleasure excursion to the Pacific, and whose anxious mothers provide them with bottled milk for the occasion, oftentimes return very respectable middle-aged gentlemen. . . .

I heard of one whaler, which, after many years' absence was given up for lost. . . . After a long interval, however, [she] was spoken somewhere in the vicinity of the ends of the earth, cruising along as leisurely as ever, her sails all bepatched and bequilted with rope-yarns, her spars fished with old pipe stores, and her rigging knotted and spliced in every possible direction. Her crew was composed of some twenty venerable Greenwich-pensioner-looking old salts, who just managed to hobble about deck. . . .

Three pet sharks followed in her wake, and every day came alongside to regale themselves from the contents of the cook's bucket, which were pitched over to them. . . .

Such was the account I heard of this vessel and the remembrance of it always haunted me; what eventually became of her I never learned; at any rate she never reached home, and I suppose she is still regularly tacking twice in the twenty-four hours, somewhere off Buggerry Island, or the Devil's-Tail Peak.[5]

Along with these thoughts must have gone some of more positive delight—reminiscences of stories told by Thomas Wilson Melville of his visit to Nukuheva in the summer of 1829 or by his uncle Captain John De Wolf, who had been there in 1804 with the expedition of Adam Johann von Krusenstern, the first Russian to circumnavigate the globe. "The Marquesas! What strange visions of outlandish things does the very name spirit up! Lovely houris—cannibal banquets—groves of cocoanuts—coral reefs—tattooed chiefs—and bamboo temples; sunny valleys planted with bread-fruit trees—carved canoes dancing on the flashing blue waters—savage woodlands guarded by hor-

[5] These impolite names disappeared after the first edition and did not return until the Everyman's issue of 1907.

rible idols—*heathenish rites and human sacrifices.*" As the *Dolly* sailed into the harbor of Nukuheva, under the ignored directions of a drunken Royal Navy ex-lieutenant who was the pilot of the port, these travel-agency-folder anticipations of Melville's were somewhat ruffled when the bay proved to be already occupied by "six vessels, whose black hulls and bristling broadsides proclaimed their warlike character". They were a fleet under Admiral Dupetit-Thouars, who had shortly before taken possession of the islands "in the name of the invincible French nation". Melville expresses considerable distaste, as a matter of principle, for these imperial proceedings—"Four heavy, double-banked frigates and three corvettes to frighten a parcel of naked heathen into subjection! Sixty-eight pounders to demolish huts of cocoa-nut boughs, and Congreve rockets to set on fire a few canoe sheds!" Bad though this business is in itself, it is that much worse when carried out by the French, of whom he has a conventional Anglo-Saxon estimate: an over-elegant and sly people. "And yet, notwithstanding their iniquitous conduct in this and in other matters, the French have ever plumed themselves upon being the most humane and polished of nations."

Ashore on leave, Melville and another young sailor named Toby took the opportunity, when the rest of the party fell asleep in a canoe shed while waiting out a shower, to steal off and make their way into the mountains, to wait there until the ship should sail. Because they thought they would then not be searched for, they intended to go close to the valley of the Typees, whose "very name is a frightful one; for the word 'Typee' in the Marquesan dialect signifies a lover of human flesh".[6] Tom (as Melville named himself on this occasion)

---

[6] According to Mr. Anderson, who quotes Abbé Boniface Mosblech, the name when used by other tribes simply meant "enemy" and when used by the Typees of themselves probably meant something highly complimentary.

and Toby had concealed a little salt meat and sea biscuit in their blouses, thinking to live chiefly on fruit. But there was nothing edible on the heights, and they were forced to descend into what they thought was the valley of the Happars, a friendly tribe. Their descent was of necessity along a stream that flowed through a deep and narrow gorge and often passed over steep falls, and their progress was much hampered by Tom's badly inflamed leg. The actual distance traveled was slight but the difficulties of the course were enormous, so that the journey took the better part of a week, and when Tom and Toby reached the valley they were half-dead with hunger and exhaustion.

This arduous descent may not be well-received by the skeptical reader and the actual topography of Nukuheva hardly makes it seem probable, but it is a cleverly placed strand in the thread of suspense that holds Melville's story together. That story is largely contrived through various devices of anticipation (Happars or Typees? preparations for a cannibal feast or not?) and delay (the introduction of informative material interesting in itself)—the same devices that, more artfully used, are the basic ones in *Moby-Dick*. If this journey down the gorge seems too difficult for credence, it is worth noting that thirty-five years later Melville still had memories of something approximate to it and asked what "truant ship-boy overworn"

> . . . now adown the mountain dell
> (Till mine, by human foot untrod—
> Nor easy, like the steps to hell)
> In panic leaps the appalling crag? . . .

In the valley Tom and Toby encountered two young natives, male and female, who led them to what they shortly discovered to be a Typee settlement, where they were received with great kindness. In this little village and its immediate environs Tommo (which was the Typee embellishment of his name) remained for four months, after the first two weeks or so the only white man there, since Toby had left to get medical aid for Tommo's infected leg at Nukuheva—the redundant name of the island's chief settlement—whence he never returned. The Typees kept Tommo in a species of protective custody, toward what end he never was entirely sure, though a tabooed native of another tribe, the only outsider Tommo saw during his stay in the valley, told him they were holding him until his leg was healed and he the suitable object of a cannibal feast. During Tommo's stay with them, the Typees had two skirmishes with their hereditary enemies the Happars, and from the second of these skirmishes Tommo saw them return with some bundles slung from poles, which presumably contained the corpses of their foes. These, everything indicated, were utilized for a ceremonial feast to which only the warriors of the tribe were invited. Whether anthropophagy was ever practised by the Marquesans has not been established, but the restriction of the diners in the case Melville describes agrees with modern knowledge of primitive cannibalism. At last, with the help of the same native, Tommo managed to effect his escape, but not before he had killed with a boat hook an old one-eyed warrior who was trying to prevent his departure.

Other than a narrow escape from being tattooed, the physical adventures in this "narrative of a four months' residence among the natives of a valley of the Marquesas Islands" are confined to what might be called a prologue and an epilogue: the descent into the valley and the escape from it. These nicely balance the lotus-eater's interlude between, but even if Melville invented both episodes, and it is possible that his historical "escape" was a perfectly polite farewell, we need not suppose that they were contrived out of considerations of form more conscious than those that appear to any good storyteller; there is no symbolism intended by them. The chief figure in that interlude, and the one who captured the fancy of Melville's contemporaries, was the girl Fayaway; and she was, again, the typical figure of irresponsible delight recurrent in masculine erotic reverie. She was the noble savage in her most luscious feminine form (of which the Polynesian style of dress left very little to be conjectured), and Tommo's relationship with her was, at least so far as the book recounts, observant of the Albany standards of propriety to the extent that time and place would allow. Whatever the fancy of his readers added to Tommo's association with Fayaway—and this addition would be so much or so little as each one needed to complete his private idyll—his own account makes plain that when they were together they were almost always attended by her brother Kory-Kory, who had been appointed by King Mehevi of the Typees as Tommo's keeper under the appearance of being his body servant.

Though everything that befell Tommo did not befall Melville, *Typee* assumes that we shall identify the two, and Fayaway is the one figure of an amorous concern in Melville's life of which he gives us any personal record. Fayaway seems to have been a real enough person, for Lieutenant Henry Wise, who visited the Marquesas in 1848 and a year later published a book about his travels, had come across a girl of that name, but aside from her physical characteristics she has no more substance than the symbolically intended Yillah of *Mardi*, and it would seem that her effect on Melville was not very different from what it was on Melville's readers, for most of whom she was what W. H. Hudson's Rima was for a later generation. "I was the declared admirer of Miss Fayaway," states Melville, but when he describes the object of his admiration, perhaps it is not only the unskillfulness of the young writer that causes him to fall back on clichés—perhaps it is a deeper defect in vision, an organic inability sympathetically to see what he cannot identify with himself.

Her free pliant figure was the very perfection of female grace and beauty. Her complexion was a rich and mantling olive, and when watching the glow upon her cheeks I could almost swear that beneath the transparent medium there lurked the blushes of a faint vermilion. The face of this girl was a rounded oval, and each feature as perfectly formed as the heart or imagination of man could desire. Her full lips, when parted with a smile, disclosed teeth of a dazzling whiteness; and when her rosy mouth was opened with a burst of merriment, they looked like the milk-white seeds of the "arta", a fruit of the valley, which, when cleft in twain, shows them reposing in rows on either side, imbedded in the rich and juicy pulp. . . [etc.].

I may succeed, perhaps, in particularizing some of the individual features of Fayaway's beauty, but that general loveliness of appearance which they all contributed to produce I will not attempt to describe. The easy unstudied graces of a child of nature like this, breathing from infancy an atmosphere of perpetual summer, and nurtured by the simple fruits of the earth; enjoying a perfect freedom from care and anxiety, and removed effectually from all injurious tendencies, strike the eye in a manner which cannot be pourtrayed. This figure is no fancy sketch; it is drawn from the most vivid recollections of the person delineated.

These vivid recollections Melville was apparently entertaining while he was courting Elizabeth Shaw, for *Typee* is "affectionately inscribed" to her father, "Lemuel Shaw, Chief Justice of the Commonwealth of Massachusetts". It may even be that Melville's Calvinism strengthened him in these recollections, though it was none of its intended offices to do so. For, if the flesh as matter is evil, and especially as it obtrudes itself in day-to-day affairs, its images of delight are nevertheless not to be completely eradicated and will be that much more readily entertained when they are located in a realm, partly ideal and partly mnemonic, which seems real but no longer material.

Tommo's attachment to Fayaway was no more finally binding than Melville's and he left her "sobbing indignantly" and to be comforted with a roll of cotton cloth, and passed on to the adventures related in *Omoo*. When fourteen months later Melville again saw Nukuheva, it was from the deck of a man-of-war as a sailor who was not given shore leave.

Not only was Fayaway's beauty owing to "an atmosphere of perpetual summer" but also nearly everything else that was enjoyable in the valley of the Typees. Though Melville's comparisons of "barbarism" and civilization are often to the disadvantage of the latter, he evidently was not proposing anything systematic: it was simply a matter of observation that certain things were better ordered in Polynesia thanks to the accident of climate. ". . . The continual happiness, which so far as I was able to judge appeared to prevail in the valley, sprung principally from that all-pervading sensation which Rousseau has told us he at one time experienced, the mere buoyant sense of a healthful physical existence." Melville added to this a recognition of the human dignity of the Marquesans, which, in practice at any rate, the white pioneers in the Pacific were inclined to overlook. He suggested that a number of Marquesans sent to the United States as missionaries might there perform as much good as an equal number of American missionaries sent to the Marquesas, but the implication in this was that the Marquesan daily behavior respected the Western ethical code better than did that of those who were the code's evangelists.

On the subject of American missionaries in Polynesia Melville was bitter and he obviously condemned them as a class despite his protest that he was rebuking only those who had failed in their duties. Possibly he believed the South Seas islanders would have been as well off without Christianity as with it, and this thought would not have been unnatural to a man who in time came to think that Christianity put an obligation on the soul that, though inescapable, was greater than it could meet. If this was his belief, it was fortified by his observation that the introduction of Christianity was always concurrent with native decay. But he did point out that the natives were only nominally Christianized; they lost the natural or pagan morality they once had; their lands were appropriated and—quite literally in Hawaii—they were degraded to the function of draught animals; syphilis was introduced among them; and in the process of extinguishing heathenism the heathens were extinguished as well.

Melville's criticism of the Protestant missionaries was made from a Protestant basis which minimized the sacramental aspect of religion, and presumably he saw the missionaries' function as one of carrying to the Polynesians the code of behavior that could be deduced from the Sermon on the Mount. Since a rather similar code is found in the teaching of most sages, the success of the missionaries was dependent on their personal virtue rather than on any unique thing they could carry to the people of the South Seas. Further, in introducing certain practices European rather than Christian, they divorced the people of the South Seas from the simple society in which the practice of their natural virtues had not been too difficult and united them to one in which the observance of the Golden Rule was all but impossible. Neither in *Typee* nor *Omoo* did Melville say this explicitly, but if we combine his skepticism about the benefits of Christianity to the Polynesians with his later questioning of religion, such a rationale for his attitude toward the missionaries seems indicated. "That greatest real miracle of all religions" was the Sermon on the Mount, he said in *Pierre*, yet he was certainly doubtful that its wisdom was applicable to this world and probably doubtful that God had spoken it. If the final wisdom was folly and carried no divine sanction, then it was just as well to keep it from the happy valley where "blue devils, hypochondria, and doleful dumps, went and hid themselves among the nooks and crannies of the rocks".

Omoo was published a year after *Typee*. It is concerned with the five or six months during which Melville sailed on the whaler that took him off Nukuheva, then lived on the Society Islands, first in jail on Tahiti as a mutineer and later as a beachcomber on the adjacent island of Imeeo. It is a "rounder" book than *Typee* for a number of reasons: Melville had had the experience of writing the earlier book; the time span of *Omoo* pretty much accorded with the actual time span of the adventures he drew on; and the characters he presented he had known longer and had not been separated from by the barrier of language. Though a large number of the characters in it are identifiable and most of its statements have been verified, the book is not especially revealing of Melville himself, and this is precisely because it adheres to the statement in its subtitle: *A Narrative of Adventures in the South Seas*. Oddly enough, in the books in which he presents himself directly to the public view—*Typee, Omoo, Redburn,* and *White-Jacket*—Melville is the least concerned with his own personality; in these books he appears merely as the observing agent and the "man who lived among cannibals" (as he later regretfully described himself to Hawthorne). When Melville came to deal with his personal problems and the metaphysical problems they entailed, the latter loomed so large that he was not much concerned to link them with the events of his day-to-day life—which has caused much puzzlement and labor to those of his critics who have sought to establish in his life and works a unity that is not there. There is a constant temptation to suppose that we shall understand a man's work better when we know more about the man, and this is accompanied by another temptation to raise a consistent, but entirely supposititious, figure of the man with which his books are made forcibly to accord. Melville, enigmatic as a person and the writer of allegorical works with no especially evident key, always invites to such an enterprise.

Melville calls the ship in which he left Nukuheva some time in August of 1842 the *Julia*—the name, it may be, of the next vessel on which he shipped and which carried him from the Society Islands to the Sandwich Islands. His account of the month or so he spent on this first ship (the *Lucy Ann*, an old Canadian-built barque, out of Sydney under Captain Vinton), sailing in a generally westward direction whither only the first mate knew, contains some of the funniest passages in Melville's writing. The captain, "quite a young man, pale and slender, more like a sickly counting-house clerk than a bluff sea-captain", was "no more meant for the sea than a hair-dresser" and had no more authority over the crew, who called him "The Cabin Boy" and "Paper Jack"—on one occasion even to his face, into which at the same time a pot of tea was thrown. This "dapper little fellow in nankeen jacket and white canvas pumps" kept pretty much to his cabin, from sickness and terror, and left the running of the ship to the chief mate, the only officer remaining, since the two other mates had deserted and the ship's doctor had exiled himself to the foc's'le after knocking out the captain in a political argument. The chief mate was "the beau ideal of the efficient race of short thick-set men" and the only man aboard who could navigate; "he abhorred all weak infusions, and cleaved manfully to strong drink" and with "his quadrant, a rusty old thing, so odd-looking that it might have belonged to an astrologer" he sometimes "went staggering about deck, instrument to eye, looking all over for the sun—a phenomenon which any observer might have seen right overhead". Next in degree of drunkenness were the carpenter and the cooper, who had found a way into the ship's store of "Pisco"—a Peruvian liquor much used in the Pacific at that time. Since the carpenter and cooper were generous in sharing what they stole, the rest of the crew were only slightly less intoxicated than they, and even the sick—some of whom may have been malingerers but two of whom died at sea—were liberally dosed with pisco. Since there seems to have been hardly any changing of sail or course and watch was kept in the most casual fashion, the crew had not much more to occupy themselves than pisco, complaints about the miserable food (condemned Navy stores auctioned off in Sydney), and conjectures as to where they were sailing—to a whaling ground, said the mate, known to no one but himself, where the whales scratched their backs on the ship's sides and a full cargo would be put away in a week.

The doctor, who was called Doctor Long Ghost because of his tall and emaciated person, apparently thought that his resignation relieved him of any duty to look after the sick sailors. Melville makes no comment on this inhumanity, even though he himself was still suffering from his inflamed leg when he came aboard, and it is interesting to reflect that not much more than a hundred years ago the idea of the self-dedication of the physician was not yet current. Indeed, the heroic and selfless man in white whose calling is a sufficient end in itself first comes into literature, so far as I know, in Somerset Maugham's *Of Human Bondage* and does not appear at all in the 19th century. However, Melville's portrait of Dr. Long Ghost is intended as that of an engaging rascal with a touch of mystery about him.

. . . From whatever high estate Doctor Long Ghost might have fallen, he had certainly at some time or other spent money, drunk Burgundy, and associated with gentlemen.

As for his learning, he quoted Virgil, and talked of Hobbes of Malmsbury, besides repeating poetry by the canto, especially Hudibras. He was, moreover, a man who had seen the world. In the easiest way imaginable, he could refer to an amour he had in Palermo, his lion hunting before breakfast among the Caffres, and the quality of the coffee to be drunk in Muscat; and about these places, and a hundred others, he had more anecdotes than I can tell of. Then such mellow old songs as he sang, in a voice so round and racy, the real juice of sound. How such notes came forth from his lank body was a constant marvel.

Dr. Long Ghost chose Melville, the only fully literate member of the crew, as his especial companion, loaned him his few books, and played chess with him. Mr. Anderson has discovered that the doctor in real life bore, for a time at any rate, the name of John Troy, and M. Simon suggests that he may have been the son of Alan Cunningham, whose "A Wet Sheet and a Flowing Sea" Melville quotes in *Redburn*. Lewis Mumford hazards that "the doctor was a capital fellow to finish off Melville's education" and a sort of "picaresque library", and doubtless he did show the young man that learning could be a considerable personal adornment for even such a laudanum-taking rogue as the doctor was. A less favorable influence is laid to the doctor by Van Wyck Brooks,[7] who thinks that Dr. Long Ghost's recitations from *Hudibras* may have decided Melville on the unhappy use of tetrametric couplets when he set out, in *Clarel*, to write a philosophical poem with the physical bulk of the contemporary two-decker novel. This would have been the most long-lasting of the doctor's influences; Melville kept in Long Ghost's company all the time he was in the Society Islands, but the period of that sojourn was perhaps the only time when Melville's behavior was not irreproachably "respectable".

Toward the end of his stay on Imeeo, Melville tells us, a kindly native produced for his reading, from the chest of a deceased sailor, copies of *Peregrine Pickle* and *Ferdinand Count Fathom*, and there is in *Omoo* what Mr. Sedgwick calls "the

[7] "Notes on Herman Melville" in *Emerson and Others* (New York, 1927: E. P. Dutton & Company).

68

broad *genre* realism of the eighteenth century" which obviously owes something to Smollett. The following scene has been quoted by Mr. Mumford as an instance of Melville's accurate ear for dialogue, and in rebuttal of Robert Louis Stevenson's statement that Melville had no ear for living speech at all,[8] but it seems worth repeating here as an example of the book's general tone and pervasive good spirits. Ropey was an unfortunate baker who had taken to sea when his wife "ran off with his till and his foreman" and who, as an irreclaimable landsman, was the butt of the crew.

The watch below, just waked from their sleep, are all at breakfast; and Ropey, in one corner, is disconsolately partaking of its delicacies. Now, sailors newly waked are no cherubs; and therefore not a word is spoken, everybody munching his biscuit, grim and unshaven. At this juncture, an affable-looking scamp—Flash Jack—crosses the forecastle, tin can in hand, and seats himself beside the landlubber.

"Hard fare this, Ropey," he begins; "hard enough, too, for them that's known better and lived in Lun'nun. I say now, Ropey, s'posing you were back to Holborn this morning, what would you have for breakfast, eh?"

"Have for breakfast!" cried Ropey, in a rapture. "Don't speak of it!"

[8] Toby addressed Tom in this fashion when they were about to climb down "a rocky precipice of nearly a hundred feet in depth . . . over which the wild stream poured in an unbroken leap": "The result of my observations you wish to know, do you? . . . Well, my lad, the result of my observations is very quickly imparted. It is at present uncertain which of our two necks will have the honor to be broken first; but about a hundred to one would be a fair bet in favor of the man who takes the first jump." Toby was supposed to be a person of some refinement, and he therefore was made to speak in the convention proper to such a person. He probably even thought of himself as speaking in this manner. When Melville recorded the speech of persons of no education, he doubtless came closer to what was actually said, though even here there had to be the observance of a convention of some kind, since the unmeditated speech of anyone is too repetitious, elliptical, and tedious for written dialogue. The good writer of dialogue of course catches the spoken rhythm and *timbre*.

"What ails that fellow?" here growled an old sea-bear, turning round savagely.

"Oh, nothing, nothing," said Jack: and then, leaning over to Rope Yarn, he bade him go on, but speak lower.

"Well, then," he said, in a smugged tone, his eyes lighting up like two lanterns, "well, then, I'd go to Mother Moll's that makes the great muffins: I'd go there, you know, and cock my foot on the 'ob, and call for a noggin o' somethink to begin with."

"And what then, Ropey?"

"Why then, Flashy," continued the poor victim, unconsciously warming with his theme; "why then, I'd draw my chair up and call for Betty, the gal wot tends to customers. Betty, my dear, says I, you looks charmin' this mornin'; give me a nice rasher of bacon and h'eggs Betty my love; and I wants a pint of h'ale, and three nice h'ot muffins and butter—and a slice of Cheshire; and Betty, I wants—"

"A shark-steak, and be hanged to you!" roared Black Dan, with an oath. Whereupon, dragged over the chests, the ill-starred fellow is pummeled on deck.

The captain's illness did not respond to a hot bath which Dr. Long Ghost at last prescribed, and Jermin, the mate, was forced to turn back from his haunt of tame whales and take the *Julia* to Papeetee. From here the crew refused to take the ship to sea again despite the injunctions of the local British consul and they were put in chains aboard one of Admiral Dupetit-Thouars' frigates that seemed always to be at Melville's ports of disembarkation in the Pacific. Next they were transferred to the "Calabooza Beretanee" or English jail, where they remained until the *Julia* had raised a new crew and sailed. Released from jail, Melville and Long Ghost wandered about Tahiti and Imeeo, putting up as the guests of the hospitable natives, making a pretense of working for a Yankee and an Englishman who were potato-growers, witnessing one of the native dances that the missionaries had forbidden, using the product of what was probably the first bootlegger to appear in American literature (the missionaries had also forbidden the Tahitians to make or use intoxicants), and attempting to gain an audience with Queen Pomaree for the purpose of getting into her employ.

Failing in this last endeavor, Melville decided to ship on a whaler that was lying by to augment her crew and he was put to some trouble to prove to her captain, a man from Marthas Vineyard, that he was an American and not one of the mutiny-provoking sort from Sydney. The captain, after a meal of taro pudding and baked pig and two bottles of wine, was convinced of Melville's American birth by feeling his pulse, but Long Ghost, he insisted, was a Sydney "bird"—which indeed he may have been. Leaving Dr. Long Ghost on Imeeo with some Spanish silver dollars the captain of the *Leviathan* had advanced, Melville once more set out on the wide Pacific to cruise "for whale off the coast of Japan". But whether he sailed on the *Leviathan* toward Japan or on the Australian brig *Julia* northward to Honolulu or on yet another ship that eventually put in at Maui is not definitely known.

From what has been said it will be evident that neither *Typee* nor *Omoo* occupies a high place in the Melville canon. Were they his only books, their chief value would be as an eyewitness' accounts of the South Seas islands before the white man had completely changed their original aspect (even allowing for Melville's use of written sources). Nor, related to the rest of Melville's work, do they seem so important as some critics estimate them. Mr. Sedgwick finds in *Typee* the expression of "a universal truth about human consciousness", the "embodiment of the world as we have all felt in the glow and rapture of youthful love, whatever the object of that love". Richard Chase [9] discovers in the captivity in the "Happy Valley" and

[9] "An Approach to Melville", *Partisan Review*, May–June, 1947.

the useless leg significances which, since he takes the Freudian approach, it would be gratuitous to point out here but which he apparently holds prevail throughout Melville's writing. And the more sociologically minded critics have found in his contrasts of Marquesan and American life a basic condemnation of the latter involving a Rousseauistic attitude toward the development of society.

Aside from Mr. Chase's analysis, which rests on a *petitio principii* with which it is impossible to argue, these estimates are not entirely wide of the mark. Both books are the products of youth; they show an appetite for new experience, a quick and skeptical eye for any contradiction in the surface aspect of things, and there is everywhere in them abundant evidence of what George Santayana, perhaps meaning something a little more subtle, has called animal faith. It is an attractive enough Melville who is seen in these pages, even though, as has been mentioned, he lacks here and there in entire objective honesty.

We may assume there was still some of Redburn's stiffness and Redburn's pretensions—when a Tahitian girl is looking at him as an object of curiosity in the stocks at the Calabooza Beretanee, he disposes himself in an attitude of Byronic melancholy —but he made a point of befriending poor Rope Yarn and he is a spokesman for the human rights of the Polynesians, pointing out "that the more ignorant and degraded men are, the more contemptuously they look upon those whom they deem their inferiors". There have been those who wished Melville had remained the joyous young traveler in "old Mendanna's sea", returning home only to bring for the less enterprising reminiscences of a whole series of valleys

> Where the breadfruit fall
> And the penguin call
> And the sound is the sound of the sea

and had not become the angry voyager of metaphysical spaces. If some of us, as Mr. Sedgwick says, know the valley of Typee in our youth, all of us ineluctably sail toward the metaphysical spaces, and it is an elementary prudence to know something of them in this life before we meet them in the next.

VI

AMONG THE PALTERERS
OF THE MART

IN 1848 BAYARD TAYLOR, ALREADY A VERY SUCCESSFUL AUTHOR
at the age of twenty-three, wrote to his fiancée telling her,
among other things, how busy he was. One of the non-remu-
nerative jobs he had on hand was to turn out a series of verses
for a Valentine's Day party that Anne Charlotte Lynch was to
give at her Waverley Place house. Miss Lynch's was perhaps
the foremost literary salon in New York; Horace Greeley
(Taylor's employer) went there, as did Poe, Bryant, Margaret
Fuller, even Emerson on at least one occasion, N. P. Willis,
and Ik Marvel (probably the first New York literary person to
"restore" a run-down Connecticut farm). Among the celebrities
attending the party was Herman Melville and for him Taylor
wrote:

> Bright painter of those tropic isles,
>   That stud the blue waves, far apart,
> Be thine, through life, the summer's smiles,
>   And fadeless foliage of the heart
> And may some guardian genius still
>   *Taboo* thy path from every ill.

Melville had only two books to his credit and his contributions to the periodical press were anonymous (and apparently
not paid for), but there was something like a vogue for those
two books: they were widely commented on in the magazines
and newspapers and even the few attacks on Melville's veracity

made by the defenders of the missionaries added to the interest in the books. Melville had engaged a nearly equal amount of attention in England in much the same proportion of praise and abuse; there had been two articles about him in a French paper which their author, Philarète Chasles, a professor in the College of France, would include in a book discussing Anglo-American literature; and the month of the party he had received an offer for a German translation of his work. The attentions he had received, or would receive, indicate that there was one of those little eddies of publicity about him such as today appear in the literary stream when a very youthful, very adventurous, or very obscene author breaks water. Melville in his time was a little of all three—though as regards the last it should be noted that the expurgations which were made for the second edition of the book (perhaps by the author himself rather than by Evert Duyckinck, who has been held responsible for them [1]) were prompted by a delicacy of which only his age was capable. Sara Jane Lippincott, under her pen name of Grace Greenwood, published an inept but friendly parody of *Typee* in *The Saturday Evening Post*; William Ellery Channing II wrote a hundred couplets called "The Island Nukuheva" with only the second quality of his "sublimo-slipshod" style; Ik Marvel spoke of a *Typee* disorder that "attacked with peculiar virulence adventurous schoolboys, and romantic young ladies who had an eye for nature"; and Willis mentioned Melville's "cigar and his Spanish eyes".

Melville's introduction to New York literary society, both in the flesh and in print, was largely the work of Evert Augustus Duyckinck. Duyckinck, who was three years Melville's senior, was the son of the first publisher in New York. He studied law

---

[1] Arthur Stedman in his introduction to an 1892 edition of *Typee* speaks of "a few paragraphs excluded by written direction of the author."

at Columbia College and took his M.A. there in 1838, in which year he made his European tour. Well off enough to take to literature yet live comfortably, he edited in 1841 and 1842 a literary monthly called *Arcturus* in association with Cornelius Mathews, a writer of wide popularity in his time but today of little interest except to literary resurrectionists. Melville, as has been said, came to Duyckinck's attention when the latter was the editor of Wiley & Putnam's Library of Choice Reading. When Duyckinck, along with his younger brother George, became an editor of *The Literary World*, the period's chief literary weekly, Melville was much dealt with in its pages; each of his books was treated sympathetically and most of them more than once. Duyckinck was a devoted collector of books and his library was one of the largest then in New York. Melville borrowed frequently from it, and his borrowings are indicated not only in the list of them which Duyckinck kept but also in Melville's own writings, where the influences of Rabelais, Browne, and Carlyle are the most obvious. We may imagine that the conversation of Duyckinck and his circle of friends had some educative value for Melville, who probably first came amongst them as a rather extraordinary sailor but for whom Duyckinck developed a very real friendship, continuing to see Melville, during the years when Melville mixed little in society of any kind, until his own death in 1878.

The man who does not understand himself—or, since no man understands himself, the man who does not understand that he cannot be an external object of his own knowledge makes an excessive demand in friendship, for he wishes his friends to realize for him the knowledge he is unable to gain alone. ("It is because we ourselves are in ourselves, that we know ourselves not," says Babbalanja the philosopher in *Mardi*.) When we come to examine Melville's association with Hawthorne, we shall see that he made a demand of this sort;

but it was apparently the only time he did so.[2] To be provoked to this demand Melville had first to overcome his prevailing reserve, and this doubtless could only be brought about by some feeling of identity, since the lonely man, of whom Melville would in later years become an almost classic figure, is nearly always the proud one who looks at others to see his own face.

At the time of his first acquaintance with Evert Duyckinck, Melville had not begun descending into "the heart of man; descending into which is as descending a spiral stair in a shaft, without any end, and where the endlessness is only concealed by the spiralness of the stair, and the blackness of the shaft". There was in 1847 and 1848 more light in his world and he moved towards objects quicker arrived at. That Duyckinck took his place as one of the solid objects in this world, definite and limited according to the kind of person he was, hardly means, as one of Melville's biographers has suggested, that he failed Melville. Duyckinck was an admirer of Coleridge, and so could hardly have been averse to the discussion of metaphysics, but he was a man for whom there were no large uncertainties; he was comfortable in his Episcopalianism and his real gentility, his collecting of books, his family (on the rare occasions he was away from his wife, he wrote her daily), his careful records of his expenses and correspondence, and in those masculine gatherings—at once social, literary, mildly alcoholic, and of an ordered informality—which seem to have disappeared with the 19th century. One of these occasions he noted on October 6th, 1847:

The Art Union opened its new rooms to night in its Broadway quarters in the rear of Mr. Cram's former dwelling house—a long

[2] Jack Chase, the British seaman on an American man-of-war whom Melville eulogized in *White-Jacket* and to whom he dedicated his last work, may have been, after Hawthorne, the friend for whom Melville had the deepest feelings. But we know no more about their friendship than will allow us to suppose it was the usual attachment of a young man to an older one, kindly and of unusual talents.

hall, well lighted, the walls covered with paintings by Cole, Page, Brown, Gignoux, Hicks &c, the floor well sprinkled with good fellows, the artists generally of fine personal appearance, a selection from the Press. Frank Parton brought me a ticket of invitation, and Herman Melville dropping in, I carried him along, introducing him to Mr. Bryant and others. One of Sully's bathing nymphs suggested Fayaway. Lanman introduced me to Mount the humorous painter, of a fine and even beautiful countenance. There was supper, and punch, a liquor according to the ordinary in Jonathan Wild nowhere spoken against in Scripture. The practice on this occasion was purely canonical. Mr. George Gibbs in a speech of solid impudence drew out Colton of the Whig Review,[3] as the head of the leading magazine. Colton, whose ordinary state is that of a crack ship under a pretty heavy press of canvas was in a state of high art. Thumping an inverted wineglass on the table he began and rivalled an infuriated Dutch windmill in the flourishes of his arms. It was a circular speech also, revolving on a single idea or rather half a dozen words loud sounding among which was Platonic—the oysters probably representing the plates and the punch, the tonic. Mount and Melville were delighted with this living tableau. Matteson told a couple of good stories, with appropriate action & told them well.

Melville's attendance at affairs of this kind was perhaps more frequent after his marriage, for in the three years between that event and his return from the Pacific he seems to have lived mainly at his mother's house in Lansingburgh, though he must have been a frequent visitor to Boston to pay his court to Elizabeth Shaw and to New York to attend his interests there. First amongst the latter there was the new edition of *Typee*, with its expurgations and a supplement containing a curious vindication

[3] Variously called *The American Whig Review* and *The American Review: A Whig Journal*, this was one of the few native periodicals to treat Melville's books unfavorably. The issue of the July before the Art Union gathering contained a personally vituperative attack on *Omoo*, written by George Washington Peck, accusing its author of pornographic intentions and sexual impotence.

of the book's authenticity. How luck attended Melville in his first book is explained in the following letter, written to Evert Duyckinck in July, 1846, from Lansingburgh:

There was a spice of civil scepticism in your manner, my dear Sir, when we were conversing together the other day about "Typee"—What will the politely incredulous Mr. Duyckinck now say to the true Toby's having turned up in Buffalo, and written a letter to the Commercial Advertiser of that place, vouching for the truth of all that part (which has been considered the most extraordinary part) of the narrative, where he is made to figure.—

Give ear then, oh ye of little faith—especially thou man of the Evangelist [4]—and hear what Toby has to say for himself.—

Seriously, my dear Sir, this resurection of Toby from the dead—this strange bringing together of two such places as Typee and Buffalo, is really very curious.—It can not but settle the question of the book's genuineness. The article in the C. A. with the letter of Toby [in which Toby had said "I am happy to testify to the entire accuracy of the work so long as I was with Melville"] can not possibly be gainsaid in any conceivable way—therefore I think it ought to be pushed into circulation. I doubt not but that many papers will copy it—Mr. Duyckinck might say a word or two on the subject which would tell . . . I have written Toby a letter & expect to see him soon & hear the sequel of the book I have written (How strangely that sounds!)

Bye the bye, since people have always manifested so much concern for "poor Toby", what do you think of writing an account of what befell him in escaping from the island—should the adventure prove to be of sufficient interest?—I should value your opinion very highly on this subject.

And in a postscript, which indicates how vexed he was by any questioning of the literal truth of his book, he added:

Possibly the letter of Toby might by some silly ones be regarded

[4] A reference to the reviewer for *The New York Evangelist*, whose skepticism about *Typee* had been more spicy than civil.

as a hoax—to set you right on that point, altho' I only saw the letter last night for the first time—I will tell you that it alludes to things that no human being could ever have heard of except Toby. Besides the Editor seems to have seen him.

Melville hurried to Buffalo—or to Darien in Genesee County, where according to the editor of *The Buffalo Commercial Advertiser* Richard Tobias Greene's father was "a respectable farmer"—to get from Toby the material for his supplement, the manuscript of which he sent to Duyckinck before the end of the month. He and Toby corresponded occasionally over the next fifteen years and Toby, who had taken to journalism, whether inspired to write by the example of his old companion or by some occult influence on the *Acushnet* and in the Marquesas, named his son Herman Melville and must have had a part in giving the same name to a nephew.

On December 7th of the same year Melville arrived in New York "from the East" (presumably Boston) and wrote to Duyckinck asking him to look at "a new book in M. S." and saying "I address you now as not being in any way connected with Messrs W & P but presume to do so confidentially as a friend". In any case, "Messrs W & P" did not publish *Omoo* but Harper & Brothers, who, according to a story reported by Victor Hugo Paltsits, had rejected *Typee* because "it was impossible that it could be true and therefore was without real value". When Melville turned up with the manuscript of his second book, Harper was at the door, leaving for Europe; a copy reader ran out with the news. " 'Take it at once,' said Mr. Harper, jumping into his carriage and driving off." [5]

With *Omoo* accepted Melville presumably did not at once

[5] "Herman Melville's Background and New Light on the Publication of *Typee*" in *Bookman's Holiday: Notes and Studies Written and Gathered in Tribute to Harry Miller Lydenberg* (New York, 1943: The New York Public Library).

begin work on his next book, which was to appear two years later and be (after the first hundred pages) so unlike his previous ones. He turned out a few reviews of books for *The Literary World* and a series of seven humorous articles for *Yankee Doodle*, an attempt at an American *Punch* edited by Duyckinck's friend Mathews. These articles were anecdotes, of Paul Bunyan-like exaggeration, about General Zachary Taylor, "the hero of Palo Alto", who was then being built up as the Whig candidate for the presidential election of 1848. They are described by Mr. Thorp, otherwise judicious in his estimates, as "hilarious", but their humor about tacks on saddles, wayward cannon-balls, and the exhibition of Old Zack's breeches at Barnum's Museum would be painful today even if one did not know by whom they had been written. Old Zack survived this kind of thing (or, the mysteries of a popular election being what they are, profited by it) and was chosen President, but *Yankee Doodle*, of which the articles were typical, did not last to celebrate the victory, expiring after a year of publication.

Authentic Anecdotes of "Old Zack" ran from July 24th to September 11th, 1847, and in all likelihood they were turned out in casual haste by their author, for on August 4th he married Elizabeth Shaw. The marriage must have seemed like the realization of a love older than both the bride and the groom and a union of the families long delayed, for Justice Shaw had once been the suitor of Nancy Melville, Herman's aunt, who had died while they were still engaged. About Melville's first love for Elizabeth we know very little; there are no surviving letters of his courtship or his early married years, and in his books the only figure that bears any sort of resemblance to Elizabeth—Lucy in *Pierre*—lacks substance as much as any other woman amongst his characters. That shortly after his marriage he should have begun writing a book about a hopeless

Melville

and impossible love seems a justification for supposing that his
life with Elizabeth failed of some rapture he had expected; but
it also seems that the expectation is far more open to criticism
than Elizabeth is. The intimacies of Melville's relationship
with his wife and his earlier attitude toward her we do not
know; what is said about them must be conjectural. We do
know, from Elizabeth's letters, that her devotion to Herman
was entire and her great repect for him enduring, and it would
be at once insolent and unjust to ascribe these to a false Victorian humility, a business of a woman's knowing "her place".
We know, too, from a group of poems Herman presented to
her in later years that his affection for her had by that time
run very deep, and the title he gave to the group recalled "how
often" he had "come . . . early in the bright summer mornings of old, with a handful of these cheap little cheery roses of
the meek, newly purloined from the fields to consecrate them
on that bit of maple-wood mantel—your altar, somebody called
it—in the familiar room facing your beloved South!" The cheap
little cheery roses were red-clover blossoms, and he reminded
her, as he had done yearly, that he had found a four-leaved one
"by the wayside on the early forenoon of the fourth day of a
certain bridal month, now four years more than four times ten
years ago".⁶

Quite possibly the love expressed here is the product of a
wisdom the young Melville did not have, which had taken a
lifetime to acquire, and, like all love, it must have rested on the
admission of man's limitation and his need of what is other than
himself. The hero of *Mardi*, seeking the lost girl Yillah
through most of the book and knowing at last he cannot have
her, ends his story with himself fleeing "over an endless sea",
pursued by the "three fixed specters" who have pursued him
through the book. Whatever the symbolism Melville intended

⁶ So that Melville wrote this the year before his death.

82

here, this is also the picture of the lover who demands that love which will make no demands on him; the fixed specters pursuing him are himself, as is the changing specter he pursues. *Mardi's* hero said that his first act as emperor of his soul was to abdicate, but his abdication involved only the duties and not the prerogatives of rule. In this monstrous attitude of Taji's— whom we need not hesitate to identify with Melville—in what Rudolf Allers has called "the revolt of the creature against his place in creation, and against the finiteness of his humanity",[7] lay the source of any dissatisfaction Melville may have felt in his life with Elizabeth.

Of *Mardi* Elizabeth wrote to her mother: "I suppose by this time you are deep in the 'fogs' of 'Mardi'—if the mist ever does clear away. I should like to know what it reveals to *you*. . . ." Elizabeth Shaw was not a Sophia Peabody, but neither was she an Olivia Langdon. Both Mrs. Hawthorne and Mrs. Clemens, in their different ways, censored their husbands' work; Mrs. Melville, her granddaughter has told Mr. Braswell, would not have dared to change so much as a comma of Herman's. If the other side of this means that she had no notion of where Herman's commas should fall, so that all his struggling was done alone, still the question remains whether anyone could have "understood" Melville. The misunderstood person, as often as not, is one who will not make himself plain to others or who demands that he be accepted on his own terms: his silences or the ellipses of his language are barriers he sets up which in being scaled stand as testimony to his worth. The allegory and symbolism in Melville's work are something of this sort in relation to the significance that lies behind them, and it is probable the same thing characterized the man.

The notion that the conventions and commonplace pieties of

[7] *The Psychology of Character* by Rudolf Allers, translated by E. B. Strauss (New York, 1943: Sheed & Ward).

his age forced him to hide his real meanings in an esoteric doctrine is hardly tenable, since the 19th century, in America as everywhere else, was filled with revolt against the accepted and established and Melville nowhere said anything that one of his contemporaries did not state less ambiguously in another place. After all, Karl Marx wrote for the same paper as Bayard Taylor. Yet it is, of course, in his very ambiguity that Melville's value lies; and he lays out no simple revolutionary dogmas precisely because his experience was too intense to allow of such partial formulations. Attended by the influences he was, Melville's intensity of experience approaches the dispersion of the neurotic rather than the recollection of the saint. Against this bafflement and waste of energies, Elizabeth, the good Unitarian, had nothing to offer intellectually, but that through her love Melville came to another kind of certitude, perhaps deeper, is shown in what may be the last poem he wrote, "L'Envoi: The Return of the Sire de Nesle".[8]

> But thou, my stay, thy lasting love
> One lonely good, let this but be!
> Weary to view the wide world's swarm,
> But blest to fold but thee.

That Elizabeth from time to time represented conjugal and domestic responsibilities from which Melville wished to flee Mr. Weaver and Mr. Mumford have both pointed out. On the three occasions that Melville took to sea after his marriage, he went alone, though one would have supposed that so accomplished a traveler might have wished to share the pleasure of traveling with his family. And there is no doubt that his rôle as a father left much to be desired. Those letters of his to his children that have been published are admonitory and instruc-

[8] This poem bears the note "A.D. 16—", but the only Sire de Nesle with whom I am acquainted is the jongleur who sang under prison windows until he discovered the one where Richard Coeur de Lion was held.

tive and singularly lacking in the expression of affection. Affection, perhaps, was implied in the care with which they were composed, but this is something the children do not seem to have gathered, here or elsewhere, for no signs of their fondness for him exist and there is much evidence that between Melville and his sons the conflicts were many. In the manner of his time, and supported by his own "reserve", Melville must have been the stern father. M. Simon, rather overrating Melville's belief in political equality, points out that "il ne lui vint pas à l'esprit que sa femme et ses enfants passent être ses égaux". Unfortunately, the years of his children's upbringing coincided with the years of his deepest gloom, when he turned into the labyrinth of his self for the answers which he could have found indicated only in external creation; and we may not be unjust in supposing that he did show a certain actual indifference to his sons and daughters, much as a man with a toothache has no eye for the beauty of the stars or synchronizes their twinkles with his own throbs. The tragedy here was for both father and children —which goes to show once more how evil a thing gloom is.

VII

A S   W I S E   A S   I   A M   N O W

AFTER A HONEYMOON TRIP WHICH TOOK THEM AS FAR AS
Montreal and during which they saw the mountain scenery of
New Hampshire and Vermont and sailed down Lake Cham-
plain, the Melvilles arrived at Lansingburgh on August 27th,
following an unpleasantly crowded night on a canal boat. Allan
Melville was married the following month and took a house
at 103 Fourth Avenue, between Eleventh and Twelfth Streets,
in New York, where Herman and Elizabeth shortly went to
join him. Here Herman started to work, and on December
23rd Elizabeth wrote to her stepmother, describing Herman's
day and the manner in which her own was ancillary to it:

We breakfast at 8 o'clock, then Herman goes to walk and I fly up
to put his room to rights, so that he can sit down to his desk immediately on his return. Then I bid him good-bye, with many
charges to be an industrious boy and not upset the inkstand and
then flourish the duster, make the bed, etc., in my own room. Then
I go downstairs and read the papers a little while, and after that
I am ready to sit down to my work—whatever it may be—darning
stockings—making or mending for myself or Herman—at all
events I haven't seen a day yet, without *some* sewing or other to
do. . . . Whatever I am about I do not much more than get
thoroughly engaged in it, than ding-dong goes the bell for lunch-
eon. This is half-past 12 o'clock—by this time we must expect
callers, and so must be dressed immediately after lunch. Then
Herman insists upon taking a walk of an hour's length at least.
. . . By the time I come home it is two o'clock and after, and then
I must make myself look as bewitchingly as possible to meet Herman at dinner. . . . At four we dine, and after dinner is over,

86

Herman and I come up to our room and enjoy a cosy chat for an hour or so—or he reads me some of the chapters he has been writing in the day. Then he goes down town for a walk, looks at the papers in the reading room, etc., and returns about half-past seven or eight. Then my work or my book is laid aside, and as he does not use his eyes but very little by candle light, I either read to him, or take a hand at whist for his amusement, or he listens to our reading or conversation, as best pleases him. For we all collect in the parlor in the evening, and generally one of us reads aloud for the benefit of the whole. Then we retire very early—at 10 o'clock we all disperse.

Early in February, 1848, Elizabeth wrote her stepmother again, saying they had been out for the evening twice that week and this night were going to the opera. "We have resolved to stop after this though and not go out at all, for while Herman is writing the effect of keeping late hours is very injurious to him—if he does not get a full night's rest or indulges in a late supper, he does not feel right for writing the next day." Though Herman did not forgo Miss Lynch's Valentine's Day party—to which he took his sister, not his wife—on May 5th Elizabeth wrote that "the book is done now, in fact (you need not mention it)[1] and the copy for the press in progress". Elizabeth explained that there would be some delay in the book's appearance, since for simultaneous publication in New York and London (by which copyright infringement was guarded against) proof sheets would have to be sent abroad, and, anyway, even the manuscript wasn't ready for the printer—she was helping to write it out. But *Mardi: And a Voyage Thither* did not appear until April of the next year, published in England by Richard Bentley and in the United States by Harper & Brothers.

In the meantime Melville had written *Redburn*, possibly a

[1] Possibly to Justice Shaw, on whose generosity Melville may have had to make a demand, since on February 1st of that year his account at Harper & Brothers was overdrawn $256.03.

good part of *White-Jacket*, and on February 16th, 1849, his first son, Malcolm, had been born at Boston, where Elizabeth had gone to be with her family at her lying-in. From Boston, a few days before the publication of *Mardi*, Melville wrote to Duyckinck with a touch of *taedium vitae*:

I am glad that you like that affair of mine. But it seems so long now since I wrote it, & my mood has so changed, that I dread to look into it, & have purposely abstained from so doing since I thanked God it was off my hands.—Would that a man could do something & then say—It is finished.—not that one thing only, but all others—that he has reached his uttermost, & can never exceed it. But live & push—tho' we put one leg forward ten miles—its no reason the other must lag behind—no, *that* must again distance the other—& so we go on until we get the cramp & die.

Mardi did not do a great deal to increase its author's reputation in the circles where it was established as a writer of adventures in the South Seas, and the extent to which it was favorably received was less than had been the case with the previous books. Evert Duyckinck had written his brother a year earlier about "a few chapters of Melville's new book, which in the poetry and wildness of the thing will be far ahead of Typee & Omoo", and *The Literary World* in due time repeated this in more formal language: "It is not worth while, at this stage of a young author's career, to pronounce definitely on his capabilities, but it is safe to say that the invention, fancy, and reflective powers of Mardi, are of a higher order, and to the reader, who is not deterred by occasional defects, sources of far higher pleasure in his last than in his earlier books." A little more than a week after *Mardi's* American appearance (it had been published about a month earlier in London), Melville wrote to his father-in-law about the book which was doubtless puzzling that kindly gentleman as much as it was his daughter and the reviewers:

As Wise As I Am Now

I see that *Mardi* has been cut into by the *London Atheneum*, and also burnt by the common hangman by the *Boston Post*. However, the *London Examiner* & *Literary Gazette* & other papers this side of the water have done differently. These attacks are matters of course, and are essential to the building up of any permanent reputation—if such should ever prove to be mine—"There's nothing in it!" cried the dunce when he threw down the 47th problem of the 1st Book of Euclid—"There nothing in it!"—Thus with the posed critic. But Time, which is the solver of all riddles, will solve *Mardi*.

A year later Melville sent Evert Duyckinck a gift of the three-volume English edition of *Mardi* (in general he seems to have preferred the handsome Bentley editions of his books for the few copies he gave away). In the letter that accompanied it, he expressed himself in a way showing that he had come to regard his intention in this book as a more serious one than had informed either *Typee* or *Omoo* and that to his mind the writer's function combined the offices of prophet and sage. In fact, the writer's function went even beyond this, as he had indicated in a letter of the year before to Duyckinck, telling him that he was making his first "close acquaintance" with Shakespeare: "I fancy that this moment Shakespeare in heaven ranks with Gabriel Raphael and Michael. And if another Messiah ever comes twill be in Shakespeare's person." It was not as the work of a "man who lived among cannibals" that Melville sent his gift of *Mardi*:

Tho' somewhat unusual for a donor, I must beg to apologize for making you the accompanying present of "Mardi". But no one who knows your library can doubt, that such a choice conservatory of exotics & other rare things in literature, after being long enjoyed by yourself, must, to a late posterity, be preserved intact by your descendants.[2] How natural then—tho' vain—in your friend to de-

[2] The library became one of the nuclei of the present collection of the New York Public Library.

sire a place in it for a plant, which tho' now unblown (emblematically, the leaves, you perceive, are uncut) may possibly—by some miracle, that is—flower like the aloe, a hundred years hence—or not flower at all, which is more likely by far, for some aloes never flower.

Again: (as the divines say) political republics should be the asylum for the persecuted of all nations; so, if Mardi be admitted to your shelves, your bibliographical Republic of Letters may find some contentment in the thought, that it has afforded refuge to a work, which almost everywhere else has been driven forth like a wild, mystic Mormon into shelterless exile.

—The leaves, I repeat, are uncut—let them remain so—and let me supplementaryly hint, that a bit of old parchment (from some old Arabic M. S. S. on Astrology) tied round each volume, & sealed on the back with a Sphynx, & never to be broken till the aloe flowers—would not be an unsuitable device for the bookbinders of "Mardi".

Nevertheless, it was the man who lived among cannibals who wrote the first forty-nine chapters of *Mardi*: from there to its final 195th chapter, the author was a voyager through Evert Duyckinck's library. This later exploring is evident in the early chapters, too, where the style has grown more complex and the literary allusions more frequent, though the intention is still, plainly enough, to create a "fiction" which will have the appearance of a "verity". In the five years between his discharge from the *United States* and his composition of *Moby-Dick*, Melville's development was powerfully influenced by his reading, in which Shakespeare's plays perhaps outrank anything else. Mr. Olson has argued that the reading of Shakespeare was Melville's pivotal experience, and there is no doubt that the qualities of the tragedy and drama in *Moby-Dick* recall Shakespeare and that, as Montgomery Belgion has said, like Shakespeare's "its language instantly fills auditor or reader with a swarm of feelings, some distinct, many indefinite, but all of the nature of exaltation".[3]

The feeling of tragedy and all the elements of drama are lacking in *Mardi*; its language attempts the evocation of grandeur but succeeds only in the early chapters where it is concerned with the substantial and concrete; yet the comprehensive vision of *Mardi*, that ultimately indefinable way of seeing things by which we know one writer's work from another, is different in degree rather than in kind from *Moby-Dick's*. What is indicated here is that Melville's reading, Shakespeare included, was perhaps less of an influence than has been thought in forming the particular conception of man's tragic lot toward which he worked over these five years. The resources for expressing his insights he garnered from his reading liberally, and, again, the conventions, the postures, it might be said, he assumed for speaking, likewise came from his reading, with the defiant stance of the Shakespearean tragic hero the one most to his purpose; but the fundamental attitude is a sort of Calvinism *bouleversé*, a deeply personal revolt in which the creature finds creation opposed to his highest moral purpose. Some personal experience may have lain behind this, but that brings us to the realm of what Mr. Freeman has called "hypothetical biography". The reading of Shakespeare surely was not it, for *Mardi* was written before Melville came across the edition of Shakespeare "in glorious great type", suitable for his eyes that were "tender as young sparrows".

Mardi, like its predecessors, begins with a whaling voyage: the whaler *Arcturion* has just left Ravavai (one of the Austral Islands) to take a circuitous course to the Galapagos, since "round about these isles, which Dampier once trod, where the Spanish buccaneers once hived their gold moidores, the Cachalot, or sperm whale, at certain seasons abounds". The *Arc-*

[3] In his introduction to *Moby-Dick* (London, 1946: The Cresset Press).

turion tacks back and forth across the Line in search of whales until the crew thinks it can feel the keel striking the Equator each time the ship crosses. It is a dreary business and the narrator, a sailor in the fo'c'sle, begins to pine "for someone who could page me a quotation from Burton on Blue Devils". This narrator is a sort of more mature Redburn: "aboard of all ships in which I have sailed, I have invariably been known by a sort of drawing-room title. . . . It was because of something in me that could not be hidden; stealing out in an occasional polysyllable; an otherwise incomprehensible deliberation in dining; remote, unguarded allusions to *Belles-Lettres* affairs, and other trifles superfluous to mention." And, like Tommo or Omoo, he insists on the captain's keeping to the letter of his contract, so when the latter turns the ship toward the Arctic "bent upon bobbing for the Right whale on the Nor'-West Coast and in the Bay of Kamschatska", like Tommo he leaves ship. Since the *Arcturion* is a thousand miles from land, he does this at night in one of the whaleboats, taking along with him his "chummy" Jarl, a "Viking" from the Isle of Skye, whom he has persuaded that by sailing due west they will sooner or later strike one of the smaller island chains of Oceania.

The escape from the whaler, the long voyage in the open boat, the encounter with an apparently unmanned brigantine are told in a leisurely and discursive manner, with a good many of the short chapters given over to reflection and generalization, but the motion and presence of the sea are in all of them. The general effect, one might say, is that of the earlier Conrad: a record of physical adventure, the sensory details sharply set down and over them a penumbra of larger significance of the vague nature of Romantic wonder. The characters in the adventure, however, have a broad 18th-century comic quality: Jarl, the taciturn, unimaginative, and very superstitious sailor; Samoa, the Polynesian brave enough to amputate his own arm but in constant terror of his wife; and the wife, Annatoo, the terrible collector of trinkets.

Annatoo is the one woman in Melville's pages, roughly drawn though she is, who has any kind of interior vitality, and when she is swept overboard in the dismasting of the brigantine in a squall, the reader feels a deeper regret than the one Melville so briefly expresses. With Annatoo goes as well the ruder vitality of the book; the men have not long abandoned the brigantine and taken to the whaleboat before they enter upon unpathed waters of allegory from which the book itself in the end insists there is no escape. We have seen that it leaves its hero fleeing over an endless sea.

The outline of the allegory is simple enough. The men in the whaleboat, nearing land, come upon a canoe occupied by a native priest, his three sons and, as they shortly discover, a beautiful blonde maiden who is being carried somewhere or other to be offered up as a sacrifice. In the course of rescuing the maiden, Taji (as the narrator shortly names himself) kills the old priest, instantly asking himself whether his is a "virtuous motive" or "some other and selfish purpose—the companionship of a beautiful maid", then makes off pursued by the priest's three sons and their curses. Taji, his Yillah, and his two comrades arrive at the archipelago of Mardi, where he is received as a god by King Media, who himself is semi-divine. On King Media's island, Taji lives for a brief space in a state of euphoria which is pretty well reflected in the style he uses to describe it: "We lived and we loved; life and love were united—in gladness glided our days." The avenging brothers appear, and shortly Yillah is gone. Taji sets out in search of her amongst the islands of the archipelago, a search that is at the same time a sort of Grand Tour in the company of Media and three others, Mohi, Yoomy, and Babbalanja, who are respectively the court chronicler, poet, and philosopher.

Yillah is all but forgotten during these travels, as Melville notes that she will be before they are begun. Nor are the travels —and Mardi stands for this world—except by a very faint implication in any way related to her; the places visited are described with but little reference to what goes on in Taji's mind. Taji, in fact, has been displaced by Babbalanja, who is the real commentator on what the tourists see, and Babbalanja is in quest of the residual truth beneath appearance, which he finds as elusive as appearance itself. He speaks like a Unitarian with painful doubts:

". . . Out of itself, Religion has nothing to bestow. Not will she save us from aught, but from the evil in ourselves. Her one grand end is to make us wise; her only manifestations are reverence to Oro [the name of God in Mardi] and love to man; her only, but ample, reward herself. He who has this, has all. He who has this, whether he kneel to an image of wood, calling it Oro; or to an image of air, calling it the same; whether he fasts or feasts; laughs or weeps—that man can be no richer. And this religion, faith, virtue, righteousness, good, whate'er you will, I find in this book I hold [by an "antique pagan"]. No written page can teach me more."

"Have you that, then, of which you speak, Babbalanja? Are you content there, where you stand?"

"My lord, you drive me home. I am not content. The mystery of mysteries is still a mystery. How this author came to be so wise, perplexes me. How he led the life he did, confounds me. Oh, my lord, I am in darkness, and no broad blaze comes down to flood me. The rays that come to me are but faint cross lights, mazing the obscurities wherein I live. And after all, excellent as it is, I can be no gainer by this book. For the more we learn, the more we unlearn; we accumulate not, but substitute; and take away more than we add. We dwindle while we grow; we sally out for wisdom, and retreat beyond the point whence we started; we essay the Fondiza, and get but the Phe. Of all simpletons, the simplest! Oh! that I were another sort of fool than I am, that I might restore my good opinion of myself. Continually I stand in the pillory, am broken on the wheel, and dragged asunder by wild horses. Yes, yes, Bardianna [the sage whom Babbalanja frequently quotes], all is in a nut, as thou sayest; but all my back teeth cannot crack it; I but crack my own jaws. All around me, my fellowmen are new grafting their vines, and dwelling in flourishing arbors; while I am for ever pruning mine, till it becomes but a stump. Yet in this pruning will I persist; I will not add, I will diminish; I will train myself down to the standard of what is unchangeably true. Day by day I drop off my redundancies; ere long I shall have stripped to my ribs; when I die, they will but bury my spine. Ah! where, where, my lord, is the everlasting Tekana? Tell me, Mohi, where the Ephina? I may have come to the Penultimate, but where, sweet Yoomy, is the Ultimate? Ah, companions! I faint, I am wordless —something—nothing—riddles—does Mardi hold her?"

Babbalanja's desperation and fainting fit follow shortly after the voyagers have visited Maramma. Maramma, the Mardian holy land, apparently derives its name from Maremma, the once-fertile region of Tuscany that in the Dark Ages reverted to marshland, and is the occasion for Melville's satire on ecclesiastics and organized religion in general, though this was softened for his particular audience by making Maramma superficially equivalent to the Catholic Church and taking a dig at Her devotional practices and claims to uniqueness. Maramma is, naturally, a great exacter of tribute, holds the poor in subjection, stifles free inquiry, and is generally bloody, perjured, and full of blame. But its Pontiff, Hivohitee, when he is at last revealed, is not found lolling at ease in a state of Sardanaplian luxury; he has more the aspect of a Hindu recluse, and the little object lesson he gives the pilgrim—by shutting himself up with him in a dark room and asking him what he sees, pointing to the moral that all is vanity and perhaps, indeed, nothing —seems more like nihilism than anything else.

Babbalanja, inspired by his demon Azzageddi, moves through a succession of discourses, a few eloquent but most sophomoric, to a conclusion that there is an eternal contradiction at the heart of things, but manages to carry on with an uneradicated belief in his own contradictory heart:

"For mirth and sorrow are kind; are published by identical nerves. Go, Yoomy; go study anatomy; there is much to be learned from the dead, and I am dead, though I live; and as soon dissect myself as another; I curiously look into my secrets; and grope under my ribs. I have found that the heart is not whole, but divided; that it seeks a soft cushion whereon to repose; that it vitalizes the blood; which else were weaker than water; I have found that we cannot live without hearts; though the heartless live longest. Yet hug your hearts, ye handful that have them; 'tis a blessed inheritance!'"

That inheritance is realized by Babbalanja when the travelers come to Serenia, where he decides to remain. Life in Serenia is lived according to the precepts of the prophet Alma (Christ), its laws "not of vengeance bred, but of Love and Alma". Love and Alma are celebrated without temples and the heart can apparently cleave to them without dogmas, though the Serenians do not subscribe to "man's perfection", believing only "in his heart, there is a germ of the good". " 'Oh, Alma, Alma! prince divine!' cried Babbalanja, sinking on his knees, 'in *thee*, at last, I find repose. . . . Gone, gone! are all distracting doubts. Love and Alma now prevail.' " Succeeding this, Babbalanja has a vision in which he is transported to Heaven in the company of a sort of Virgilian guide who, as they return to earth, tells him: "Beatitude there is none. And your only Mardian happiness is but exemption from greater woes—no more. Great Love is sad; and heaven is Love. Sadness makes the silence throughout the realms of space; sadness is universal and eternal; but sadness is tranquility; tranquility the most that souls may hope for." A hope of this negative definition ends Babbalanja's torment; Melville has Media, Mohi, and Yoomy accept it too; but Taji it will not compensate for the loss of Yillah.

Melville himself, it is plain, could not accept what Babbalanja took for an answer, though in the philosopher's acceptance he appears to have seen something that was impossible only in a personal way. It was his heart that would not submit, as he thought: there would be no more questions once one had the right *feelings*. That was another way of putting what his age saw as the conflict between faith and reason. Behind this conflict lay the conviction that faith and reason necessarily came out at different termini. The sadness which is the dark area behind the sparkling vitality of so many Victorian figures—Tennyson, Arnold, Browning, Carlyle—spread from the fact that they thought the terminus at which faith arrived was the more desirable but were prevented from reaching it because man cannot live by faith alone. Here, of course, each man must be taken in his historical and psychological complex, and it should be borne in mind that the more intellectually inadequate the object of his faith, the greater will be a man's difficulty in living by it.

When the demands of the personality are split between faith and reason, the world itself is soon split into two antipathetic realms in which the being of the creature is involved. One of these is the realm that is open to exploration by reason and it is, to use something like Manichaean terminology, the created and dark realm. Anomalously enough, the realm of faith and light transcending this dark realm is then identified with non-rationality, and the universe—the whole complex of things, material and non-material, open to reason and not—becomes a basically irrational affair, so that those who reject faith because they cannot reconcile it with reason must still admit that reason can never reveal to them what they most wish to know. For many who arrive at this dilemma, the next step is a strategic retreat in which they announce that what reason cannot answer is not worth asking. Melville did not do this; he could not harmonize, but neither would he limit, his experience. He would not make a comfortable denial of the basic conflict, and all through his work the conflict is maintained, appearing now in one set of symbols and now in another, a recurrent pattern of irreconcilables.

A universe of this kind must be an anguish to the man who postulates and faces it, and his torment can only be made supportable by defiance. Defiance was Taji's answer. While he had been cruising through Mardi, not only had the three avengers appeared from time to time but also three maidens with gifts of flowers. They were the emissaries of Queen Hautia, who had seemingly become enamored of Taji by his mere repute and wished him to join her on her island of Flozella-a-Nina, a place of every sensual delight. When Taji arrives at Flozella-a-Nina, in the course of his wanderings rather than in response to the maidens' invitations, Queen Hautia greets him most fondly: "Come! let us sin, and be merry. Ho! wine, wine, wine! and lapfuls of flowers!" Taji, remembering Yillah, resists her blandishments, and finally she shows him the rose pearl Yillah had worn. ". . . She lies too deep for answer," says Hautia; "stranger voices than thine she hears: bubbles are bursting around her." Taji rushes to the sea, on which—despite the pleas of Mohi and Yoomy to embark with them for Serenia —he sets out alone, saying " 'By Oro! I will steer my own fate. . . . Mardi, farewell!' " " 'Now, I am my own soul's emperor; and my first act is abdication! Hail! realm of shades!' and turning my prow into the racing tide, which seized me like a hand omnipotent, I darted through." It has been suggested that Taji's abdication is suicide,[4] and certainly his act is intended as one of revenge on a world that will not live up to his expectations. A first-person narrative by a suicide would not be the only violation of the conventions of story-telling in *Mardi*.

There is no reason for assuming any greater coherence in the second part of *Mardi* than in the whole book. On the contrary, the reasons for not doing so are numerous and plain: the influences of Rabelais, Swift, Browne, William Beckford, Thomas Moore, Jean-Paul Richter, and Carlyle are among them, reflected in the grab-bag of styles and subject-matters which the book is.[5] Mr. Brooks has said that Melville, like many self-educated men, was at the mercy of his reading, and *Mardi*, smelling of the lamp as it does, reflects his excitement in books; it tries again and again to reproduce his own experience with literature by presenting "equivalents" of what he has read. This latter, and difficult, part of *Mardi* is composed of three elements: the romantic and fanciful for its own sake, the satirical, and the allegorical. The three elements appear according to Melville's inspiration of the moment, and the allegorical, which is much deeper in intention than in achievement, only becomes impenetrable if we attempt to make it entirely consistent with the other elements. In the merely fanciful Melville fails dismally, because his imagination nowhere in his works operates successfully without a starting point in the concrete and "given"; in order to arrive at the universal reference which the imagination at its best has, he must start with the particular, whether he takes it out of his own experience or from the many books whose use scholars have been delighted to trace in his works.

[4] See "Taji's Abdication in Herman Melville's *Mardi*" by Tyrus Hillway, *American Literature*, November, 1944.

[5] Of Melville's reading during the composition of *Mardi* there is documentary evidence (in Duyckinck's record of books borrowed) only for Browne and Rabelais among the names I have cited, though others of these are recorded at later dates by Duyckinck or among books bought by Melville.

What Ernst Jünger has called Melville's "erzählendes und fabulierendes Talent" [6] is not exercised in *Mardi* precisely because he is free in the book to make his myths up out of the whole cloth and they lack the appeal of either exceptional ingenuity or general relevance. Melville did not have the ability to work from the idea to its fictional embodiment; he worked at his best when his fiction was the area in which he discovered the idea; and consequently *Mardi*, as Mr. Sedgwick observes, "has no sensational body".

The satire is more often successful than the fantasy. Some of it deals with particular foibles, each given its place of habitation; then, on the other hand, certain of the islands represent the nations of the world and there is a fair measure of topical allusion, for the book was written in '48, when even New Yorkers had gone into the streets, not to man the barricades but, as seems to be the custom with humane-minded Americans, to show their approval of violence and revolution abroad. Melville's satire is, on the whole, Rabelaisian rather than Swiftian —by which I mean he follows Rabelais' method of achieving absurdity by stating things in another set of terms rather than Swift's method of demonstrating it by an out-of-scale logic. At the same time, the political satire owes much to Carlyle, a good many of whose stylistic eccentricities are also sadly evident. Melville may have been a staunch republican; it could hardly be otherwise in the American milieu, where any different form of government is not even a possible consideration; but so early as *Mardi* he had become quite skeptical of democratic optimism.

In present-day political simplism, democracy stands as an equivalent for anything that is good in human nature or history, and because Melville objected to flogging in the United States navy, saw an injustice in the condition of the 19th-century poor,

---

[6] Commenting on "Bartleby the Scrivener" in *Gärten und Strassen* (Berlin, 1942: E. S. Mittler & Sohn).

considered Negro slavery "a vast enormity", and held a common sailor might be a better man than the Commodore, some of his critics assume that he was an impassioned prophet of the Century of the Common Man a century before its radioactive dawn. But Melville's praise of the common man on examination always turns out to be praise of the exceptional man of lowly circumstance or origins, and when in a famous passage he speaks of "that democratic dignity which, on all hands, radiates without end from God", the examples he instances of it are Bunyan, Cervantes, and Andrew Jackson. Subscription to mass democracy does not necessarily follow from a belief in "that abounding dignity which has no robed investiture", and Melville took pains to point out that even in his earthly paradise of primitive Christianity, Serenia, the inhabitants did not "by annulling reason's laws, seek to breed equality, by breeding anarchy". And it is amusing to note how he insists on the importance of family or, more properly, blood: he suggests that two of his heroes who are of the common people—Jack Chase and Billy Budd—may be the bastards of gentlemen.

Obviously, a great deal depends on the definition one gives to democracy as Melville uses the word: he was certainly for "democracy" in so far as it meant a recognition of men's equality before God and the charity this entails; in a democracy that posited the infallibility of majority rule he did not believe, and he was constantly alert to the danger of such democracy's causing man to rebound "whole aeons back in nature". When he was almost sixty, Melville saw "the Dark Ages of Democracy" drawing close; nearly thirty years before, he had caused King Media to write a warning to the people of Vivenza (the Mardian United States) which might have come from Cheyne Row:

Sovereign Kings of Vivenza! . . . Well aware . . . that as freemen, you are free to hunt down him who dissents from your majesties; I deem it proper to address you anonymously. . . .

And, may it please you, you are free, partly because you are young. Your nation is like a fine, florid youth, full of fiery impulses and hard to restrain; his strong hand nobly championing his heart. . . . The oppressor he defies to his beard; the high walls of old opinions he scales with a bound. In the future he sees all the domes of the East. . . .

In nations, sovereign kings! there is a transmigration of souls; in you, is a marvelous destiny. The eagle of Romara [ancient Rome] revives in your own mountain bird, and once more is plumed for her flight. Her screams are answered by the vauntful cries of a hawk; his red comb yet reeking with slaughter. And one East, one West, those bold birds may fly, till they lock pinions in the midmost beyond.

But, soaring in the sky over the nations that shall gather their broods under their wings, that bloody hawk may hereafter be taken for the eagle.

And though crimson republics may rise in constellations like fiery Aldebarans, speeding to their culminations; yet, down must they sink at last, and leave the old sultan-sun in the sky; in time, again to be deposed.

For little longer, may it please you, can republics subsist now, than in days gone by. For, assuming that Mardi is wiser than of old; nevertheless, though all men approached sages in intelligence, some would yet be more wise than others; and so, the old degrees be preserved. And no exemption would an equality of knowledge furnish from the inbred servility of mortal to mortal; from all the organic causes, which invariably drive mankind into brigades and battalions with captains at their head.

Civilization has not ever been the brother of equality. Freedom was born among the wild eyries in the mountains; and barbarous tribes have sheltered under her wings, when the enlightened people of the plain have nestled under different pinions. . . .

And better, on all hands, that peace should rule with a scepter, than that the tribunes of the people should brandish their broadswords. Better be the subject of a king, upright and just, than a freeman in Franko [France], with the executioner's axe at every corner.

It is not the prime end, and chief blessing, to be politically free. And freedom is only good as a means; is no end in itself. Nor, did man fight it out against his masters to the haft, not then, would he uncollar his neck from the yoke. A born thrall to the last, yelping out his liberty, he still remains a slave unto Oro; and well it is for the universe, that Oro's scepter is absolute.

World-old the saying, that it is easier to govern others, than oneself. And that all men should govern themselves as nations, needs that all men be better, and wiser, than the wisest of one-man rulers. But in no stable democracy do all men govern themselves. Though an army be all volunteers, martial law must prevail. Delegate your power, you leagued mortals must. The hazard you must stand. And though unlike King Bello of Dominora [Great Britain], your great chieftan, sovereign kings! may not declare war of himself; nevertheless, has he done a still more imperial thing—gone to war without declaring intentions. You yourselves were precipitated upon a neighboring nation [Mexico], ere you knew spears were in your hands. . . .

It is not gildings, and gold maces, and crown jewels alone, that make a people servile. There is much bowing and cringing among you yourselves, sovereign kings! Poverty is abased before riches, all Mardi over; anywhere it is hard to be a debtor; anywhere, the wise will lord it over fools; everywhere, suffering is found.

Thus, freedom is more social than political. And its real felicity is not to be shared. *That* is of a man's own individual getting and holding. It is not, who rules the state, but who rules me. Better be secure under one king, than exposed to violence from twenty millions of monarchs, though oneself be of the number. . . .

Now, though far and wide, to keep equal pace with the times, great reforms, of a verity, be needed; nowhere are bloody revolutions required. Though it be the most certain of remedies, no prudent invalid opens his veins, to let out his disease with his life. And though all evils may be assuaged; all evils cannot be done away. For evil is the chronic malady of the universe; and checked in one place, breaks forth in another.

A wide number of interpretations have been offered as to the meaning of Yillah or her genesis. It has been suggested that she is an etherealized compensation for what Elizabeth proved to be within the closer confines of marriage; that she is "an insistent image of the full human life"; that she represents "the rejection of mature passion"; that she is a "symbol of faded ecstasy"; that she is somehow connected with Melville's enduring resentment at having been weaned from his mother's breast. Barring the last, which must assume more than it can ever explain, there is probably something of all of these in the Yillah-Hautia antithesis. What Yillah represents was stated in a general, but nearly sufficient, way by Philarète Chasles in 1851. "Aylla," said Chasles, without correction from his American translator, "or Human Happiness, is lost forever; Mr. Melville is resigned to do without her." Yillah represents, then, all the aspirations toward happiness, perfection, and certainty that, differently in degree and kind, men everywhere entertain, while Hautia is a meaner level of satisfaction and apparent success.

If by some necromancy that is given to no biographer we could discover why Melville's symbol of happiness took just the form it did, we should still not know a great deal more about the happiness that Melville sought, for his quest is not to be understood genetically but teleologically. It is easy enough to say that both Yillah and Hautia are images of delight taken from the sphere of sex and both to be enjoyed only at a great cost in guilt, the one rejected because of the cost and the other pursued exactly because the pursuit is hopeless. And it is possible that some intimacies of which we know nothing and a puritanical attitude toward sex combined in Melville to give this form to his myth of man's hunger. But did the same combination drive him to say that what he sought would be found in none of the islands of this world and that what he was assured of in the next still did not give him what he asked? The answer depends on our conception of the human situation: whether we think that situation justifies itself when man functions in it at a maximum efficiency in attaining those satisfactions which are assumed to be their own criterion; or whether we think the human situation is necessarily one of dissatisfaction short of the absolute. If it is the latter, no genetic approach to the problem of the mind will tell us what Melville's problem was. As Aristotle observed, in the wide view, the primary thing is not the seed but its perfection.

Melville, speaking through Babbalanja, said that he would prune his vine to the stump, whittle himself away to the backbone, in his attempt to define what he wanted. The statement shows both the depth and the misdirection of his perception. He was deep in apprehending that what he looked for was unique, that his inquiry must increasingly tend toward the singular; he was misdirected in seeking that unique thing in some as yet untouched portion of himself. Mistakenly locating it there, he could not of course rest in Serenia; but even had his vision been turned outward, it is doubtful that Serenia would have been his goal, since the love which was the benevolent ruling principle there was far short of the individual experience he sought: it is not abstract and universal principles but persons that are truly unique, and one Person Who is finally so. Although Yillah is devoid of any memorable lineaments and as much a general token as Serenia's love, yet it appears valid to read a deeper level of meaning into Melville's allegory, which is there whether he intended it or not, and to see in Taji's refusal to abandon the hopeless pursuit of Yillah a last underscoring of the fact that the dénouement must be personal. Taji, however, is resolved that all shall be decided on his own terms, and this places him within the limits of his own imperfection, helplessly caught and bound by what is personal to himself. If his putting to sea means suicide, it means that because he must destroy his solipsistic world, which cannot meet his most earnest demand on it.[7]

Why are the old priest's avenging sons symbols of guilt? Once more, it would be easy enough to find here indications of the sexually illicit—and naturally it has been done. But if Yillah stands for what I have tried to suggest above, Taji's guilt is something of larger implication. Guilt, after all, is a healthy and normal reaction of the human mind, and it is the pervading atmosphere of the mind, no longer healthy but nevertheless still "normal", when the complete independence of the will is insisted upon. Guilt (or the sense of sin or, in currently fashionable language, *Angst*) is the feeling in the individual that he stands outside of the order of things, that even his own sickness, however it may be in contradiction to the rest of the world, has an absolute claim to existence. Yillah—"the earthly semblance of that sweet vision that had haunted my earliest thoughts"— was really Taji's own creation, and the guilt he felt at having slain her guardian was also a guilt following on his having usurped the creative function. But Taji elects eternally to bear this guilt rather than forswear the autonomy of his will and the

---

[7] About the time Melville had Taji make his decision, Sören Kierkegaard in *The Sickness unto Death* wrote of the despairing man's attitude of defiance: "That self which he despairingly wills to be is a self which he is not (for to will to be that self which one truly is is indeed the opposite of despair); what he really wills is to tear his self away from the Power which constituted it. But notwithstanding all his despair, this he is unable to do; notwithstanding all the efforts of despair, that Power is the stronger, and it compels him to be the self he does not will to be. But for all that he wills to be rid of himself, to be rid of the self which he is, in order to be the self he himself has chanced to choose. To be *self* as he wills to be would be his delight (though in another sense it would be equally despair), but to be compelled to be *self* as he does not will to be is his torment, namely, that he cannot get rid of himself."

primacy of his own splendid isolation. The demon Azzageddi, who cannot follow Babbalanja into Serenia, still has a subject.

The most haphazardly written of Melville books, *Mardi* was yet the one whose worth he most protested. Some of this no doubt was the reaction of an author who, having had two lesser efforts well received, was hurt in his pride when a more serious book did not get an equal reception. Nevertheless, his disappointment was connected with the larger pride which the book expressed. A short time before he sent his gift copy of *Mardi* to Duyckinck, he wrote a letter (also to Duyckinck) showing how close the book stood to him and how charged it was with his concern:

—What madness & anguish it is, that an author can never— under no conceivable circumstances—be at all frank with his readers. —Could I, for one, be frank with them—how would they cease their railing—those at least who have railed.—In a little notice of "The Oregon Trail" [8] I once said something critical about another's book—I shall never do it again. Hereafter I shall no more stab at a book (in print, I mean) than I would stab at a man.—I am but a poor mortal, & I admit that I learn by experience & not by divine intuitions. Had I not written & published "Mardi", in all likelihood I would not be as wise as I am now, or may be. For that thing was stabbed *at* (I do not say through)—& therefore, I am the wiser for it.—But a bit of note paper is not large enough for this sort of writing—so no more of it.

There is an ambiguity in the letter, and it is hard to say whether Melville meant that social circumstances or the innate conditions of writing precluded complete frankness. We may assume he did not imply that he chose allegory solely for the

[8] He had reviewed Parkman's book in *The Literary World* for March 31st, 1849, and had in particular objected to Parkman's low opinion of Indians as a failure in charity.

purposes of disguise; his book is too confused for that, and there are signs he followed after the figures of his allegory to discover whatever meanings they would reveal to him. The meanings are in a measure obscure to us because they are parts of a system, unlike Bunyan's in *The Pilgrim's Progress* or Spenser's in *The Faery Queene*, which is the private creation of its author, and equally because there can be no "precise" meanings in these matters—any more than there can be a complete prose transcription of a poem. "I've chartless voyaged," says Melville toward the end of his book. "And though essaying but a sportive sail, I was driven from my course by a blast resistless. . . . So, if after all these fearful, fainting trances, the verdict be, the golden haven was not gained; yet, on bold quest thereof, better to sink in boundless deeps, than float on vulgar shoals; and give me, ye gods, an utter wreck, if wreck I do."

A partial wreck in a literary way *Mardi* must surely be judged, though Melville's talents left much for us to salvage. We cannot do the salvaging without some daring in surmise, but perhaps we had better temper this surmise by keeping in mind a passage Melville cannot have pondered long when he took inspiration from Rabelais:

Do you believe, upon your conscience, that Homer, whilst he was couching his Iliads and Odysses, had any thought upon those allegories, which Plutarch, Heraclides, Ponticus, Eustathius, Cornutus, squeezed out of him, and which Politian filched again from them? If you trust it, with neither hand nor foot do you come near to my opinion, which judgeth them to have been as little dreamed of by Homer, as the gospel sacraments were by Ovid in his Metamorphosis; though a certain gulligut friar, and true bacon-picker would have undertaken to prove it, if, perhaps, he had met with as very fools as himself, and as the proverb says, "a lid worthy of such a kettle".

VIII

HUMMING ALE FOR A PONDERING MAN

IN SEPTEMBER, 1849, MELVILLE WAS CORRECTING THE PROOFS of *Redburn*, and *White-Jacket* was probably already in proof, for he was planning to set out "in a London packet in a few weeks carrying the proof of his new book 'The White Jacket' with him", according to a letter of Evert Duyckinck's. The sale of his book to a London publisher was the formal reason of the trip on which Melville started on the 11th of the next month, but that he had rather more in mind is shown by Duyckinck's reference to "a cheap adventurous flying tour of eight months, compassing Rome", in which Melville wished his friend (and possibly his brother George) to join him. Five days out at sea on the *Southampton*, Melville had even farther goals to look toward: with a fellow passenger, he noted in his journal, he had "sketched a plan for going down the Danube from Vienna to Constantinople; thence to Athens on the steamer; to Beyrouth & Jerusalem—Alexandria & the Pyramids. . . . I am full (just now) of this glorious *Eastern* jaunt. Think of it! Jerusalem & the Pyramids—Constantinople, the Aegean, & old Athens!"

Lack of funds and homesickness were to start him back toward New York near the year's end, the second a more compelling force than the first, but it is strange how little he foresaw of this. The Holy Land prevailed upon his imagination as it did on that of so many of his time, who made their pilgrimage there, wandering over its stony ground to verify in their own experience the geography of Scripture and half hoping, one thinks, for some material sign to stay the faith materialism had sapped. Just seven years later, Melville would sail again and this time reach Jerusalem; and in another twenty years he would publish a long verse narrative in which his questionings were personified in a group of pilgrims making a similar journey.

Melville's books seem to have had a way of anticipating life. He had scarcely published *Moby-Dick* when an account came out of Panama of a whaler actually rammed and sunk by a whale; he had only been three days aboard the *Southampton* when a steerage passenger threw himself overboard and drowned, just as had a sailor on Redburn's first night at sea. The passenger, it was decided, had been mad, but another madman in the steerage it turned out was suffering, as a result of "keeping drunk for the last two months", from delirium tremens—which had been the trouble with the *Highlander's* suicide.

One more of the *Southampton's* passengers would in time go mad, but during Melville's acquaintance with him was only addicted to German metaphysics. This was a young man named George Adler, a professor of German language and literature at New York College, with whom Melville remained up more than once "till a late hour, talking of 'Fixed Fate, Free will, foreknowledge absolute' ". They were joined in these discussions by two other passengers—Franklin Taylor, a cousin of Bayard Taylor's, who had been a student at Heidelberg and, so far as this kind of conversation went, had "not been in Germany in vain"; and "a lisping youth of genteel capacity" named McCurdy, the son of a wealthy merchant, who was liberal in treating the others to drinks but who bored Melville "terribly" when he later called on him in London. At least one of these symposia they held in Melville's stateroom—"as big almost as my own room at home; it has a spacious berth, a large washstand, a sofa, glass, &c., &c."—mixing Hegel, Schlegel, and Kant with whisky punch. Of the punch "Adler drank about three table spoons full—Taylor 4 or five tumblers" and Melville, we may suppose, even more, since when he went to bed "after two in the morning" he put down "Can not remember what happened today" and did not account for things until his entry of the day following.

The trip took twenty-five or -six days. No longer a member of the Junior Total Abstinence Society who could barely be persuaded to take Jamaica rum for seasickness, Melville had mulled wine, London stout, claret, and champagne. The man whom a later generation would call a Jeremiah climbed in the rigging, played shuffle board, chess, and cards, and joined in the various social doings on the ship. Doubtless Jeremiah had his light moments, too, but then Jeremiah was inspired of God. Head winds prevented the *Southampton's* putting into Portsmouth—where Melville had hoped to go ashore instead of staying aboard until the ship reached London Dock—and, impatient to "press English earth after the lapse of ten years— *then* a sailor, *now* H. M. author of 'Peedee', 'Hullabaloo' & 'Pog-Dog' ", he took off in a cutter with Adler and Taylor, landing at Deal on Guy Fawkes day.

From Deal they set out on foot for the long walk to Canterbury but, stopping at Sandwich for a breakfast that "finished with ale & pipes", they continued the pilgrimage by train. The cathedral much impressed Melville and he noted that the place where Thomas à Becket had been killed was an ugly one. The next morning, after breakfasting on ale again (but nothing else), he took the train to London, secured a room there at 25 Craven Street, the Strand, for a guinea and a half a week, went to a concert, inquired after *Redburn* at a bookshop, then looked up notices of the book in *Bentley's Miscellany* and

Blackwood's, wondering "that the old Tory should waste so many papers upon a thing that I, the author, know to be trash, & wrote it to buy some tobacco with". Bentley—to whom Melville evidently wished first to offer *White-Jacket*—would not be in town for five days and Melville spent his time sightseeing and at the theater.

"While on one of the Bridges," he wrote in his journal, "the thought struck me again that a fine thing might be written about a Blue Monday in November London. . . ." A later entry indicates that he already had in mind what would be his eighth book, *Israel Potter,* in which this thought would be incorporated. Whether he stood on London Bridge in the "green coat [that] plays the devil with my respectability here" and saw the Thames and High Street through a damp and smoky melancholy, or whether he summoned up the mood six years later to invest the scene of his hero's sad expatriation, there is no certain way of knowing. But the description is superlative of its kind, in whatever frame of mind Melville first saw its subject.

Hung in long sepulchral arches of stone, the black, besmoked bridge seemed a huge scarf of crape, festooning the river across. Similar funeral festoons spanned it to the west, while eastward, toward the sea, tiers and tiers of jetty colliers lay moored, side by side, fleets of black swans.

The Thames, which far away, among the green fields of Berks, ran clear as a brook, here, polluted by continual vicinity to man, curdled on between rotten wharves, one murky sheet of sewerage. Fretted by the ill-built piers, awhile it crested and hissed, then shot balefully through the Erebus arches, desperate as the lost souls of the harlots, who, every night, took the same plunge. Meantime, here and there, like awaiting hearses, the coal-scows drifted along, poled broadside, pell-mell to the current.

And as that tide in the water swept all craft on, so like a tide seemed hurrying all men, all horses, all vehicles on the land. As ant-hills, the bridge arches crawled with processions of carts, coaches, drays, every sort of wheeled, rumbling thing, the noses of the horses behind touching the backs of the vehicles in advance, all bespattered with ebon mud—ebon mud that stuck like Jews' pitch. At times the mass, receiving some mysterious impulse far in the rear, away among the coiled thoroughfares out of sight, would start forward with a spasmodic surge. It seemed as if some squadron of centaurs, on the thither side of Phlegethon, with charge on charge, was driving tormented humanity, with all its chattels, across.

Whichever way the eye turned, no tree, no speck of any green thing was seen—no more than in the smithies. All laborers, of whatsoever sort, were hued like the men in foundries. The black vistas of streets were as the galleries in coal mines; the flagging, as flat tombstones, minus the consecration of moss, and worn heavily down, by sorrowful tramping, as the vitreous rocks in the cursed Gallipagos, over which the convict tortoises crawl.

As in eclipses, the sun was hidden; the air darkened; the whole dull, dismayed aspect of things, as if some neighboring volcano, belching its premonitory smoke, were about to whelm the great town, as Herculaneum and Pompeii, or the Cities of the Plain. And as they had been upturned in terror toward the mountain, all faces were more or less snowed or spotted with soot. Nor marble, nor flesh, nor the sad spirit of man, may in this cindery City of Dis abide white.

As retired at length, midway, in a recess of the bridge, Israel surveyed them, various individual aspects all but frighted him. Knowing not who they were; never destined, it may be, to behold them again; one after the other, they drifted by, uninvoked ghosts in Hades. Some of the wayfarers wore a less serious look; some seemed hysterically merry; but the mournful faces had an earnestness not seen in the others; because man, "poor player", succeeds better in life's tragedy than comedy.[1]

---

[1] The debt here to Dante's description of the Dark Plain is obvious; in his notes Melville had written: "a city of Dis (Dante's)—clouds of smoke—the

When Bentley came up to London from Brighton, he paid Melville £100 on *Redburn* and made him a very handsome offer on *White-Jacket*: £200 for the first edition of a thousand copies and such terms as they might agree on for further editions. But he could make no advance. Melville then tried other publishers, among them Murray, Longmans, and Moxon. Though Melville had a letter of introduction to him from Richard Henry Dana, Moxon's greeting was "very stiff, cold, clammy, & clumsy" (Melville complained of the "damned nonsense . . . there is about so many of these English"). Fortunately Melville had just read Charles Lamb on the *Southampton* and when he spoke of the essayist, whose foster-daughter Emma Isola Moxon had married, Moxon unbent and "said he had often put Lamb to bed—drunk". Later he sent Melville as a gift Thomas Talfourd's *Final Memorials of Lamb* and an octavo edition of Lamb's works—which may have influenced Melville toward some purchases of Tudor-Stuart dramas he shortly made. Though the other publishers equaled Moxon's eventual courtesy, they, like him, could not take on *White-Jacket*, all offering the copyright situation as their reason; and it was not till five weeks after his first arrival in London that Melville sold his book, to Bentley, with the £200 advanced in the form of a six-months note.

Again in Melville's dealings with a publisher, we apparently find him assuming that truth and fact are, for the author in his public character, on two different planes, though this time an elementary vanity may be the explanation. Less than three weeks after his return from London, there appeared in *The*

---

damned. . . ." In T. S. Eliot's *The Waste Land*, the mention of London Bridge also has its echo of Canto III of the *Inferno*:

> Under the brown fog of a winter dawn,
> A crowd flowed over London Bridge, so many
> I had not thought death had undone so many.

Literary World a letter signed "K," the original of which is in Melville's hand:

> Without going into the question of international copy right raised by the correspondence in the London "Times" copied into your journal of the 23rd inst; I believe injustice may be done Mr. Melville as well as his publishers by allowing the statement that the former "wearily hawked his unpublished *White Jacket* from Piccadilly to White Chapel calling upon every publisher in his way" &c to pass uncontradicted. It is simply untrue. But that is not all. Mr. Melville had not the slightest difficulty in making an arrangement for the publication of *White Jacket,* with Mr. Bentley, the publisher of Mr. Melville's previous work, & what is more, such arrangement was concluded promptly, without impediment or finesse. Mr. Melville is not the man to "hawk" his wares in any market & Mr. Bentley not the Publisher to allow so capital a book to escape him.

The letter went on to say that Mr. Bentley's "liberality to Authors is proverbial" and to instance some of the large royalties he had disbursed.

While Melville waited out the time in which his contract was negotiated without the "slightest difficulty", he was entertained as generously as though he had been an English author visiting modern America. At Murray's he dined waited upon by a "footman . . . habited [redundantly] in small clothes & breeches, revealing a despicable pair of sheepshanks" and met Lockhart, "in a prodigious white cravat, (made from Sir Walter's shroud, I suppose). . . . I sat next to Lockhart, and seeing that he was a customer who was full of himself & expected great homage; & knowing him to be a thorough-going Tory & fish-blooded Churchman & conservative, & withal, editor of the Quarterly—I refrained from playing the snob to him like the rest—& the consequence was he grinned at me his ghastly smiles." At the house of Joshua Bates—whom Gansevoort had found so standoffish when he called at Baring Brothers to discount the note advanced for *Typee*—he dined on "sundry mysterious French dishes" and "an indefinite quantity of Champagne, Sherry, Old Port, Hock, Madeira, & Claret", and "saw a copy of Typee on a table".

In America he had asked Judge Shaw to request of Emerson an introduction to Carlyle, but in the journal there is no mention at all of the Scotsman. Though he did not see Carlyle, he much topped his father's call in Liverpool on "the eminent Mr. Roscoe, the historian, poet, and banker", for he twice sat at the famous breakfasts of the banker-poet Samuel Rogers. The first time he was the only guest and the second time he had the company of Bryan W. Proctor (at whose poem "The Sea" Melville had poked fun in a *Literary World* review) and Alexander Kinglake (the dragoman of whose *Eöthen* Melville himself would encounter seven years later in the Near East).[2] Apparently he did not achieve the final honor of dinner at Rogers's, though he had been introduced to the old man by a letter of Edward Everett's, but he had a number of pleasant enough evenings in the company of different journalists and minor literary figures. Some five years afterwards, in the New England winter where his house seemed a ship on a sea of snow, he set down his memory of an evening in the Temple:

The apartment was well up toward heaven; I know not how many strange old stairs I climbed to get to it. . . .
The furniture was wonderfully unpretending, old, and snug. No new shining mahogany, sticky with undried varnish; no uncomfortably luxurious ottomans, and sofas too fine to use, vexed you in this sedate apartment. . . .
If I remember right, ox-tail soup inaugurated the affair. Of a

[2] There was a third banker-poet in Melville's life—Edmund Clarence Stedman, whose son Arthur was Melville's literary executor.

rich russet hue, its agreeable flavor dissipated my first confounding of its main ingredients with teamster's gads and the rawhides of ushers. (By way of interlude, we drank a little claret.) Neptune's was the next tribute rendered—turbot coming second; snow-white, flaky, and just gelatinous enough; not too turtleish in its unctuousness. (At this point we refreshed ourselves with a glass of sherry.) After these light skirmishers had vanished, the heavy artillery of the feast marched in, led by that well-known English generalissimo, roast beef. For aids-de-camp we had a saddle of mutton, a fat turkey, a chicken-pie, and endless other savory things; while for avant-couriers came nine silver flagons of humming ale. This heavy ordnance having departed on the track of the light skirmishers, a picked brigade of game-fowl encamped upon the board, their camp-fires lit by the ruddiest of decanters.

Tarts and puddings followed, with innumerable niceties; then cheese and crackers. (By way of ceremony, simply, only to keep up good old fashions, we here each drank a glass of good old port.)

. . . The spirits of the company grew more and more to perfect genialness and unconstraint. They related all sorts of pleasant stories. Choice experiences in their private lives were now brought out, like choice brands of Moselle or Rhenish, only kept for particular company. One told us how mellowly he lived when a student at Oxford; with various spicy anecdotes of most frank-hearted noble lords, his liberal companions. Another bachelor, a gray-headed man, with a sunny face, who, by his own account, embraced every opportunity of leisure to cross over into the Low Countries, on sudden tours of inspection of the fine old Flemish architecture there—this learned, white-haired, sunny-faced old bachelor, excelled in his descriptions of the elaborate splendors of those old guild-halls, town-halls, and stadhold-houses, to be seen in the land of the ancient Flemings. A third was a great frequenter of the British Museum, and knew all about scores of wonderful antiquities, of Oriental manuscripts, and costly books without a duplicate. A fourth had lately returned from a trip to Old Granada, and, of course, was full of Saracenic scenery. A fifth had a funny case in law to tell. A sixth was erudite in wines. A seventh had a strange characteristic anecdote of the private life of the Iron Duke. . . . An eighth had been lately amusing his evenings, now and then, with translating a comic poem of Pulci's. He quoted for us the more amusing passages.

And so the evening slipped along, the hours told, not by a water-clock, like King Alfred's but a wine-chronometer. . . . And throughout all this nothing loud, nothing unmannerly, nothing turbulent. . . .

The celebration of this vinous "Paradise of Bachelors" (Melville said that he did not believe in "a Temperance Heaven"), it has been argued, is meant to point up the burdens of marriage, for it appeared in *Harper's Magazine* of April, 1855, as a companion-piece to "The Tartarus of Maids", which has been interpreted as a symbolic presentation of the "biological burdens" of women. Yet if Melville intended this subtlety in printing the pieces together, we are not much rewarded by reading them in the terms thus suggested. A task of exegesis is placed on us that predicates an obscurity in Melville that is no less an artistic fault for being intended, if intended it is.

If we take the two sketches for what they present themselves as, they cover a wider area and, it seems to me, more profoundly. The first, with a legitimate heightening of tone, gives a picture of the life of pseudo-celibate luxury which the 19th-century Englishman brought to perfection. The implications of all that went into it are there in Melville's sketch, possibly more as observed detail than as general analysis: the self-indulgence sustained by a pagan decorum, the irresponsibility hidden by a sincere feeling of obligation to convention, and the convention founded on the conviction that those following it are of their nature superior. The claret, the tarts, and the potatoes in a napkin supply the flesh and blood of all this in the literal and metaphorical sense. The picture of the paper factory in which what 19th-century New England called "Lowell girls" carry on their enervating jobs poses a contrast whose moral reference is more rewarding to contemplation than any private discontent of the author which may be deduced from the same contrast. It may well be that but for the private discontent the two sketches would not have been written, but surely their meaning, as writing, is in their public statement. Otherwise all psychoanalyses would be, *per se,* works of art.

Besides dining-out Melville had more vulgar amusements. He went to the Zoölogical Gardens in Regent's Park, visited the Royal stables at Windsor, saw the Queen drive by, witnessed the public hanging of a man and wife, and watched the Lord Mayor's show. The day after the latter, accompanied by a fire officer, he went "through cellars & anti-lanes into the rear of the Guildhall, with a crowd of beggars going to receive the broken meats & pies from yesterday's grand banquet"; and this became another meal that he wrote of, though as a spectator. He looked at the frescoes in the House of Lords with a young painter called Mr. John Tenniel for his guide.

He made at least ten visits to the theater, seeing contemporary plays of little merit and second-rate 18th-century pieces, excepting for Macready in *Othello.* Macready would make his entrance in the rôle of Richelieu in still another story. Melville, however, must have been acquainted with his acting before his London visit, for he had been one of the signers of the open letter to Macready that appeared the day of the extraordinary Astor Place riots. The two Shakespearean plays whose influence is most evident in his work, *King Lear* and *Hamlet,* were performed during his stay in London but, oddly enough, he seems not to have seen them.

On November 27th, he left for Paris, where he took a room in the rue de Bussy. There his landlady's practice of leaving brandy and sugar on the mantelpiece, to be charged for according to the amount used (as Melville learned from experience), provided further material for *Israel Potter* (whose hero was denied a similar experience by the intervention of Benjamin Franklin). The adventures of Israel Potter in Paris have an insubstantial quality that must reflect Melville's feeling of dislocation in the great city whose language he could not speak. A visit to the Hôtel de Cluny gave him one of the quincuncial metaphors of *Moby-Dick*,[3] and the same book has a souvenir of a day spent at Versailles: "Go and gaze upon all the paintings of Europe, and where will you find such a gallery of living and breathing commotion on canvas, as in that triumph hall at Versailles; where the beholder fights his way, pell-mell, through the consecutive great battles of France; where every sword seems a flash of the Northern Lights, and the successive armed kings and emperors dash by, like a charge of crowned centaurs?" This describes the most obvious aspect of the baroque art that so fascinated Melville: its swirl and motion.

F. O. Matthiessen has pointed out how much those whom we now loosely call the metaphysicals influenced American thought in the age of Emerson, how creative writing in America in good measure bypassed the neo-classical period which developed out of one facet of the work of Milton and Dryden.[4] The baroque age was longer-lived on this side of the water, and, as Austin Warren has said, "politically, theologically, and morally out of sympathy with the age which followed the collapse of their hopes for England, the colonists of Massachusetts Bay took

[3] The one, in Chapter XLI, beginning "Winding far down from within the very heart of this spiked Hôtel de Cluny. . . ."

[4] See "The Metaphysical Strain" in *American Renaissance* by F. O. Matthiessen (New York, 1941: Oxford University Press).

little interest in the literature which was its product. . . . For American literary history the century constitutes a unit" of the baroque.[5] Needless to say, Melville did not derive quite the same thing from the metaphysicals as did Emerson. "Nay, I do not oscillate in Emerson's rainbow," said he in 1849. "His belly . . . is in his chest, & his brains descend down into his neck, & offer an obstacle to a draught of ale or a mouthful of cake." And some years later he annotated a statement of Emerson's on the easy routing of evil: "God help the poor fellow who squares his life according to this."

The fact is that in using the 17th-century "conceit"—as a habit of thought rather than as a verbal device—Melville was the more successful of the two. The conceit, in this sense, was an attempt to reconcile the various planes of experience and being, to mount by an analogical ladder from the physical world of the senses to the metaphysical world—the world beyond or above the physical, as the Greek preposition suggests. Emerson indeed got to the metaphysical world, but once there, he seems to have kicked his ladder away, content to abide in that sort of Oriental vacuity with which today the word "metaphysics", in part thanks to Emerson's own interest in Eastern thought, is popularly associated.

Melville, though his metaphysical clarity was nothing singular, retained a firm hold on both terms of the conceit and, in his writing, it provided him with the "mechanism of sensibility which could devour any kind of experience", as Mr. Eliot's famous phrase has it. This sensibility the early 19th-century Romantics tried to revive, and for their model of the poet (who, for them, was also the sage) Coleridge, Lamb, Hunt, and Hazlitt turned to the 17th century. But their attempt was vitiated by a distrust of reason, which the Romantic mind thought gave

[5] *Rage for Order* by Austin Warren (Chicago, 1948: The University of Chicago Press).

ideal essence rather than reality, so that, where its model was almost ludicrously exact, the Romantic mind was vague. Great age of antinomianism though it was, in practice the 17th century observed no antinomy of faith and reason, as no theologically-minded age could. It tried after a universe of a logical coherence that surprises us today. Henry More and Robert Burton, those ardent Platonists, studied the physiology of angels with detailed inquisitiveness and arrived at the conclusion that angels produced excrement—an opinion that Disraeli in his *Curiosities of Literature* would falsely ascribe to St. Thomas Aquinas. Thomas Browne, the author of a book that submitted vulgar errors to the analysis of reason, was glad to use his powers of intellect and wealth of learning in a court of law to secure the condemnation of two persons tried for witchcraft. Isaac Newton considered himself less a theorist of physics than an interpreter of Scriptural prophecy, on which subject he wrote what he believed to be his most important book. Descartes put both the beginnings of scientific optics, in which he was a careful experimenter, and of idealistic epistemology, which opposes reason to common sense, into the Cartesian vortices that, typical of the age, were like inverted funnels aimed at the Platonic Oneness which so fascinated it. This wholehearted commitment to unity in some cases placed unity before the variety of matters to be unified, and Hobbes and Locke, for example, attaining their coherent systems by excluding all that was not amenable to the direction of their reasoning, started atheism's claim to rationality.

Yet the very involution and elaborateness of the baroque mentality, we may guess, proceeded from a deep fear, growing in the European mind since the rejection of the mediaeval synthesis, that man had his being on two realms which could not be reconciled. The 17th century perhaps saw more practice of magic than any other time, and what is magic but the placation of the powers of Darkness on their own terms? The Manichaean strain appears again and again—in the Plotinian philosophy and in Calvinist theology, in figures as far apart as the two Dutchmen Bayle and Jansen. With his conviction of the "unknown but still reasoning thing . . . behind the unreasoning mask", Melville's temperament found its affinities in the baroque age. Of course, it is not historically true that all was tormented movement there; and when Melville in his last years came to collect engravings of paintings, he prized above any others those of the long autumnal perspectives of Claude Lorraine.

From Paris he went on to Brussels, which he found to be just what Baudelaire would later understand by the word "Belgian". His next stop was Cologne, where he took in the Cathedral, the Maria Himmelfahrtskirche, and St. Peter's. "In this antiquated gable-ended old town," he wrote, "—full of Middle Age, Charlemagne associations—where Rubens was born & Mary De Medici died—there is much to interest a pondering man like me." Then he went up the Rhine to Coblenz, and there noted in his journal, and may have experimentally verified, "that the finest wine of all the Rhine is grown right under the guns of Ehrenbreitstein". "This frowning fortress" commanded a generalization in *Pierre:* "As the vine flourishes, and the grape empurples close up to the very walls and muzzles of cannoned Ehrenbreitstein; so do the sweetest joys of life grow in the very jaws of its perils." Thoroughly homesick, under Ehrenbreitstein his sweetest joy was thought of Lizzie, and December 13th saw him back in London.

Awaiting him was an invitation from the Duke of Rutland, the father of Lord John Manners, Disraeli's friend and sponsor, to visit Belvoir Castle some time in January. He was much tempted to accept, arguing to himself that here was a chance "to know what the highest English aristocracy really & practically is" and to acquire "material", but after meditating over a cigar, the longing to see his wife and child and the necessity of saving money won out: he took "a pair of pants to be altered to a tailor" and sent his regrets to the Duke. He booked his passage home, then waited a few days until his ship would sail and read De Quincey's *Opium Eater*—"the marvellous book". In the new coat he had bought on the Strand and with the gifts picked up for those in America—shoes and gloves for his wife, a fork for his son, a cigar case for his brother Allan, and medals and a bottle-stopper for the Duyckincks—he went to Portsmouth, whence he sailed on Christmas Day, as the *Pequod* later would, toward the white whale.

THE WORLD IN A MAN-OF-WAR

THE BOOK MELVILLE HAD CARRIED TO LONDON APPEARED there in January, 1850, and the American edition followed in March. *White-Jacket* shows Melville in complete command of the resources of his art, the narrative style precise or evocative at need and the rhetorical flights confined to the possible. Melville's ambitions were less in this book than they had been in *Mardi,* and he may have written it, as he had written *Redburn,* to take the cash and let the credit go for being one of the "men who *dive*". He was rather diving into the pork barrel of his nautical experiences and coming up with the last that was there in point of time. Added to his account of his adventures as a seaman in the American Navy from August, 1843, to October, 1844, was a propagandizing intention, directed particularly against the practice of flogging. Melville's protest against corporal punishment was neither original nor, at the time, especially daring, since agitation for the abolition of flogging had been going on for some years. Dana's book, as we have noted, was published the year Melville set out for the Pacific, and it contained an account of flogging—though aboard a merchantman—as eloquent in its own way in condemning the brutal custom as Melville's treatment of the subject. Before going abroad, Melville had written to Dana about "this man-of-war book", asking him to say a word for it if it were "taken hold of in an unfair or ignorant way". Melville's protest at the use of the cat came rather late in his own work, for in *Omoo* he had hazarded that flogging might be a means of securing the necessary toughness of sailors, though he wished it understood that he approved neither of means nor end. Flogging was abolished by an act of Congress about six months after the publication of Melville's book and, he said in a letter, he offered up "devout jubilations". Beginning a year before Congress's action, *The United States Magazine and Democratic Review* had run a series of articles agitating against flogging which in all likelihood was of more influence than *White-Jacket*.

Melville's criticism of naval practice included more than flogging. The *United States* (which sailed under the name of the *Neversink* in the book) had fought in the War of 1812, and thirty-one years later cannot have been the best-arranged of warships, so far as the comfort and well-being of her crew were concerned. As Melville points out, the hardships attendant on crowding five hundred men into something the size of a 19th-century frigate were much increased by the observance of a naval discipline that had been promulgated in the 17th century. The physical unpleasantness of seafaring was, by all accounts, no greater in the navy than in the merchant marine or the whale fishery, nor can the distinction drawn between officers and crew have been so very much sharper, but in the case of the navy hard treatment and depressed station carried a governmental sanction which made for a sense of final injustice hardly conducive to good morale. Melville, naturally enough, suffered from this feeling of injustice more strongly than the majority of his shipmates, and it may be that he therefore exaggerates the prevalence of the feeling. When he speaks of the officers' ideal of the sailor, it is not improbable that he thought of himself in contrast to that ideal. What they want, he says, is

a fellow without shame, without a soul, so dead to the least dignity of manhood that he could hardly be called a man. Whereas, a seaman who exhibits traits of moral sensitiveness, whose demeanor shows some dignity within; this is the man they, in many cases, instinctively dislike. The reason is, they feel such a man to be a continual reproach to them, as being mentally superior to their power. He has no business in a man-of-war; they do not want such men. To them there is an insolence in his manly freedom, contempt in his very carriage. He is unendurable, as an erect, lofty-minded African would be to some slave-driving planter.

But that the American Navy of his time was dominated by a spirit derived from that of the British Navy in the days of press gangs, not meliorated by any common acceptance of the hereditary aptitude of some men for rule, seems beyond dispute. The abuse of authority was frequent, as is usually the case where authority merely obtains from the book. "My own soul now sinks at what I myself have portrayed," says Melville near the end of his reminiscences, and he does indeed give a complete and explicit catalogue of horribly crowded quarters, abominable food, uncleanliness, medical care more an exercise in brutality than anything else, thieving, drunkenness, sodomy, indifference by the men in command to everything but insubordination, plus the stultification and going-by-the-rules that are endemic in navies. Though these evils could be lessened by curtailing "powers which exceed the due limits of reason and necessity" and though "most of the sailor iniquities . . . are indirectly to be ascribed to the morally debasing effects of the unjust, despotic, and degrading laws under which the man-of-war's-man lives", Melville disclaims any "sentimental and theoretic love for the common sailor". "The knotted, trebly intertwisted villainy, accumulating at a sort of compound interest in a man-of-war" was not determined solely by the organization under which the ship was run; it was the increment of a capital that the sailors, like all men, carried aboard with them. Or, since Melville himself is not consistent in these matters, we might lay a different emphasis in interpreting him and say that the evil and the organization are fundamental to the man-of-war's world in which they both exist and that the small floating world is in this the simulacrum of the bigger one.

Around the trope suggested by its subtitle, *The World in a Man-of-War*, the book is organized, and the *Neversink* is taken as a figure of the universe, foreshadowing the concept that was to be worked out with greater consistency and detail in *Moby-Dick. White-Jacket* is of course much closer to autobiographical fact than the work that followed it—though here, again, the author re-arranged and invented according to his needs and drew on written sources—but its allegorical strain is more patent just to the extent that it is more arbitrary. A ship at sea and the world are both societies; the analogy is immediately to be seen, but the correspondence of the two societies is not necessarily illuminating, and a certain amount of what Melville has to say lacks the quality of inevitability which a good story always has. A sort of wit-writing ensues which, though evidence of a real skill, remains a little bare in its contrivance:

In truth, a man-of-war is a city afloat, with long avenues set out with guns instead of trees, and numerous shady lanes, courts, and byways. The quarter-deck is a grand square, park, or parade ground, with a great Pittsfield elm, in the shape of the main-mast, at one end, and fronted at the other by the palace of the Commodore's cabin.

Or, rather, a man-of-war is a lofty, walled, and garrisoned town, like Quebec, where the thoroughfares are mostly ramparts, and peaceable citizens meet armed sentries at every corner.

Or it is like the lodging houses in Paris, turned upside down; the first floor, or deck, being rented by a lord; the second, by a select club of gentlemen; the third, by crowds of artisans; and the fourth, by a whole rabble of common people. . . .

And with its long rows of port-hole casements, each revealing the muzzle of a cannon, a man-of-war resembles a three-story house in a suspicious part of town, with a basement of indefinite depth, and ugly-looking fellows gazing out at the windows.

Among the rabble of common people, the narrator is distinguished by his white jacket—the substitute reefer or grego he made for himself out of canvas because he had been refused a proper one from the ship's stores. This jacket is another device for artistic unity, its manufacture given in the first chapter and the penultimate chapter recounting how the jacket caused him to fall into the sea, where he cut himself free of it with his knife. The fall from the weather-top-gallant yardarm is obviously susceptible of symbolic interpretation: the moment of awful peril met with a moral act by which Melville is freed from the garment that had marked him among the crew, hampered his movements, and given him so little protection against the weather, each in its turn understood as the token of a wider meaning. Equally, the significance of the fall may be accepted as wholly aesthetic, with no wider frame of reference than the series of events of which it is one: the dramatic and perilous moment in which the narrator cuts away the identity that has given us his story and takes his leave. No matter how received, the incident is an occasion of acute and vivid observation, so that it had been generally assumed that here Melville surely wrote of a terrifying experience of his own, until Mr. Anderson discovered the original of it in an unexceptional work called *A Mariner's Sketches* written by one Nathaniel Ames and published in 1830. Ames is not worth quoting here even to establish the parallel, but two paragraphs of what he contributed toward may be given as an example of Melville's art in recording exact sensory observation in a way to suggest something large and portentous in and beyond what the senses touch and, as is often the case in his purple passages, the prose submits to a nearly regular scansion:

As I gushed into the sea, a thunder-boom sounded in my ear; my soul seemed flying from my mouth. The feeling of death flooded over me with the billows. . . . I sank almost feet foremost through a soft, seething, foamy lull. Some current seemed hurrying me away; in a trance I yielded, and sank deeper down with a glide. Purple and pathless was the deep calm now around me, flecked by summer lightnings in an azure afar. The horrible nausea was gone; the bloody, blind film turned a pale green; I wondered whether I was yet dead, or still dying. But of a sudden some fashionless form brushed my side—some inert, coiled fish of the sea;' the thrill of being alive again tingled in my nerves, and the strong shunning of death shocked me through. ·

For one instant an agonizing revulsion came over me as I found myself utterly sinking. Next moment the force of my fall was expended; and there I hung, vibrating in the mid-deep. What wild sounds then rang in my ear! One was a soft moaning, as of low waves on the beach; the other wild and heartlessly jubilant, as of the sea in the height of a tempest. Oh soul! thou then heardest life and death: as he who stands upon the Corinthian shore hears both the Ionian and the Ægean waves. The life-and-death poise soon passed; and then I found myself slowly ascending, and caught a dim glimmering of light.

The white jacket also brought Melville to the especial attention of Jack Chase. The actual existence of a person of that name has been proven by Mr. Anderson from the muster rolls of the *United States*, and there is testimony that he was in real life the curious combination of the carefree sailor, the lover of poetry, and the born leader of men that he is in the book. Jack—"better than a hundred common mortals; Jack . . . a whole phalanx, an entire army"—who recited Byron and Camoëns in the maintop, who, "a stickler for the Rights of Man, and the liberties of the world", had once deserted the *Neversink* "to draw a partisan blade in the civil commotions of Peru" and become a gold-braided officer on a Peruvian sloopof-war, then with a gallant gesture resigned his commission to return to his humble place on the American frigate, who cried out against the captain when the crew was mustered to see the flogging of an old sailor "By Heaven! it's only a halter; I'll strike him!", who was nature's nobleman and civilization's democrat in proclaiming "The public and the people! Ay, ay, my lad, let us hate the one and cleave to the other", who announced " 'I've that here, White-Jacket'—touching his forehead—'which, under happier skies—perhaps in yon solitary star, peeping down from the clouds—might have made a Homer of me' "—this Jack Chase is the first of Melville's heroic figures to carry any meat on his bones. Taji, the moment he enters Mardi, becomes the wraith into which his author in the end avowedly transforms him, but, however highflown Jack's apostrophes in the maintop on starlit nights, we do catch the gleam of his white-duck trousers and the motion of the salt air in his "abounding nut-brown beard". Nevertheless, the approach to Jack is mainly external; he is there to be observed, an "incredible" object in the popular sense of something that is seen but not explained.

White-Jacket eschews the depths with a certain wariness, "for after all, philosophy—that is, the best wisdom that has ever in any way been revealed to our man-of-war world—is but a slough and a mire, with a few tufts of good footing here and there". It is this determination to keep to the solid surface that explains Melville's advocacy of a sort of evangelical Christianity. The tenets of Alma and Serenia are openly subscribed to, not, as some critics have thought, out of hypocrisy and as a sop to convention, but because the subscription is allowed by a duality in the author's mind. Melville's thought posed two levels of experience, on the upper one of which Alma's teachings were sufficient. But that what Christ said had of its nature to be either inclusively sufficient or not at all Melville felt and knew beyond any overt formulation, and when in his epilogue he once more used the metaphor of the man-of-war world, his uneasiness at having placed himself where ethics were divorced from just that world he pictured compelled him to give warning: "whatever befall us, let us not train our murderous guns inboard; let us not mutiny with bloody pikes in our hands".

In his attempt to remain on the surface of things, Melville in *White-Jacket* also rested on the doctrine of predestination in which he had been brought up. Fatalism and determinism may be essentially joyless, but the limits they put on inquiry make for a type of somnolent contentment, a spiritual laziness happy to suppose that there are no answers because that saves asking questions. Toward that curious equipoise—in a mood approaching despair, one imagines—Melville strove, saying that we "sail with sealed orders, and our last destination remains a secret to ourselves and our officers; yet our final haven was predestinated ere we slipped from the stocks at Creation". Within this scheme, the heart's moral aspirations are troublesome, always asking for more than the course of things appears to allow and unable to be taken for wholly rational while evil comes within the same scheme. Evil moves in the world like an independent agent, traveling everywhere in the complex web on the dark underside of life where "the heartless necessities of the predestination of things" are worked. And, strangely, there are some who are in accord with this dark agent and who find in it nothing of woe. Such was the sergeant-at-arms, Bland, "an organic and irreclaimable scoundrel, who did wicked deeds as the cattle browse the herbage, because wicked deeds seemed the legitimate operation of his whole infernal organization". At last, the demanding heart can be served only by a Titanism that will create its own world; caught in the indifferent progress of events, each man must turn inward to realize what he most aspires after and, by affirming

the articles of his belief, assert the independence of his will
from all the restraints his intellect has woven around him.

. . . All events are mixed in a fashion indistinguishable. What
we call Fate is even, heartless, and impartial; not a fiend to kindle
bigot flames, nor a philanthropist to espouse the cause of Greece.
We may fret, fume, and fight; but the thing called Fate everlast-
ingly sustains an armed neutrality.

Yet though all this be so, nevertheless, in our own hearts, we
mold the whole world's hereafters; and in our own hearts we
fashion our own gods. Each mortal casts his vote for whom he will
to rule the world; I have a voice that helps to shape eternity; and
my volitions stir the orbits of the furthest suns. In two senses, we
are precisely what we worship. Ourselves are Fate.

A man may well arrive at a desperate point in his philosophy
and make a public statement of it before he himself is involved
in it; and it is likely that at the time of writing *White-Jacket*
Melville had achieved a temporary equilibrium. It is likely, too,
that he enjoyed recalling his days as a man-of-war's man, for
hardship, danger, and toil are always pleasant objects of contemplation once safely passed. Though Melville's soul might
sink as he looked back on what he had written, there is a
quality of high spirits in the book and an outward-moving
tendency of the mind. The latter not only embraced the events
and sights of Melville's fifteen months aboard the *United
States* but also went on to a number of matters, entirely peculiar
to the *Neversink*, which are the book's highest manifestations
of literary skill. One, we have seen, is the fall from the mast
and is expertly fitted into the structure of the book. Another,
an occasion on which the narrator is about to be unjustly flogged,
adds a personal poignancy to the indictment of corporal punishment, besides stating in terms of dramatic conflict the moral
insight which is the book's leitmotif—the individual's inalien-
able right to be considered as one. The celebrated scene in

which the Surgeon of the Fleet, Dr. Cadwallader Cuticle, after divesting himself of his coat, neckerchief, wig, false teeth, and glass eye, demonstrates to a gathering of Navy doctors his skill at amputation obviously is derived from 18th-century models as much as is the doctor's name. Its macabre humor and broad satire, however, are brought out with an economy of touch and detail (allowing for the essential grisliness of the thing) that more than justify the imitation. In a similarly restrained style, Melville achieves another effect in recounting a death at sea:

. . . A dim lamp was burning on the table, which was screwed down to the floor. This light shed dreary shadows over the white-washed walls of the place, making it look like a whited sepulchre under ground. The wind-sail had collapsed, and lay motionless on the deck. The low groans of the sick were the only sounds to be heard; and as I advanced, some of them rolled upon me their sleepless, silent, tormented eyes. . . .

Shenly was lying on his back. His eyes were closed, forming two dark-blue pits in his face; his breath was coming and going with a slow, long-drawn, mechanical precision. It was the mere foundering hull of a man that was before me; and though it presented the well-known features of my mess-mate, yet I knew that the living soul of Shenly never more would look out of those eyes.

So warm had it been during the day, that the Surgeon himself when visiting the sick-bay, had entered it in his shirt sleeves; and so warm was now the night, that even in the lofty top I had worn but a loose linen frock and trowsers. . . . I sat by the side of the cot, and with a bit of crumpled paper—put into my hand by the sailor I had relieved—kept fanning the motionless white face before me. . . .

At last the heavy breathing grew more and more irregular, and gradually dying away, left forever the unstirring form of Shenly. . . .

It was placed on the death-board (used for that purpose), and we proceeded with it toward the main hatchway, awkwardly crawling under the tiers of hammocks, where the entire watch-below was sleeping. As, unavoidably, we rocked their pallets, the man-of-war's-men would cry out against us; through the mutterings of curses, the corpse reached the hatchway. Here the board slipped, and some time was spent in adjusting the body. At length we deposited it on the gundeck, between two guns, and a union-jack being thrown over it for a pall, I was left again to watch by its side.

I had not been seated on my shot-box three minutes, when the messenger-boy passed me on his way forward; presently the slow, regular stroke of the ship's great bell was heard, proclaiming through the calm the expiration of the watch; it was four o'clock in the morning. . . .

Hardly had the brazen din died away, when the Boatswain and his mates mustered round the hatchway, within a yard or two of the corpse, and the usual thundering call was given for the watch below to turn out.

"All the starboard-watch, ahoy! On deck there, below! Wide awake there, sleepers!"

While this is not writing that can't be equaled in many a lesser man's books, it is worth quoting to show that Melville had a firm grip on the more elementary details of his art, that he did not depend on the weaving of great verbal arabesques over subject-matters thrown to him by chance. Possibly the useless fanning in the hot sick-bay, the passage of the corpse under the sleepers, and the calling of the watch took place as described, but even the selection of these things from memory is the conscious action of the artist who knows what it is he would make. The exterior world is mastered in *White-Jacket* and marshaled into order on the written page, and on the weight and substance conveyed there the simpler (which are not necessarily the lesser) emotions attend, but the world beyond the senses is riven too deep and we are asked to believe it is brought to port merely because the frigate was.

THE BURNING OF CORINTH

AFTER MAJOR THOMAS MELVILLE THE YOUNGER HAD LEFT Pittsfield, the ownership of Broadhall passed from the Melville family, but the Major's son Robert continued to work the farm and take in summer boarders, as the Major himself is said to have done. Here, in the summer of 1850, came Melville with his wife and child to escape what he later described as "the Babylonish brick-kiln of New York". Shortly afterwards, Evert Duyckinck and his friend Mathews visited Broadhall and Duyckinck reported to his wife that "the house . . . is a rare place—an old family mansion, wainscoted and stately, with large halls and chimneys—quite a piece of mouldering rural grandeur" and spoke appreciatively of "Mrs. Herman Melville in a great flopping straw hat tied under the chin, floating about with the Zephyrs, in blue, pink, or lilac". He thought Melville might turn out a book about Broadhall, and this may have prophesied *Pierre,* in which the ancestral Saddle Meadows was modeled on Broadhall as much as on any of the Gansevoort houses around Albany. *Pierre,* however, must still have been entirely *in ovo,* for three days later Duyckinck wrote to his brother that "Melville has a new book mostly done—a romantic, fanciful & literal & most enjoyable presentment of the Whale Fishery—something quite new". If, after Duyckinck returned to New York and there was less gadding about the countryside, Melville settled down to his book again, it was, as he described the writing of a letter, under the garret near a "little embrasure of window" commanding "so noble a view of Saddleback" and at an old desk of his uncle's that he had rescued from the corn loft, marked by fowls and with eggs in the pigeon-holes.

The general vicinity of Pittsfield, which included the towns of Stockbridge and Lenox, had become the summer gathering-place of the figures of the literary efflorescence of the 40's and 50's. In the middle of the previous century, Jonathan Edwards had urged repentance on the Housatonic Indians in the forest about Stockbridge, riding over the forest paths with his notes for his great work disproving the freedom of the will pinned to his coat; a hundred years later, the thinkers of the day came there more willingly than he: the wilderness was re-asserting itself in second-growth timber, in the swift American pace the section already had an air of age, and the decaying farms were being taken over by people whose means came from cotton mills, journalism, and the colleges which were already a major New England industry. Among the summer visitors were Longfellow, Lowell, Dr. Holmes, Charles Sumner, Emerson, Agassiz, G. P. R. James, Fanny Kemble, Harriet Beecher Stowe, and a host of others whose names now mean nothing without the obscure information that was once their fame. William Cullen Bryant had been born in Cummington, some twenty miles from the three more noted towns, had practised law nearby in Great Barrington, and often returned to the Berkshire country. The Sedgwicks, a continuingly prominent name in New England, had long been established at Stockbridge, where Catherine Sedgwick wrote novels that are still readable to the sufficiently curious and where she maintained a literary salon, to which came Harriet Martineau, Washington Irving, and some of the Italian political refugees who, at the period, were almost as numerous in Boston as the American cultural refugees in Italy. But the most noted—as it eventually proved—of the Berkshire literary colonists was Nathaniel Hawthorne, who in May of the year of Melville's visit left

Salem and its customs house for the little red farmhouse near
Lenox that would become Mr. and Mrs. Pringle's place in
A Wonder-Book and *Tanglewood Tales*.

A month after Hawthorne's arrival, Melville's Aunt Mary
Melville, likewise staying at Broadhall, gave her nephew a
copy of *Mosses from an Old Manse*. Though he had possibly
read a few of the *Twice-Told Tales* and *The Scarlet Letter*,
his reading of the *Mosses* had a unique impact on him, moving
him to write an enthusiastically eloquent appreciation, which
was published in *The Literary World*. The weight of the
evidence is that Melville wrote his panegyric before meeting
Hawthorne. The first part of "Hawthorne and his Mosses"
by "a Virginian Spending July in Vermont" (the disguise was
even extended to Aunt Mary, who became "a mountain girl"
with cheeks like "strawberry beds") appeared in the August
17th issue of Duyckinck's magazine, and from one of the latter's
missives to his wife we know that he, Mathews, Fields (the
Boston publisher), Dr. Holmes, Melville, and Hawthorne
had been on a mountain hike on, at the latest, the 5th, during
which they were caught in a shower and drank champagne from
a silver mug. In the essay, Melville denies any personal
acquaintance with Hawthorne. Five days after the appearance
of the second part, Mrs. Hawthorne wrote to Duyckinck,
unable to "speak or think of anything but the extraordinary
review of Mr. Hawthorne" and asking of the author: "Who
can he be, so fearless, so rich in heart, of such fine intuition?
Is his name altogether hidden?" In a letter accompanying his
wife's Hawthorne, after referring to Melville's books with
approval, goes on to mention the author of the "Mosses",
plainly unaware of his identity: "But he is no common man;
and, next to deserving his praise, it is good to have beguiled
or bewitched such a man into praising and more than I deserve."
It is plain enough that the Hawthornes had no idea they were

personally acquainted with the author of the extraordinary review. Nevertheless, this continuing anonymity is a little curious. The protest of a Virginian in Vermont that he doesn't know so retiring a New Englander as Hawthorne does seem superfluous. Further, the statement in part one of the essay that it was written in a day allows that it may have been done at a later date than its by-line indicates. From what we know of Melville's fondness for mystification, it could be that he had written his piece after he had drunk champagne with its subject in a shower on Monument Mountain.

Hawthorne's characterization of the essay as a banquet too lavish in its hospitality for him to accept everything offered at it is a sounder judgment on what Melville had done than Melville's judgment on what Hawthorne had done. The passages in which Hawthorne is compared to Shakespeare and the dramatist analyzed, Edmund Wilson has said, "must have been inspired by [Melville's] sense of his own genius rather than by any clear conception of the quality of Hawthorne's".[1] The very fact that Melville chose *Mosses from an Old Manse,* which had appeared in 1846, instead of the just-published *Scarlet Letter* for his encomium is puzzling, as Mr. Wilson also notes, though the lesser work may have been chosen because a lesser work is often more attractive to the critic with a "message"— which in this case concerned, though unconsciously, the critic himself. It is not that what Melville said about Hawthorne was irrelevant; he was quick to apprehend what distinguished Hawthorne's work, but his praise blew it up to a dimension it simply did not have and his emphases were his own preoccupations. What so fixed and fascinated him, as he said, in Hawthorne was the dark side of Hawthorne's soul, "shrouded in a black-

[1] *The Shock of Recognition,* edited by Edmund Wilson (Garden City, N. Y., 1943: Doubleday & Company).

ness, ten times black" in contrast to "all the Indian-summer sunlight on the hither side".

Certain it is . . . that this great power of blackness in him derives its force from its appeals to that Calvinistic sense of Innate Depravity and Original Sin, from whose visitations, in some shape or other, no deeply thinking mind is always and wholly free. For, in certain moods, no man can weigh this world without throwing in something, somehow like Original Sin, to strike the uneven balance. . . . Still more: this black conceit pervades him through and through. You may be witched by his sunlight . . . but there is the blackness of darkness beyond; and even his bright gildings but fringe and play upon the edges of thunderclouds. In one word, the world is mistaken in this Nathaniel Hawthorne. He himself must often have smiled at its absurd misconception of him. He is immeasurably deeper than the plummet of the mere critic. For it is not the brain that can test such a man; it is only the heart. You cannot come to know greatness by inspecting it; there is no glimpse to be caught of it, except by intuition; you need not ring it, you but touch it, and you find it is gold.

How far Melville had come from Christian orthodoxy—in the entire scheme of reference, of course, since he personally had never rested in it—this passage makes plain. The pervading black conceit is indeed a long way from all that is implied when the paschal candle is lighted in the darkest night and it is said: "O certe necessarium Adae peccatum, quod Christi morte deletum est! O felix culpa, quae talem ac tantum meruit habere Redemptorem! O vere beata nox! . . ." The belief in the Redemption allows of no fascination with darkness, but the man for whom darkness is—and the contradictory metaphor has a quality of rightness—one of "those occasional flashings forth of the intuitive Truth in him", and for whom this intuition seems complete, will always find it hard to turn his eyes toward the light. And this is probably because, without the idea (really, the fact) of Redemption, blackness represents the extreme limit of human perception and the dark is the fittest symbol of what the solitary, the completely self-reliant, man faces. Wherever the Christian illumination has spread but is still denied, darkness is accepted only in a kind of despair. The Oriental with the same intuition, supposing he is untouched by Christianity, appears to escape despair, as Western man knows it, because of his inability to conceive of the notion of hope, and the terrors of darkness are for him in some degree mitigated because the ultimately desirable is Nirvana—which no argument that I know allows to be taken for anything but Nothing. But the mind which has been touched by Christianity cannot escape the notion of being—not necessarily as a metaphysical concept but as, at the least, an awareness of some external and enduring reality. If the conviction of the Redemption of the created part of this reality is lost—as that conviction was lost as early as the teachings of Manes and is still lost in those moderns for whom original sin is merely a "psychological datum"—but the fact that it is "being" is still kept in view, the imperfection of this being becomes something independent and in the end, its signs found everywhere, an omnipresent force with an intelligence of its own, like Ahriman.

Melville's thought would shortly so develop that it might be interpreted thus; Hawthorne's thought perhaps contained the germ of the same development but, for all his constant use of allegory and the very simple nature of the characters in his novels and stories, his interest did not extend much beyond the psychological, and he was content to observe the patterns of the New England consciousness without pushing beyond them to "ontological heroics". "All over him, Hawthorne's melancholy rests like an Indian-summer," Melville said quite correctly; but the "him" was his works and, though we know from his *Notebooks* how large a part of each day went into his writing, Hawthorne had sufficiently isolated his melancholy so that his son Julian, when he read the romances after his father's death, was amazed the man he had known could have written books so informed with sadness. Sharp as his perceptions were on the level to which he confined himself, or to which his type of vision confined him, Hawthorne certainly did not have "a great, deep intellect, which drops down into the universe like a plummet"; that sort of mind was rather his critic's. Melville's intellect was never a superbly ordered one, moving through experience with the constant power of making subtle distinctions; he was neither the mystic nor metaphysician he has been called; but his mind was one that at no point would arrest its own momentum and could not stop short of "the unspeakable foundations, ribs, and very pelvis of this world" and his genius was his ability to report his soundings as the experience of the whole man.

It was the recognition that the sincere artist is totally committed to what he says that lay back of his remarks on the brain and the heart. The "great, deep intellect" was "indispensable" to the "man in whom humor and love are developed in that high form called genius", but "only the heart" could test him. A year after the *Literary World* essay, Melville wrote to Hawthorne:

It is a frightful poetical creed that the cultivation of the brain eats out the heart. But it's my *prose* opinion that in most cases, in those men who have fine brains and work them well, the heart extends down to hams. And though you smoke them with the fire of tribulation, yet, like veritable hams, the head only gives the richer and better flavor. I stand for the heart. To the dogs with the head! I had rather be a fool with a heart, than Jupiter Olympus with his head. The reason the mass of men fear God, and *at bottom dislike* Him, is because they rather distrust His heart, and fancy Him all brain like a watch. (You perceive I employ a capital initial in the pronoun referring to the Deity; don't you think there is a dash of flunkeyism in that usage?)

Just what distinction Melville intends both here and in his essay between the heart and the brain is rather obscure, even as it is in all his writing. Heart and brain must stand for something more than any set of contrary tendencies a man may feel, for more than desire and reason in opposition. "The heart is the feminine in man," said a character who spoke for the author in Melville's last story, and long before Melville had described the mind as a China subject to constant invasions from the Tartar hordes of truth. There is, plainly enough, some tension between the two and they have not a common goal. This conflict Melville assumed to be a necessary condition of human existence, but the tension and anxiety it gave rise to he inevitably sought to escape. The conflict is, of course, not inevitable, and to state it as one between heart and head confuses its real nature. St. Augustine's description of the conflict as one between two wills is more revealing and indicates how the desired unity is to be found: in singleness of will. Singleness of will implies a singleness of vision as well. Ultimately the matter is one for what Melville called "psychologic theologians", but when he wrote of Hawthorne, the exploration of reality was presenting itself to him as a problem in his art—not a simply technical problem but also a question of what was to be found in this exploration, for his writing was for him, as it is for any serious artist, a vehicle of knowledge, not merely an instrument for displaying foregone conclusions. And the conflict that so troubled him had its surface equivalent in the fact that he had to write for money the sort of books he felt least moved to write: "What I feel most moved to write," he said in the letter just quoted, "that is banned,—it will not pay. Yet, altogether, write the *other* way I cannot. So the product is a final hash, and all my books are botches." But his disgust with the business of

writing he expressed when he was driving himself to finish
Moby-Dick; when he was at the beginning of the book and also
writing the essay on Hawthorne, the figure of Shakespeare had
suggested to him something better. Shakespeare, too, had made
his concessions to popular taste, but blackness remained

that background, against which Shakespeare plays his grandest
conceits, the things that have made for Shakespeare his loftiest but
most circumscribed renown, as the profoundest of thinkers. For by
philosophers Shakespeare is not adored as the great man of tragedy
and comedy.—"Off with his head; so much for Buckingham!"
This sort of rant, interlined by another hand, brings down the
house,—those mistaken souls, who dream of Shakespeare as a mere
man of Richard-the-Third humps and Macbeth daggers. But it is
those deep far-away things in him; those occasional flashings-forth
of the intuitive Truth in him; those short, quick probings at the
very axis of reality;—these are the things that make Shakespeare,
Shakespeare. Through the mouths of the dark characters of Hamlet, Timon, Lear, and Iago, he craftily says, or sometimes insinu-
ates the things which we feel to be so terrifically true, that it were
all but madness for any good man, in his own proper character, to
utter, or even hint of them. Tormented into desperation, Lear, the
frantic king, tears off the mask, and speaks the same madness of
vital truth. . . . In Shakespeare's tomb lies infinitely more than
Shakespeare ever wrote. And if I magnify Shakespeare, it is not so
much for what he did as for what he did not do, or refrained from
doing. For in this world of lies, Truth is forced to fly like a scared
white doe in the woodlands; and only by cunning glimpses will
she reveal herself, as in Shakespeare and other masters of the great
Art of Telling the Truth,—even though it be covertly and by
snatches.

Yet "Richard-the-Third humps and Macbeth daggers" were
to have their equivalents in *Moby-Dick*, and though Melville
complained of "those Americans who look forward to the coming of a great literary genius among us . . . in the costume of

Queen Elizabeth's day", in the full expression of his own genius he would use the language and postures of the Elizabethan stage, while the Renaissance hero, even to his rhetoric, would provide him with the model for his protagonist. Ironically enough, "the popularizing noise and show of broad farce and blood-besmeared tragedy", of which *Moby-Dick* has its due share, would account for perhaps the majority of the book's readers when at last it gained a wide audience. The irony went even beyond this: like *Gulliver's Travels*, the book would be turned over to children (instead of *Typee*, which Melville thought might be given to "the babies who will probably be born in the moment immediately ensuing upon my giving up the ghost. . . . Given to them, perhaps, with their ginger-bread") and appear in a children's series along with Hawthorne's *Wonder-Book*. Crowning it all, a future poet laureate would foresee a Judgment Day with "Moby-Dick, towing the ship Our Lord was in, with all the sweet apostles aboard of her". This is a strange picture indeed to draw from any possible reading of Melville's text, but Doomsday too will be strange, and it may be that in his simplicity Mr. Masefield saw better the end for which Moby-Dick was made than did Melville when he sent Captain Ahab to challenge the whale.

In October the Melvilles settled as year-round residents in Pittsfield. With the help of Justice Shaw, Herman bought a house about a mile from Broadhall in the direction of Lenox and within sight of the summer place of Dr. Holmes. Because of the Indian relics he found there, Melville named the place Arrowhead. More than fifty years earlier, the house had been a tavern; it was a central-chimney farmhouse of a type common in the region, but much larger than most—providing accommodation for the female relatives who, one or another, seem to have been constant guests there. Three mountains—Greylock,

Washington, and October—dominated the prospects from the house, "sitting as in a grand Congress of Vienna of majestical hilltops, and eternally challenging our homage". Toward Greylock Melville's own workroom on the second floor faced, and on the same side of the house, the north, he later built the porch that gave its name to *The Piazza Tales* (1856) and where, sitting in the summer, he was reminded of the sea: "For not only do long groundswells roll the slanting grain, and little wavelets of the grass ripple over upon the low piazza, as their beach, and the blown down of dandelions is wafted like the spray, and the purple of the mountains is just the purple of the billows, and a still August noon broods upon the deep meadows, as a calm upon the Line; but the vastness and lonesomeness are so oceanic, and the silence and the sameness, too, that the first peep of a strange house, rising beyond the trees, is for all the world like spying, on the Barbary coast, an unknown sail."

Through all the seasons and from attic to cellar, the house and its surroundings served Melville well, though in the end he would learn from it the sad lesson, which literary men are taught recurrently, that writing and farming can only be combined when the writing subsidizes the farming. The first autumn at Arrowhead he described in a letter to Duyckinck, remarking that he had "cruelly bruised" his pen-finger with a hammer:

It has been a most glowing & Byzantine day—the heavens reflecting the hues of the October apples in the orchard—nay, the heavens themselves looking so ripe and ruddy, that it must be harvest-home with the angels, & Charle's Wain be heaped as high as Saddle-Back with Autumn's sheaves. You should see the maples— you should see the young perennial pines— the red blazings of the one contrasted with the painted green of the others, and the wide flushings of the autumn are harmonizing both. I tell you that sunrises and sunsets grow side by side in these woods, & momentarily moult in the falling leaves.

In December he wrote again:

I have a sort of sea-feeling here in the country, now that the ground is all covered with snow. I look out of my window in the morning when I rise as I would out of a port-hole in a ship in the Atlantic. My room seems a ship's cabin; & at nights when I wake up & hear the wind shrieking, I almost fancy there is too much sail on the house, & I had better go on the roof and rig in the chimney. Do you want to know how I pass my time?—I rise at eight—thereabouts—& go to my barn—say good-morning to the horse, & give him his breakfast. (It goes to my heart to give him a cold one, but it can't be helped) Then, pay a visit to my cow—cut up a pumpkin or two for her, & stand by to see her eat it—for its a pleasant sight to see a cow move her jaws—she does it so mildly & with such a sanctity.—My own breakfast over, I go to my workroom & light my fire—then spread my M. S. S. on the table—take one business squint at it, & fall to with a will. At 2½ P.M. I hear a preconcerted knock at my door, which (by request) continues till I rise & go to the door, which serves to wean me effectively from my writing, however interested I may be. . . . My evenings I spend in a sort of mesmeric state in my room—not being able to read—only now & then skimming over some large-printed book.

Two years later the hero of *Pierre* sat down to a day of writing—which in Pierre's case Melville extended until half-past-four—in a similar north bedroom, where the drafts were as cold as any in the Berkshires. Here Pierre sat in deep layers of clothes, his feet on hot bricks and a hot brick under his ink-well and a crooked cane by his side so he could reach for his needs without "sadly impairing his manifold intrenchments, and admitting the cold air into their innermost nooks". Melville's lamentation over this scene no doubt derives more from the mood in which it was written than from any he felt when he was writing *Moby-Dick* in surroundings that held the Alpine cold in which the artist always works:

Now look around in that most miserable room, and at that most miserable of all the pursuits of man, and say if here be the place, and this be the trade, that God intended him for. A rickety chair, two hollow barrels, a plank, paper, pens, and infernally black ink, four leprously dingy white walls, no carpet, a cup of water, and a dry biscuit or two. Oh, I hear the leap of the Texan Camanche, as at this moment he goes crashing like a wild deer through the green underbrush; I hear his glorious whoop of savage and untamable health; and then I look in at Pierre. If physical, practical unreason make the savage, which is he? Civilization, Philosophy, Ideal Virtue! behold your victim!

Pierre's labors in New York, aside from the demands of the story, were necessarily less than his author's, the literary farmer's, in Pittsfield, and Melville reported himself busy at different times with woodcutting, "building and patching and tinkering away in all directions . . . corn and potatoes . . . and many other things to attend to. . . . I work myself; and at night my bodily sensations are akin to those I have so often felt before, when a hired man, doing my day's work from sun to sun." The famous horny-handedness of the sailor he had long since lost and he complained of blisters.

The scenery around Arrowhead also was utilized in *Pierre*, the first of Melville's "land pieces"; the house itself appeared in two sketches he contributed to *Putnam's Magazine* for March and May of 1856. In "The Apple-Tree Table" a garret is described which we may presume is drawn from the one at Arrowhead since it is typical of the unfrequented attics of country houses:

The roof shedding the water four ways from a high point in the center, the space beneath was much like that of a general's marquee —only midway broken by a labyrinth of timbers, for braces, from which waved innumerable cobwebs, that, of a summer's noon, shone like Bagdad tissues and gauzes. On every hand some strange insect was seen, flying, or running, or creeping on rafter and floor.

Under the apex of the roof was a rude, narrow, decrepit step-ladder, something like a Gothic pulpit-stairway, leading to a pulpit-like platform, from which a still narrower ladder—a sort of Jacob's ladder—led somewhat higher to the lofty scuttle. The slide of this scuttle was about two feet square, all in one piece, furnishing a massive frame for a single small pane of glass, inserted into it like a bull's eye. The light of the garrret came from this sole source, filtrated through a dense curtain of cobwebs. Indeed, the whole stairs and platform, and ladder, were festooned, and carpeted, and canopied with cobwebs; which, in funereal accumulations, hung, too, from the groined, murky ceiling, like the Carolina moss in the cypress forest. In these cobwebs, swung, as in aerial catacombs, myriads of all tribes of mummied insects. . . .

The sun was about half-way up. Piercing the little sky-light it slopingly bored a rainbowed tunnel clear across the darkness of the garret. Here, millions of butterfly moles were swarming. Against the sky-light itself, with a cymbal-like buzzing, thousands of insects clustered in a golden mob.

The passage is worth quoting less for its vividness—which many a present-day writer devoted to the housewifely polishing of minutiae could surpass—than for the fact that it was written about the time of which Elizabeth Melville later noted "we all felt anxious about the strain on his health" [2] and when, it has been suggested, Herman's behavior was so abnormal as to make his family fear for sanity. The ability to write exact and well-ordered observation is, of course, no proof that a man is not inwardly much disturbed, but that ability does show that the personal disturbance is not the substance of what the man is saying. The more eccentric works of the same period—notably

[2] "In the Spring of 1853" concludes Elizabeth's sentence. However, Melville's trip to the Holy Land in 1856 was for his "health".

Pierre and *The Confidence-Man*—are concerned with matters of greater spiritual significance than the appearance of dusty attics, but the command of writing in them, *quâ* writing, is just as great as in "The Apple-Tree Table", from which the necessary conclusion appears to be that Melville remained equally in command of his experience so far as it went into his books. "Abnormal" this experience possibly was, yet it is wholly consistent with the general estimate of the human condition given in both books, and we can, I think, judge his works in their own terms, without insisting that their chief value is as symptoms of a personal difficulty he could or would not state directly.

The other of the *Putnam's* sketches dealing with Arrowhead is "I and My Chimney", in which the house's big central chimney is celebrated. Merton Sealts [3] has proposed an ingenious explanation of this otherwise meandering, informal essay by which the chimney is translated into Melville's fortitude or soul and its supposed secret chamber into his father's insanity or his own and various characters concerned with the chimney are shown, through the use of anagrams, to be persons concerned with Melville's insanity in real life. Mr. Sealts's theory has the neat articulation of similar ones relating the measurements of the Great Pyramid to the ruins of Tiahuanaca and the sages of Thibet, and, its premises granted, is no easier to refute. However, it is interesting to remark that Elizabeth noted that the wife of the essay—who is all for pulling down or breaking into the chimney—was not herself but Maria Melville. It is not possible to say whether Maria, during her stay at Arrowhead, was doubtful of her son's sanity, but it does seem a safe inference, from what is known of her character and of such domestic arrangements generally, that she had ideas about the management of the house not always in agreement with those

[3] See his "Herman Melville's 'I and My Chimney'" in *American Literature*, May, 1941.

of the owner. At any rate, the chimney was not touched, except for the saws and witticisms Melville painted over the main fireplace, and it still stands today, soaring "from the cellar, right up through each successive floor, like an anvil-headed whale, through the crest of a billow".

However things were later, the first year or two at Pittsfield were active and pleasant enough. By the middle of December, eighty-five chapters of the book about the whale fishery were done. In March Hawthorne came for a short stay at Arrowhead. He and Melville retired to the barn, sat on the carpenter's bench, and talked philosophy. Toward the end of July, Melville was getting the last of the manuscript of *Moby-Dick* off to the printer (typesetting had begun before the book was finished) and getting in his hay. The Duyckinck brothers made a visit in August. In his *Notebooks* Hawthorne recorded an excursion made with them and Melville to a nearby Shaker settlement and spoke his distaste for the Shakers—like so many persons of puritanical habit, he appears to have been repelled by an open and avowed asceticism. Evert Duyckinck promptly wrote to his wife of more mountain climbing—an overnight ascent of Greylock or Saddleback, made along with a horse-drawn wagon, presumably to carry the roasted chicken, ham sandwiches, brandied fruit, champagne, port, rum, and cognac which he told his wife he had had on the trip. Around this time Mrs. Hawthorne described Melville in a letter to her mother:

He has very keen perceptive power; but what astonishes me is, that his eyes are not large and deep. He seems to me to see everything accurately; and how he can do so with his small eyes, I cannot tell. They are not keen eyes, either, but quite undistinguished in any way. His nose is straight and handsome, his mouth expressive of sensibility and emotion. He is tall and erect, with an air free, brave and manly. When conversing, he is full of gesture and force, and loses himself in his subject. There is no grace or polish. Once in a while his animation gives place to a singularly quiet expression, out of these eyes to which I have objected; an indrawn, dim look, but which at the same time makes you feel that he is at that moment taking deepest note of what is before him. It is a strange, lazy glance, but with a power in it quite unique. It does not seem to penetrate through you, but to take you into itself.

Under Bentley's imprint, *Moby-Dick* appeared as *The Whale* in London on October 18th, and early the next month it was brought out in New York by Harper & Brothers. Between the two publication dates, Melville's second son was born, and Peter Gansevoort's martial exploits were recalled in the boy's name—Stanwix. Almost at once, Melville got to work on *Pierre*. The wife of J. R. Morewood—a neighbor whose son married a niece of Melville's—reported that he remained at work in his room until dusk, "when he for the first time in the whole day partakes of solid food". The Morewoods' was a house where there were much social goings-on, and as a visitor there Melville cannot have been quite the recluse that Mrs. Morewood, according to a letter she wrote to Duyckinck in December, reproached him for being:

Mr Herman was more quiet than usual—still he is a pleasant companion at all times and I like him very much—Mr Morewood now that he knows him better likes him much more—still he dislikes many of Mr Hermans opinions and religious views—It is a pity that Mr Melville so often in conversation uses irreverent language—he will not be popular in society here on that very account—but this will not trouble him. . . . I . . . told him the recluse life he was leading made his city friends think he was slightly insane—he replied that long ago he came to the same conclusion himself but if he left home to look after Hungary the cause in hunger would suffer. . . .

The month before Sarah Morewood wrote her letter, Hawthorne had permanently quitted the Berkshires. The relationship between Hawthorne and Melville has been pictured as one in which Melville pursued and Hawthorne cautiously side-stepped, if he did not flee. That Melville both derived and sought more from their friendship than could ever occur to Hawthorne there was in it is plain. His own remoteness as a person Hawthorne was well aware of; "I have been carried apart from the main current of life," he remarked rather sadly years before he knew Melville, and Melville observed that "there is something lacking—a good deal lacking—to the plump sphericity of the man. . . . He doesn't patronize the butcher—he needs roast-beef, done rare." Nevertheless, loyalty and kindness Hawthorne had; six years after his first acquaintance with Melville, he would reproach himself that he had not succeeded in getting the younger man (Melville was fifteen years his junior) a consular appointment and he noted down that Melville was "better worth immortality than most of us". At the same time he recorded Melville's "characteristic gravity and reserve of manner", so that it cannot be that at any time he had felt himself compelled to retreat from his friend's importunate demands for attention and regard. It is possible that, during the first summer in the Berkshires, Melville was an indiscreetly frequent caller at the little red farmhouse, but if Hawthorne was caused any worry by this, it was probably for the responses of Mrs. Peters, the colored cook, and not for the intrusion on his own retirement.

The excessive demand made on friendship by Melville, spoken of earlier, was not an explicit due bill presented to Hawthorne for affections rendered which the latter found intolerable. That demand was exorbitant rather in the return Melville expected from himself—from the self which it is impossible for a man objectively to experience, but which, so long as, "like Russia or the British Empire, he declares himself a sovereign nature (in himself) amid the powers of heaven, hell, and earth", will seem to him the fit object of his deepest longing. Naturally, such a man does not recognize "the tormenting, mild image in the pool" for his own; that is why he thinks it possible to embrace it; but we may say that the fit object of his longing "seems" to be his self because perfection and delight as he conceives them are conditions created out of the self even in its longing. All the soul's desires tend, in their converging routes, toward perfection, a goal which it apprehends with no more prescience than does the body the satisfaction striven toward by any one of its active longings, and all human experience of that perfection shows it to be a contact with something wholly other than the self. When Hawthorne wrote to Melville his appreciation of the just-published *Moby-Dick*,[4] and Melville replied in a letter that is one of the great classics of auctorial gratitude, it is peculiarly noticeable that the figure of Hawthorne somehow fails to appear in the letter. An expression of gratitude is a gift made in recognition of a gift received, and the whole meaning of a gift is that it should in some fashion be the token of the recipient's worth; what Melville celebrates so eloquently is the moment when on the road to the Morewoods' he felt his and Hawthorne's identity:

Your letter was handed me last night on the road going to Mr. Morewood's, and I read it there. Had I been at home, I would have sat down at once and answered it. In me divine magnanimities are spontaneous and instantaneous—catch them while you can. The world goes round, and the other side comes up. So now I can't write what I felt. But I felt pantheistic then—your heart beat in my ribs and mine in yours, and both in God's. A sense of unspeakable

---

[4] When Julian Hawthorne issued in 1885 his father's biography, in which first appeared Melville's letters, he said that "Hawthorne's answers, if he wrote any, were unfortunately destroyed some years ago"—presumably by Melville himself. The internal evidence is that there were letters from Hawthorne, but the fact that only one side of the correspondence has survived has probably tended to make the relationship of the two men look far more one-sided than it was.

security is in me this moment, on account of your having understood the book. I have written a wicked book, and feel spotless as the lamb. Ineffable socialities are in me. I would sit down and dine with you and all the gods in old Rome's Pantheon. It is a strange feeling—no hopefulness is in it, no despair. Content—that is it; and irresponsibility; but without licentious inclination. I speak now of my profoundest sense of being, not of an incidental feeling.

Whence come you, Hawthorne? By what right do you drink from my flagon of life? And when I put it to my lips—lo, they are yours and not mine. I feel that the Godhead is broken up like the bread at the Supper, and that we are the pieces. Hence this infinite fraternity of feeling. Now, sympathizing with the paper, my angel turns over another page. You did not care a penny for the book. But, now and then as you read, you understood the pervading thought that impelled the book—and that you praised. Was it not so? You were archangel enough to despise the imperfect body, and embrace the soul. Once you hugged the ugly Socrates because you saw the flame in the mouth, and heard the rushing of the demon, —the familiar,—and recognized the sound; for you have heard it in your own solitudes.

My dear Hawthorne, the atmospheric skepticisms steal into me now, and make me doubtful of my sanity in writing you thus. But, believe me, I am not mad, most noble Festus! But truth is ever incoherent, and when big hearts strike together, the concussion is a little stunning. Farewell. Don't write a word about the book. That would be robbing me of my miserly delight. I am heartily sorry I ever wrote anything about you—it was paltry. Lord, when shall we be done growing? As long as we have anything more to do, we have done nothing. . . .

The divine magnet is on you, and my magnet responds. Which is the biggest? A foolish question—they are *One*.

All affection and love involve some feeling of identity; in a sense, we love others because they are like us, and in that likeness, our common creation by God, is the very obligation to love. And, in the practical mechanics of human relationships, we find it easier to develop our liking with those who resemble us because the resemblance gives us one or more avenues of daily approach. Their insight into, and their possession of, the Calvinist mind were at least one point of resemblance between Melville and Hawthorne; and the fact that Melville saw, not incorrectly, in Hawthorne an intelligence that could grasp the terms of his own discourse released his eloquence, allowing him to act out an inner person who developed in expression. Soliloquies posit an audience of some sort, and even the interior monologue supposes an unknown ear which appreciates the last nuance. Stanley Geist, in an unusually perceptive essay, has summarized quite aptly Hawthorne's meaning to Melville: "How haunting, how insatiable was his wish to speak to another human being across the eternity of space which encompassed his derelict planet, one comprehends perhaps most of all in the essay on 'Hawthorne and His Mosses', where Melville created his own image, named it Nathaniel Hawthorne, and stretched out his arms to embrace it in a fraternal compact with himself and Shakespeare. Eventually, of course, the illusion of Hawthorne crumbled before the reality, and Melville was left to consort with the ghosts of men who had died hundreds of years before—they alone (with Shakespeare at their head) affording him that sense of spiritual affinity which he sought vainly in the universe of the living." [5]

Somewhere from ten to twenty-five years after first meeting him, Melville put Hawthorne's portrait into *Clarel*. While, as I have tried to show, he confused the essential Hawthorne with himself, the man given to everyday observation he saw clearly enough, and the character depicted in *Clarel* agrees with the one generally allowed to Hawthorne. Hawthorne appears as

[5] *Herman Melville: The Tragic Vision and the Heroic Ideal* (Harvard Honors Theses in English No. 12) by Stanley Geist (Cambridge, Mass., 1939: Harvard University Press).

Vine, one of the doubting and troubled pilgrims in the mid-Victorian Holy Land. To the Arabs attending the caravan of Europeans, he seems "some lord who fain would go, for delicate cause, incognito", and to his companions his real identity is even more obscure, for he rarely speaks and he rides "o'ercast, estranged . . . in thought's hid repast", good-fellowship "a chord long slack in him". In the desert he rides like one "at home in dearth" and he has

> No trace
> Of passion's soil or lucre's stain,
> Though life was now half-ferried o'er.
> If use he served not but forbore—
> Such indolence might still but pine
> In dearth of rich incentive high. . . .
> A charm of subtle virtue shed
> A personal influence coveted,
> Whose source was difficult to tell. . . .
> Under cheer
> Of opulent softness, reigned austere
> Control of self. Flesh, but scarce pride,
> Was curbed: desire was mortified;
> But less indeed by moral sway
> Than doubt if happiness thro' clay
> Be reachable. . . .
> And yet
> Not beauty might he all forget,
> The beauty of the world, and charm:
> He prized it tho' it scarce might warm.
> Like to the nunnery's denizen
> His virgin soul communed with men
> But thro' the wicket.

Clarel, the tormented young divinity student who may not be Melville throughout the poem but certainly represents him at this point, tries to get beyond the wicket. On only one occasion will Vine make conversation at any length, and he is then facetious, though in a kind enough way:

> Divided mind knew Clarel here;
> The heart's desire did interfere.
> Thought he, How pleasant in another
> Such sallies, or in thee, if said
> After confidings that should wed
> Our souls in one:—Ah, call me brother!—
> So feminine his passionate mood
> Which, long as hungering unfed,
> All else rejected or withstood. . . .
> Does Vine's rebukeful dusking say—
> . . . . Art thou the first soul tried by doubt?
> Shalt prove the last? Go, live it out.
> But for thy fonder dream of love
> In man toward man—the soul's caress—
> The negatives of flesh should prove
> Analogies of non-cordialness
> In spirit.

Clarel wonders if Vine is merely exercising his power of charm as "pride's pastime" or if he would let go "his nature but for bar". Then the young man recalls his fiancée in Jerusalem:

> Nay, dizzard, sick these feelings are;
> How findest place within thy heart
> For such solicitudes apart
> From Ruth? [6]

But for the unhappy Clarel there was to be no wedding of souls in one: returning to Jerusalem, he met Ruth's funeral

[6] Amateur psychopathology has been current in literary biography and criticism for a quarter-century now, and with texts like these to go on, some of his critics have of course found evidences of homosexuality in Melville. Lloyd Morris in *The Rebellious Puritan: Portrait of Mr. Hawthorne* (New York, 1927: Harcourt, Brace & Co.) says: "Melville's agonized skepticism was, in all likelihood, not the cause but the symptom of his malady. That malady was undoubtedly an intolerable loneliness; a hopeless awareness of the necessity for a companionship

cortege. In middle life Melville knew this had to be, though he might not know the reason why. In his thirty-second year, he had held "the strange fancy, that, in all men, hidden, reside certain wondrous, occult properties—as in some plants and minerals—which by some happy but very rare accident (as bronze was discovered by the melting of the iron and brass at the burning of Corinth) may chance to be called forth here on earth; not entirely waiting for their better discovery in the more congenial, blessed atmosphere of heaven". Hawthorne, quite by accident, was the catalyst; the transmutation was unstable, but it lasted long enough to make possible one of the strangest of books.

---

so intimate and understanding that it could have been satisfied only by love. Melville's marriage was scarcely happy; it is probable that he was unsuited to marriage and it is likely that he was incapable of being physically attracted to women."

The assumption here seems to be that a sexual maladjustment necessarily precedes a deeply felt philosophical confusion. But the reverse can just as well be argued: after all, one of our vulgar terms for the pederast derives from the place-name of certain mediaeval heretics. That Melville sought in his association with Hawthorne (as Clarel did in his with Vine) a satisfaction that many persons only get incidentally to sexual love is obvious; but if the analysis I have given above of just what it was that Melville sought is approximately correct, then no love of any kind could have given it to him. The same longing, differently directed, could only have been satisfied in God. Melville does display many of the traits to be found in the contemporary homosexual neurotic as the type appears in psychiatric case histories; but the ideal type of the neurotic—homosexual or otherwise—seems to have many points of correspondence, as Dr. Rudolf Allers has observed, with the person who has an unresolved metaphysical problem. Of this Melville had his share.

Both women and sex simply as such are not well evoked in Melville's work, yet if anything so particular as women and sex were concretely presented in the work of an allegorical novelist, it would be even more worthy of comment. The celebration of male beauty, of which there are a few instances in Melville's work, is common to the literature of his time, a good many of whose heroes are, by present-day standards, androgynous in appearance. Finally, there seems to be no satisfactory definition of the homosexual except as the person who has, or wishes to have, physical relations with his kind. The "unconscious" homosexual seems a term about as meaningful as the teetotaling alcoholic.

MOST MONSTROUS AND MOST MOUNTAINOUS

WHEN MELVILLE'S PIERRE WAS ENGAGED IN WRITING A BOOK "which the world should hail with surprise and delight", his author wrote of him that "that which now absorbs the time and the life of Pierre, is not the book, but the primitive elementalizing of the strange stuff, which in the act of attempting that book, has upheaved and upgushed in his soul. Two books are being writ; of which the world shall only see one, and that the bungled one. The larger book, and the infinitely better, is for Pierre's own private shelf. That it is, whose unfathomable cravings drink his blood; the other only demands his ink. But circumstances have so decreed, that the one can not be composed on the paper, but only as the other is writ down in his soul. And the one of the soul is elephantinely sluggish, and will not budge at a breath." The complaint about slowness of composition could not have been made justly with *Moby-Dick* in mind, which, though it ran to more than nine hundred pages in the first edition, was written, either in two versions or one, in no more than eighteen months, as we have seen. Melville was describing what the writing of a book must be for any writer of serious intentions, but the notion that *Moby-Dick* is in fact two books, the profounder of which he had to couch in an esoteric language, has increasingly developed, and the result is a vast amount of exegetical literature in which the whale of the title is identified as representing everything from Fate to a vested interest in property.

It is true, certainly, that the story of *Moby-Dick* proceeds on two levels. On one level, as Melville himself wrote to Richard Bentley when offering him the still-unfinished novel, "the book is a romance of adventure, founded upon certain wild legends in the Southern Sperm Whale Fisheries, and illustrated by the author's own personal experience, of two years & more, as a harpooner". On the other level, it tells of an attempt at "an audacious, immitigable, and supernatural revenge" and is a terrible essay in blasphemy.

In his copy of the Psalms, Melville at some time marked the verse "The fool hath said in his heart, There is no God", and in the first of his more ambitious books Babbalanja said there were no atheists, "for in things abstract, men but differ in the sounds that come from their mouths, and not in the wordless thoughts lying at the bottom of their beings". "Take God out of the dictionary," Melville wrote to Hawthorne, "and you would have Him in the street." The blasphemy in *Moby-Dick* primarily intends no insult to other people's conception of God; it is not, like the blasphemy of Voltaire or the Victorian Samuel Butler, a mockery of beliefs assumed to be ridiculous, but an attempt on Melville's part to insult and assail the God of his own belief by confronting Him as an equal.

There are many men (perhaps, as Melville suggested, this is true of all men) for whom there is no question of God's existence; what concerns them is the way in which they will accept their relationship to God. Nor, once it is admitted, does it seem possible to conceive of this relationship as other than a personal one. No man can escape the awareness of his own personality, however elusive and beyond final analysis that personality must always be, and his awareness is accompanied by another of something not himself, by a less immediate, but no less certain, sense of a further personality that the existence of his own must assume. All this can be stated in metaphysical terms, but it is also a psychological datum, which men can treat in various ways, some choosing to act in their daily lives as though they had no such perception and some developing it toward the awful clarities of mysticism.

There is little evidence, I have already said, that Melville was either the mystic or metaphysician he has been called. He did, as Hawthorne remarked, reason much "of Providence and futurity, and of everything that lies beyond human ken", but he seems neither to have attempted nor approached anything like a system in these matters, for the individual human experience always took precedence in his interest over any explanation of why it should be so. "I stand for the heart," he said, and despite their many speculative generalizations his books are concerned with the heart's obstinacy in specific situations. Because his central characters lack communion with other persons, they are all Ishmaels of a sort, driven into what is, in the sight of the rest of humanity, a desert, but in this waste they are still persons, acting as much from the heart's prompting as from the head's guidance. This constant reference to the experiencing agent and insistence that no problem is solved if the solution does not reckon in the questioner to whom it is addressed might have been preliminary to mystical experience. Unfortunately, the personality that Melville glimpsed beyond his own seemed antipathetic to it; he would have to find his answers in the sovereign self, since the God of Calvinism forbade any closer approach.

By the time he sat down to write *Moby-Dick,* Melville of course professed no sort of formal religion. There is not any evidence that he underwent a struggle in relinquishing the Calvinism—Presbyterian, Congregationalist, or Dutch Reformed —in which he had been brought up; sailing about the Pacific had been enough to win him from Protestant orthodoxy. To the contented disbelief of his earliest manhood, succeeded the kind of inquiry he undertook in *Mardi*, where he arrived at the incompatible conclusions of Babbalanja and Taji—though a despair like Taji's has more than once developed out of a natural religion like Babbalanja's. But there is little need to give a precise formulation of Melville's creed at the period when he was writing his one great book. The general attitude, the *Weltanschauung*, attaching to religious dogmas will often remain long after the dogmas have been abandoned, and Melville's continued to be the Calvinist mentality, whatever his articulate credo was.

Had Melville been writing a theological thesis, the image of God appearing there doubtless would have been different from the one in *Moby-Dick*. Novelists, however, write not as they wish to but as they must; their material, in the sense of something more than the mere paraphernalia of their stories, is given to them and they set it down, voluntary agents only in their submission to their genius. The genius is less than the whole man, who may reject what it offers or, if he has the unusual powers, direct it to other ends within a range still predetermined by that genius. Melville consented to what his genius offered and, convinced of a boundless energy in himself, was ready to have his perception of God, his whaling adventures, and his recent reading transmuted into the stuff of "a hideous and intolerable allegory".

When Melville used those words, he applied them to the whale itself, not the story about it, for he was aware that real whales would have to swim and sound in real seas in *Moby-Dick* if the book were to answer its own imperatives. God could not be directly assaulted, but His creation could, and the whale was hunted not only as a symbol of creation but also as part of it. E.-D. Forgues, a contemporary reviewer in *la Revue des Deux Mondes*, said that Ahab tried to harpoon *Moby-Dick* because he could not harpoon God.[1] The quarrel with God is always the quarrel with the world as a man finds it or as he thinks he finds it. Another American of great talent, Mark Twain, who pursued the same quarrel at last ended it by destroying creation, taking the solipsistic attitude and declaring only the observer existed. "Nothing exists but you," the Devil, who was thus the boy's own making, told Theodore Fischer in *The Mysterious Stranger*. "And you are but a *thought*—a vagrant thought, a useless thought, a homeless thought, wandering forlorn among the empty eternities!" In Melville's story, at the close "all collapsed, and the great shroud of the sea rolled on as it rolled five thousand years ago"; not the whale but his pursuers had disappeared.

Father Mapple's sermon, delivered early in the book, sets the tone of what might be called the book's orthodoxy, for there are at least two kinds of conflict in the story. One is Ahab's conflict with the powers and Power he is defying and the other is the conflict between Ahab's heterodox religious ideas, largely Manichaean, and the more "prudent" and submissive notions originally announced by Father Mapple and later exemplified in Starbuck, the first mate. Father Mapple's sermon provides the initial crescendo in *Moby-Dick* and is the first of those meditations which give as much an impression of motion as the scenes of action themselves. To what extent Melville consciously set it there as a preliminary statement of his book's theme is a question that probably will never be fully resolved. The extent to which every last thing in *Moby-Dick* is knowingly contrived toward a foreseen end has been much debated, and more recently the general tendency has been to regard the work as a sort of Chinese carving in which one intricacy is contained within another, with hardly a sentence that will not reveal further and deeper meanings to patient inquiry.

[1] Referred to by William Braswell in *Melville's Religious Thought*.

The truth seems to be that no great deal of painstaking artistry went into *Moby-Dick*; Melville himself complained that the book was written in such haste that he could give less than his best to it, and the 19th-century practice of setting type while the writing was still in progress prevented any major revision. Broiled in hell fire, as Melville said the book was, the remarkable thing is that it fired with so few crazes. A singleness of vision does prevail throughout the book, and there can be no question of Melville's having merely blundered into his best passages. Yvor Winters points out that the earliest scenes in the book, laid in New Bedford, are painted in sombre gothic tones and are full of shadowed corners that hold dim auguries of the things that are to come.[2]

Moby-Dick is a sustained effort and a unified work; Melville's main purpose in writing it was surely clear to himself; and that a book is variously interpreted is as much a sign of its vitality as of its ambiguity. Yet, in the end, there remains some quality of the accidental about this book's greatness, for never again would Melville accomplish so brilliantly any task to which he addressed himself. Writing to Mrs. Hawthorne shortly after the book's publication, he made a statement which indicates that his must in some measure have been the case of the poet who, amazed, takes his pen and writes the inevitable word. "I had some vague idea while writing it," he said, "that the whole book was susceptible of an allegorical construction, and also that parts of it were—but the speciality of many of the particular subordinate allegories were first revealed to me after reading Mr. Hawthorne's letter, which, without citing any particular examples, yet intimated the part-and-parcel allegoricalness of the whole."

Whether or not Melville designed as much in his story as

[2] See "Herman Melville and the Problems of Moral Navigation" in *Maule's Curse* by Yvor Winters (Norfolk, Conn., 1938: New Directions).

has been found there, Father Mapple's sermon sets forth a standard to which Melville must have felt that he, as an author, would in a degree conform and which Ahab, in another fashion, would reject. The preacher is presumably drawn from two persons in real life, the famous Father Taylor who preached the Gospel in nautical language on the Boston waterfront and the chaplain of the seamen's bethel in New Bedford when Melville was there. Standing in a pulpit shaped like a ship's prow, to which he has climbed by way of a rope ladder, Father Mapple speaks in the little chapel whose walls are covered with plaques memorializing whalemen lost at sea. He tells how Jonah has sought to flee the obligation placed upon him by God and how at last "Jonah, bruised and beaten—his ears, like two seashells, still multitudinously murmuring of the ocean—Jonah did the Almighty's bidding". Woe to those, he says, who will not preach the truth.

"But oh! shipmates! on the starboard hand of every woe, there is a sure delight; and higher the top of that delight, than the bottom of the woe is deep. Is not the main-truck higher than the kelson is low? Delight is to him—a far, far upward, and inward delight—who against the proud gods and commodores of this earth, ever stands forth his own inexorable self. Delight is to him whose strong arms yet support him, when the ship of this base treacherous world has gone down beneath him. Delight is to him, who gives no quarter in the truth, and kills, burns, and destroys all sin though he pluck it out from under the robes of Senators and Judges. Delight,—top-gallant delight is to him, who acknowledges no law or lord, but the Lord his God, and is only a patriot to heaven. Delight is to him, whom all the waves of the billows of the sea of the boisterous mob can never shake from this sure Keel of Ages. And eternal delight and deliciousness will be his, who coming to lay him down, can say with his final breath—O Father! —chiefly known to me by Thy rod—mortal or immortal, here I die. I have striven to be Thine, more than to be this world's or mine own. Yet this is nothing: I leave eternity to Thee; for what is man that he should live out the lifetime of his God?"

This sermon—whose level of eloquence perhaps had not been reached since Edwards alienated his congregation at Northampton (for true eloquence does not always persuade)—preaches a stern God whose commands are hard and the reward for serving whom is not the delight offered by love but the one which a man may take in his own rectitude. There is no Christianity in the sermon and, indeed, very little concern anywhere in the book with anything that could be called specifically Christian: in neither is there a recognition of salvation as a freely bestowed gift. The orthodoxy of *Moby-Dick* is the orthodoxy of the Old Dispensation, and it is not surprising that 1,851 years after it had been set aside a man should find it intolerable. Captain Ahab's (and probably Melville's) world is ruled by an "army of inalterable law" which his heart calls on him to defy since his head can find no reason in its demands. Ahab was to be a sort of Jonah-in-reverse, standing forth "his own inexorable self" and slaying the whale rather than being swallowed by him. In his world where evil was as potent as good and where all had been pre-ordained, God could have designed him for his blasphemous rôle.

And Ishmael, in the same anomalous way, would do "the Almighty's bidding. . . . To preach the Truth to the face of Falsehood!" This truth might be in its various parts inconsistent—which Melville did not see—and therefore "mortally intolerable"—which Melville saw most clearly—but it rested on the authority of

a man of greatly superior natural force, with a globular brain and a ponderous heart; who has also by the stillness and seclusion of many long night-watches in the remotest waters, and beneath constellations never seen here in the north, been led to think untraditionally and independently; receiving all nature's sweet or

savage impressions fresh from her own virgin voluntary and con-
fiding breast, and thereby chiefly, but with some help from accidental advantages, to learn a bold and nervous lofty language—
that man makes one in a whole nation's census—a mighty pageant
creature, formed for noble tragedies. Nor will it at all detract from
him, dramatically regarded, if either by birth or other circumstances, he have what seems a half wilful over-ruling morbidness
at the bottom of his nature. For all men tragically great are made
so through a certain morbidness. Be sure of this, O young ambition,
all mortal greatness is but disease.

That morbidness Ahab's very name announces, for Ahab was
the worst of the kings of Israel, the apostate who worshiped
Baal. When Ishmael engaged himself and Queequeg, the tattooed Polynesian harpooner with whom he had made friends in
New Bedford, to sail on the strangely named skipper's *Pequod*,
he was assured that despite the name and "stricken, blasted, if
he be, Ahab has his humanities". Though the "certain wild
vagueness of painfulness concerning him" which Ishmael felt
was further stirred when a stranger appositely called Elijah
warned against the voyage, the young man had signed to sail
and in the cold dawn of a Christmas day, warned once more
by Elijah, he and Queequeg boarded the ship, which was preparing to put out while Captain Ahab remained "invisibly enshrined within his cabin". Toward nightfall, the *Pequod* sailed
out of Nantucket Harbor and the sun was gone when she was
headed into the open sea with "vast curving icicles" hanging
from her bows "like the white ivory tusks of some huge ele-
phant". The Quaker pilot, a part-owner of the ship, was
dropped. "Ship and boat diverged; the cold, damp night breeze
blew between; a screaming gull flew overhead; the two hulls
wildly rolled; we gave three heavy-hearted cheers, and blindly
plunged like fate into the lone Atlantic."

In the next brief chapter, a curious apostrophe to a character called Bulkington who has appeared once before and does not appear again, Melville announces what is to be the added dimension of the *Pequod's* voyage and what the meaning of the seas on which she ventures. He says that "all deep, earnest thinking is but the intrepid effort of the soul to keep the open independence of her sea. . . . In landlessness alone resides the highest truth, shoreless, indefinite as God. . . ." What Bulkington represents is not said. It has been suggested that he stands for human rationality, quite lost in the *Pequod's* strange voyage, and perhaps no harm is done if he is allowed to be that in "this six-inch chapter [that] is the stoneless grave of Bulkington". Yet, as Mr. Belgion has pointed out, nothing is added to the story if every person and thing in it is given an abstract equivalent that is its true "meaning". Certainly, all things in the book point to something beyond themselves, for, as Melville has Ahab say, "some certain significance lurks in all things, else all things are little worth, and the round world itself but an empty cipher to sell by the cartload, as they do hills about Boston, to fill up some morass in the Milk Way". But all things also have their situation in time and place; they are particular, as they must be for the purposes of drama, since there is no drama in a conflict of generalities and abstractions, but only in what concretely exemplifies them. The certain significance that Ahab seeks he wants so he may bend things to his private purposes; and all the reflections and generalizations Melville makes on the human state are incidental to the tale of one man and the men who attend him—a "grey-headed, ungodly old man, chasing with curses a Job's whale round the world, at the head of a crew . . . chiefly made up of mongrel renegades, and castaways, and cannibals".

Using the device of anticipation and delay which is employed throughout the book, Melville puts off the actual appearance of

Captain Ahab for some time. When the ship, sailing southward, passes out of winter, Ahab at last comes on deck, looking "like a man cut away from the stake, when the fire had overrunningly wasted all the limbs without consuming them, or taking away one particle from their compacted aged robustness". His face marked with a horizontal, livid scar, he stands partly supported by a "barbaric white leg. . . . fashioned from the polished bone of the sperm whale's jaw". This is the substitute for the leg he has lost to Moby-Dick, the white whale, and he has gone to sea to avenge that loss. But before this intention is made known, Ahab has been often seen on deck, his ship is approaching tropical waters, and the wide-spreading sea has made itself felt not only all about the *Pequod* but also in Melville's most discursive chapters. He calls all hands aft and, nailing a golden doubloon to the mainmast, promises it to the first man who raises "a white-headed whale with a wrinkled brow and a crooked jaw"—Moby-Dick. Wasn't this, Starbuck asks Ahab, the whale that has taken off his leg. "Aye, aye!" cries Ahab, "and I'll chase him round Good Hope, and round the Horn, and round the Norway maelstrom, and round perdition's flames before I give him up. And this is what ye have shipped for, men! to chase that white whale on both sides of land, and over all sides of earth, till he spouts black blood and rolls fins out." Starbuck, who alone amongst the crew dares to offer any opposition to the captain, objects: "To be enraged with a dumb thing, Captain Ahab, seems blasphemous." Answering him in a terrible speech, Ahab makes quite plain the reason for his rage:

All visible objects, man, are but as pasteboard masks. But in each event—in the living act, the undoubted deed—there, some unknown but still reasoning thing puts forth the mouldings of its features from behind the unreasoning mask. If man will strike, strike through the mask! How can the prisoner reach outside except by thrusting through the wall? To me, the white whale is that wall, shoved near to me. Sometimes I think there's naught beyond. But 'tis enough. He tasks me; he heaps me; I see in him outrageous strength, with an inscrutable malice sinewing it. That inscrutable thing is chiefly what I hate; and be the white whale agent, or be the white whale principal, I will wreak that hate upon him.

Starbuck at the time does not persist in his objections, but makes his own silent reservations. The other two mates are not given much to imagination and they do not speculate at all; if there is a whale to be hunted, they will hunt him: in so far as Ahab's purpose is the death of a whale, it accords with theirs. The crew—belonging to "the unreckoning and unworshipping things, that live; and seek, and give no reasons for the torrid life they feel"—are one with Ahab in the matter of the whale, won over by the mere display of his energy. At Ahab's order, the three harpooners toast his endeavor, drinking from the sockets of their harpoons. They are unbaptized savages—a Polynesian, an African, and an American Indian—and for them, children of darkness, there is not too great an audacity in Ahab's striking at the whale; used in their worship to placating whatever inimical powers are contained in the whale, why should they not thrust their steel at the same powers when the order to do so is as inspired as Ahab's appears to be?

There is not much to wonder at if Starbuck's arguments cannot prevail here. He does represent a sort of sanity as against Ahab's monomania, but his is "mere unaided virtue or right-mindedness", a quality of what would be comfortable prudence in any but these most uncomfortable circumstances. Unable to meet Ahab on an equal plane of argument or eloquence, to sway the old man from his mad purpose he can only urge the satisfactions of home, wife, and child. If he is the book's Christian champion, he champions a kind of cosy domesticity in which worldly foresight moderates each action. Melville was obviously more ambitious for Starbuck and intended him to have a nobler stature than this suggests. Nevertheless, it remains significant that Ahab's Christian antagonist is the brave but cautious sailor, the good husband and father, and the man whose final allegiance is to "the treacherous, slavish shore". One might half suppose that "orthodoxy" was connected with Lizzie and the two boys in the farmhouse in the Berkshires.

Ishmael joined with the crew in the oath Ahab asked them to swear: "God hunt us all, if we do not hunt Moby Dick to his death!" Although there was dread in his soul, there was also "a wild, mystical, sympathetical feeling": "Ahab's quenchless feud seemed mine". Ahab's feud could not have been to Ishmael the simple contagion it was to the rest of the crew, for when Ishmael mounted to the mast-head it was, by his own confession, less to sight sperm whales than to revolve in his head the problem of the universe. When Ishmael tells what the white whale was to Ahab, there seems to be as much agreement as sympathy in his exposition:

The White Whale swam before him as the monomaniac incarnation of all those malicious agencies which some deep men feel eating in them, till they are left living on with half a heart and half a lung. The intangible malignity which had been from the beginning; to whose dominion even the modern Christians ascribe one half of the worlds; which the ancient Ophites of the east reverenced in their statue devil;—Ahab did not fall down and worship it like them; but deliriously transferring its idea to the abhorred white whale, he pitted himself, all mutilated, against it. All that most maddens and torments; all that stirs up the lees of things; all truth with malice in it; all that cracks the sinews and cakes the brain; all the subtle demonism of life and thought; all evil, to crazy Ahab, were visibly personified and made practically assailable in Moby Dick. He piled upon the whale's white hump the sum of all the general rage and hate felt by his whole race from

Adam down; and then, as if his chest had been a mortar, he burst his hot heart's shell upon it.

And in the next chapter, the celebrated one on "The Whiteness of the Whale", Ishmael tells what the whale meant to him. "It was the whiteness of the whale that above all things appalled me," he says, for, despite its happier associations, "there yet lurks an elusive something in the innermost idea of this hue, which strikes more of panic to the soul than the redness which affrights in blood". What in him responded with horror to whiteness was "the instinct of the knowledge of the demonism in the world". The obsession with evil and the attendant notion of God's remoteness or even indifference arrives sooner or later at some form of Manichaeanism. There is no question of Melville's having been a formal Manichaean: his theology appears not to have been well developed enough for that. But Manichaeanism, in its different kinds, did have a fascination for him. Long after the writing of *Moby-Dick*, Clarel would cry out (though with reference to a particular Manichaean proscription of the flesh):

> Nay, nay: Ah! God, keep far from me
> Cursed Manes and the Manichee!

In *Moby-Dick*, the Manichaean doctrine that the visible world is the work of a lower and malignant power is more than once referred to, and Manichaeanism as a poetic myth is everywhere congenial to the story.

When Ahab brings out the whaleboat-crew which he has smuggled aboard and concealed below decks to serve in his own boat, the oarsmen are seen to be "aboriginal natives of the Manilas;—a race notorious for a certain diabolism of subtilty, and by some honest white mariners supposed to be the paid spies and secret confidential agents on the water of the devil, their lord", while the harpooner, Fedallah, is a Parsee and so a believer in the two Principles. He is described as "such a creature as civilized, domestic people in the temperate zone only see in their dreams, and that but dimly" and his descent is traced from the days "when though, according to Genesis, the angels indeed consorted with the daughters of men, the devils also, add the uncanonical Rabbins, indulged in mundane amours". Fedallah is meant to make our flesh creep and he plays a rôle like that of the witches in *Macbeth*, but he is also more deeply involved in the story.

Fedallah is a fire-worshiper and a practitioner of magic. Toward the end of the book, Ahab reveals himself as likewise a worshiper of fire and explains his scar: "Oh! thou clear spirit of clear fire, whom on these seas I as Persian once did worship, till in the sacramental act so burned by thee, that to this hour I bear the scar; I now know thee, thou clear spirit, and I now know that thy right worship is defiance." The god who can be defied can also be placated, for if in the first action men can oppose their integrity to his, in the second they can oppose their ingenuity. This placation is magic.

There is, indeed, an atmosphere of magic throughout *Moby-Dick*, not alone in the recurrent portents of what is to come in its predestined world (where such portents are rationally quite plausible) but also in Ahab's endeavor so to use these portents that he can slip through the interstices of the pre-ordained. Before Ahab announces his fire-worship or -defiance, he has destroyed his quadrant and resolved to steer the *Pequod* by dead reckoning. His throwing-down of the quadrant has been interpreted as his abandonment of reason by his rejection of science, though the fact remains that the seas into which Ahab wishes to sail were never open to science, practical or theoretical. On those seas, as Ahab conceives them, magic is not an irrational aid. "Ahab is Conjur Man," says Mr. Olson (rather like a black cook in a dialect story of the 70's). Ahab's world is an arbitrary one (for his moral imperatives are not connected with things as they are) whose forces may be propitiated or counteracted in kind, as one roll of the dice may be by another. In this malignant universe, man in his despair and exasperation may, like Ahab, be defiant or he may, again like Ahab, seek to manipulate for his own ends a realm that is nevertheless hostile to human values. Thus Ahab takes a Parsee as his adviser, a proclaimer of omens, who by his magian lore will enable Ahab to circumvent the demands of evil necessity. Ahab's attempt at appeasing the dark powers is, of course, a deception, as is all magic, which tries to cheat the forces it deals with by conceding less than it gains.

In the mysteries of literary creation, an author may come to serve his characters, and the suggestion of fetishism there is in the regard with which Melville turns over brute facts in his hands may be derived from Ahab. In any case, the chapters on cetology and on the mechanics of whaling (still full and reliable sources of information) are not mere catalogues of facts: they are the body from which the book's air of magic rises. Further, they contribute to the evocation of size and vastness which is fundamental to the book. This sense of physical largeness is, at its simplest, found in the book's length, nearly a quarter of a million words, and again in its scene, the oceans of the world, and in the creature which is there pursued—"the mightiest animated mass that has survived the flood; most monstrous and most mountainous!" While we are aboard the *Pequod*, Mr. Brooks has observed, "we are living from first to last in a world one degree larger than life", and the language by which this effect is achieved is one that has drawn on a wide range of literature and nature for images of the colossal. Melville has that concern with "amount and number" to which Thomas Wolfe's hero would later confess, and in this preoccupation with size there is perhaps something specifically American.

The huge has, to be sure, always fascinated man, whose constant essays in the enormous are probably a compensation for his own tininess in the scale of nature; but the American mind has a tendency toward the abstract which makes the colossal especially attractive to it. The exaggerated dualism of Puritanism inclines those who entertain it to place all worthwhile reality on the plane of the ideal, away from the corruptions of the material world. Since, however, the images of thought must still come from the world of sense, there seems to be no other vision of the ideal except as the particular inflated to gigantic size. Democracy, too, with its norm of the mathematical average, prompts toward a thinking in terms of vast aggregates. Melville's thought, however, was saved from being filled with featureless immensities by his interest in what I have called the magical; in his quest for the cunning duplicates in mind of each atom that stirs in matter, in what was rather like a search for those secret names which primitive people suppose give one power over things, he examined the various faces of matter with painstaking care. "From his mighty bulk," he said, "the whale affords a most congenial theme whereon to enlarge, amplify, and generally expatiate." Then to this he added: "Since I have undertaken to manhandle this Leviathan, it behooves me to approve myself omnisciently exhaustive in the enterprise; not overlooking the minutest seminal germs of his blood, and spinning him out to the uttermost coil of his bowels."

As he pursues this inquiry, or relates his story, one term of his free-tumbling metaphors is again and again an American phenomenon. The whaleman drags out the teeth of his catch "as Michigan oxen drag stumps of old oaks out of wild woodlands" and a solitary old whale, "like venerable moss-bearded

Daniel Boone . . . will have no one near him but Nature herself; and her he takes to wife in the wilderness of waters". Describing Ahab's retired state, he writes: "He lived in the world, as the last of the Grisly Bears lived in settled Missouri. And as when Spring and Summer had departed, that wild Logan [3] of the woods, burying himself in the hollow of a tree, lived out the winter there, sucking his own paws; so, in his inclement, howling old age, Ahab's soul, shut up in the caved trunk of his body, there fed upon the sullen paws of its gloom!" And in some lofty souls there is a Catskill eagle, and "even if he forever flies within the gorge, that gorge is in the mountains; so that even in his lowest swoops the mountain eagle is still higher than the other birds upon the plain, even though they soar". The river most familiar to Melville before he went to live by the Housatonic, the Hudson, gave its name to a school of painters who saw the native scene under an aspect of baroque grandeur and whose most celebrated member, Frederick Edwin Church, could equally encompass the Palisades, the Ecuadorean Andes, and a volcano in eruption.

Some of Melville's prose is indeed volcanic and overblown, written in what Mr. Blackmur has called "the gothic convention of language with all its archaisms and rhetorical inflations".[4] Yet the very looseness of the convention makes it a receptive vehicle for the jostling insights which Melville's imagination contained rather than ordered. The pragmatic test

[3] Willard Thorp's excellent edition of *Moby-Dick* (New York, 1947: Oxford University Press) contains the following note: "James Logan (*c.* 1725–80), an Indian leader at first friendly to the colonists, turned against the white man because of the slaughter of members of his family. His name was familiar to school children in Melville's time because they had to recite a supposed speech of Logan's made famous by Jefferson's use of it in his *Notes on the State of Virginia* (ed. of 1800)."

[4] See "The Craft of Herman Melville" in *The Expense of Greatness* by R. P. Blackmur (New York, 1940: Arrow Editions).

of his success in using it is the comparison with someone like Beddoes: Melville managed the adaptation of this style to a new subject-matter so well that his story has become the classic of whaling, while *Death's Jest-Book* is only a cleverly faked antique, interesting not because it deceives but because of the mistaken ingenuity that has gone into it. Though Beddoes wrote verse, the comparison is valid because in many passages in *Moby-Dick* the distinction between prose and verse is very thin indeed. Shakespeare gave to Melville not only "the prevailing black conceit" which he had ascribed to Hawthorne and perhaps the conception of Ahab himself, the manner of much of the dialogue, the inspired madness of Pip the black cabin-boy, and the fulfillment of Fedallah's impossible-seeming prophecies, but Shakespeare also gave him something of his language.

Besides those reminiscences of his reading that had already appeared in his writing, there must have been present in Melville's mind as he worked on *Moby-Dick* the echoes of Shakespeare's language, especially as it is used in the later plays, where sense and rhythm run over the iambic line and toward the greater flexibility of prose Shakespeare had shown him that language could enlarge perception as well as record it. There is in *Moby-Dick* much straightforward prose, in which we see through the writing to the object described, but the passages uniquely Melville's are those in which the apprehension of the thing spoken of cannot be divorced from the words used. In these Melville writes a far better poetry than any he would later write in regular meters. The first ship which the *Pequod* meets at sea is the occasion for a short chapter that, in its kind and allowing for the relative wastefulness of prose, seems equivalent to a sonnet. It is worth quoting in full here not only to isolate it in the perfection of its form, but also to illustrate the manner in which ordinary incidents of whaling are made significant in the story of Ahab:

The Albatross

South-eastward from the Cape, off the distant Crozetts, a good cruising ground for Right Whalemen, a sail loomed ahead, the Goney (Albatross) by name. As she slowly drew nigh, from my lofty perch at the fore-mast-head, I had a good view of that sight so remarkable to a tyro in the far ocean fisheries—a whaler at sea, and long absent from home.

As if the waves had been fullers, this craft was bleached like the skeleton of a stranded walrus. All down her sides, this spectral appearance was traced with long channels of reddened rust, while all her spars and her rigging were like the thick branches of trees furred over with hoar-frost. Only her lower sails were set. A wild sight it was to see her long-bearded look-outs at those three mast-heads. They seemed clad in the skins of beasts, so torn and be-patched the raiment that had survived nearly four years of cruising. Standing in iron hoops nailed to the mast, they swayed and swung over a fathomless sea; and though, when the ship slowly glided close under our stern, we six men in the air came so nigh to each other that we might almost have leaped from the mast-heads of one ship to those of the other; yet, those forlorn-looking fishermen, mildly eyeing us as they passed, said not one word to our own look-outs, while the quarter-deck hail was being heard from below.

"Ship ahoy! Have ye seen the White Whale?"

But as the strange captain, leaning over the pallid bulwarks, was in the act of putting his trumpet to his mouth, it somehow fell from his hand into the sea; and the wind rising now amain, he in vain strove to make himself heard without it. Meantime his ship was still increasing the distance between. While in various silent ways the seamen of the Pequod were evincing their observance of this ominous incident at the first mention of the White Whale's name to another ship, Ahab for a moment paused; it almost seemed as though he would have lowered a boat to board the stranger, had not the threatening wind forbade. But taking advantage of his windward position, he again seized his trumpet and knowing by her aspect that the stranger vessel was a Nantucketer and shortly bound home, he loudly hailed—"Ahoy there! This is the Pequod, bound round the world! Tell them to address all future letters to the Pacific ocean! and this time three years, if I am not at home, tell them to address them to—"

At that moment the two wakes were fairly crossed, and instantly, then, in accordance with their singular ways, shoals of small harmless fish, that for some days before had been placidly swimming by our side, darted away with what seemed shuddering fins, and ranged themselves fore and aft with the strangers' flanks. Though in the course of his continual voyagings Ahab must often before have noticed a similar sight, yet, to any monomaniac man, the veriest trifles capriciously carry meanings.

"Swim away from me, do ye?" murmured Ahab, gazing over into the water. There seemed but little in the words, but the tone conveyed more of deep helpless sadness than the insane old man had ever before evinced. But turning to the steersman, who thus far had been holding the ship in the wind to diminish her headway, he cried out in his old lion voice,—"Up helm! Keep her off round the world!"

Round the world! There is much in that sound to inspire proud feelings; but whereto does all that circumnavigation conduct? Only through numberless perils to the very point whence we started, where those that we left behind secure, were all the time before us.

Were this world an endless plain, and by sailing eastward we could ever reach new distances, and discover sights more sweet and strange than any Cyclades or Islands of King Solomon, then there were promise in the voyage. But in the pursuit of those far mysteries we dream of, or in tormented chase of that demon phantom that, some time or other, swims before all human hearts; while chasing such over this round globe, they either lead us on in barren mazes or midway leave us whelmed.

The *Pequod* comes the full circle of her isolation with the last ship but one she meets—the *Rachel*, also out of Nantucket, whose captain begs Ahab's aid in searching for his young son, adrift in a whaleboat. Ahab, driving the *Pequod* toward the season-on-the-line (the time when sperm whales frequent equatorial waters in the Pacific) where he knows Moby-Dick will be found, refuses help, and Melville's description of the parting vessels is again poetry. Again, it is not in those polyphonic sonorities in which the marked rhythms are most obviously "poetic" but in the manner in which the thing is seen:

Soon the two ships diverged their wakes; and long as the strange vessel was in view, she was seen to yaw hither and thither at every dark spot, however small, on the sea. This way and that her yards were swung around; starboard and larboard, she continued to tack; now she beat against a head sea; and again it pushed her before it; while all the while, her masts and yards were thickly clustered with men, as three tall cherry trees, when the boys are cherrying among the boughs.

But by her still halting course and winding, woful way, you plainly saw that this ship that so wept with spray, still remained without comfort. She was Rachel, weeping for her children, because they were not.

Before this encounter, Captain Ahab has completed his alienation from ordinary humanity. The elements have conspired to drive him back, but without success: he has kept all sails set in a typhoon; he has defied the lightning and the St. Elmo's fire which has danced on his mast-heads; he has replaced his reversed compass-needle with a sail-maker's needle; he has substituted a coffin for the sunken lifebuoy. Against every obstacle, he is determined to make known the rights of his "queenly personality", asserting its sovereignty "in the midst of the personified impersonal". At the same time, that very personality is the heaviest of the burdens he has to bear, and as he labors to carry out its dictates, it becomes as elusive and ambiguous as what he would oppose. After all, it is a creature as much as the whale and it is made by the same hand. The dominion of his queenly personality is limited, perhaps it and its realm are illusions, and he cries out: "What is it, what nameless, inscrutable, unearthly thing is it; what cozening, hidden lord and master, and cruel, remorseless emperor commands me; that against all natural loving and longings, I keep so pushing, and crowding, and jamming myself on all the time, recklessly making me ready to do what in my own proper, natural heart, I durst not so much as dare? Is Ahab, Ahab? Is it I, or God, or who, that lifts this arm?" God has done all this, he says, not he, reducing his world of evil to its final irrationality and implying that Omnipotence assaults itself. As to all for whom existence is evil, annihilation seems sweet to him: "But it is a mild, mild wind, and a mild looking sky; and the air smells sweet now, as if it blew from a far-away meadow; they have been making hay somewhere under the slopes of the Andes, Starbuck, and the mowers are sleeping among the new-mown hay. Sleeping? Aye, toil we how we may, we all sleep at last on the field. Sleep? Aye, and rust amid greenness; as last year's scythes flung down, and left in the half-cut swaths—Starbuck!"

Ahab, though his final gesture seems a larger one, like Taji is driven to embracing death. Knowing that in the end the whale cannot be conquered, he elects his own destruction, since he can work his vengeance on himself alone. Self-love is ineradicable, as modern psychiatry has shown in tracing out all its contradictory expressions, though the psychiatrists were hardly the first to understand that a self-love which falsely estimates its object will defeat its own aim. The exasperated Manichaean finally comes to prize himself above all the other parts of creation, but, since he too is a part of creation, he too partakes of evil and ultimately he must sacrifice himself, laying down his life not for another but only because it is not what he demands it should be; in a world that is evil, he offers his life up out of hate. He sees a hideous contradiction in the heart of everything, yet how can a contradiction exist? That it cannot is the first of the mind's certainties. "But it is this *Being* of the matter; there lies the knot with which we choke ourselves," Melville told Hawthorne, and just before the fouled harpoon-line choked Ahab the old man, unrelenting in his pride, cried out the same thing: "Oh, now I feel my topmost greatness lies in my topmost grief."

This, of course, is madness, and so much Melville knew: when he called Ahab mad, it was not merely to excuse him to his audience. The truth for Melville *was* madness when compared with the religious orthodoxy familiar to him (though this orthodoxy held the germ of the madness, as I have tried to show) and with the Unitarian and Transcendentalist optimism that was succeeding orthodoxy, the bump of which the orthodoxy was the hollow. The one person on the *Pequod* with whom Ahab had any human contact was the negro cabin-boy Pip, who had been driven mad when in a fit of cowardice he jumped from a whaleboat and thought himself abandoned in the sea. The prototype of Pip, as I have said, is Shakespeare's wise fool and more particularly Lear's poor Tom, but Pip is considerably more than an archaic ornament. Pip consistently speaks of himself in the third person as someone who has died— "poor little Pip, whose drowned bones now show white, for all the blackness of his living skin". Perhaps what is implied in this—rather than the "fadeless fidelity of man" that the boy showed toward his captain—endeared the little black to Ahab. "Like cures like," said Ahab in explaining his affection; both he and the boy had arrived at the same wisdom, though by different routes. When Pip jumped from the boat,

the sea had jeeringly kept his finite body up, but drowned the infinite of his soul. Not drowned entirely, though. Rather carried down alive to wondrous depths, where strange shapes of the un-warped primal world glided to and fro before his passive eyes; and the miser-merman, Wisdom, revealed his hoarded heaps; and among the joyous, heartless, ever-juvenile eternities, Pip saw the multitudinous, God-omnipresent, coral insects, that out of the firmament of waters heaved the colossal orbs. He saw God's foot upon the treadle of the loom, and spoke it; and therefore his ship-mates called him mad. So man's insanity is heaven's sense; and wandering from all mortal reason, man comes at last to that celestial thought, which, to reason, is absurd and frantic; and weal or woe, feels then uncompromised, indifferent as his God.

Ahab had come to the celestial thought that was also absurd and frantic as the servitor of his queenly personality, compelled to the discovery in a servitude which he could not escape; but Pip had attained it by the loss of his personality. "Ahab is for ever Ahab, man," declared the captain, and though, as "the Fates' lieutenant", he acted under orders, his bravery, which was his pride, made his service possible. Pip, in his cowardice, had descended into the element in which Ahab would be lost, the sea, whence he had come back with a knowledge which other men did not have but which had been so gained that he was no longer able to meet the demands of the "real" world. A knowledge that is crippling is madness. Pip's wisdom, "un-compromised, indifferent as his God", was as ineffective in the created world as its description implied his God was. The sub-stance of his wisdom was that good and evil are equal forces and that everywhere the latter bears on man more directly. Pip could tolerate this knowledge because, so to speak, there was no Pip. "Monsieurs, have you seen one Pip?—a little negro lad, five feet high, hang-dog look, and cowardly? . . . Seen him? No!" And Ahab, before all else insisting that he would be him-self, how should he tolerate it except by coming not to be?

You cannot catch Leviathan with a hook, and no one theory will fully account for *Moby-Dick*. Made of a strange stuff upheaved by the act of writing, it must, as Thoreau said of a very different man's writing, "be approached and studied like a natural object". It is not unprofitable to know that Melville perhaps first imagined the ending of his story when he read Owen Chase's account of the sinking of the Nantucket whaler *Essex* in 1820 by an enraged whale, that he scoured Thomas Beale's *The Natural History of the Sperm Whale* and other whaling books for his cetology and hunted down the whale in John Kitto's *Cyclopaedia of Biblical Literature*, that *Lear* is among the most marked of his copies of Shakespeare's plays, and that his knowledge of Gnostic and Manichaean heresies probably came from Pierre Bayle's *Dictionary*. None of this, however, will enable us to penetrate any deeper into the mystery of *Moby-Dick*. The mystery, it will do no harm to repeat, is not one of some secret doctrine worked into the parable of the white whale: what the story means was clear from the beginning and the English publishers deleted the most forthright blasphemies from the first edition. The mystery is rather the simple fact of Melville's success, the power of his strange and monstrous book.

Circumstances of time and place helped him. The immensity of the whale and the vastness of the sea, both of which he knew intimately, were equivalents of what he had to say—"objective correlatives" in Mr. Eliot's phrase. They were more, certainly, than just counters to put forth his meaning, for finally a great deal of what he had to say was derived from the things through which he said it. His Protestant heritage, the insistent dualism in whose extremes of light and darkness Calvinism saw all things, gave him his conception of the human lot and within the strait limits thus set on his thoughts and feelings he dived deep, to soundings where he saw no light but whose enveloping horror he was determined to report. Since the truths of art are not the truths of morals, and even less the truths of theology, what Melville came back to tell has its own particular verity: given his assumptions, this is what the world must seem, and also what the world *is* for a man of those assumptions. In Melville's world, Mr. Olson has noted, Noah and Moses were his contemporaries, and we have seen that Christ hardly figured there at all. Melville never fully understood Christianity. "Let faith oust fact," cried Starbuck, the only Christian on the *Pequod*, though no fact of any kind is perceived except through faith.

XII

THE AMBIGUITY *

HOWEVER DESPAIRING THE ESSENTIAL NOTION OF "MOBY-DICK" is, Melville had been filled with a re-assuring sense of his own creative energies during the writing of the book. "Oh, Time, Strength, Cash, and Patience!" he had exclaimed in an early chapter, and by the time the book was finished he found himself badly tried for all four, but this he could properly ascribe to external circumstances rather than to any deficiency of his own. In the last month of 1850, he had written to Duyckinck asking him if he could not send him "about fifty fast-writing youths, with an easy style & not averse to polishing their labors". He had need of them, he said, "because since I have been here I have planned about that number of future works & cant find enough time to think about them separately". Weary in mind with the last pages of his book and in body with the farm work at Arrowhead, he might write to Hawthorne: "My dear Sir, a presentiment is on me,—I shall at last be worn out and perish, like an old nutmeg-grater, grated to pieces by the constant attrition of the wood, that is, the nutmeg"; but when the book had appeared, he was, as we know, buoyed up with a sense of accomplishment: "I have written a wicked book, and feel spotless as the lamb." He felt capable of further wickedness, too: "So, now, let us add Moby Dick to our blessing, and step from

* The present book had been sent to the printer before I had read Henry A. Murray's introduction to *Pierre* (New York, 1949: Hendricks House, Farrar Straus). There are a number of parallels between Dr. Murray's estimate and mine of Pierre's character—especially in the way we both find Romanticism, neuroticism, and Manichaeanism compounded there. Perhaps this analysis is that much more credible in being separately arrived at by persons whose assumptions are as different as Dr. Murray's and mine probably are.

that. Leviathan is not the biggest fish;—I have heard of Krakens."

Almost at once, he began another book. It must have been well advanced by the first week of 1852, when he wrote from New York to Mrs. Hawthorne describing it as "a rural bowl of milk". It appears to have been finished by the middle of April, for he was then negotiating by letter its sale to Bentley in London, who had already lost more than £400 on Melville's works and apparently was not willing to offer much for the rights of what the author described as "my new book possessing unquestionable novelty, as regards my former ones,—treating of utterly new scenes & characters;—and, as I believe, very much more calculated for popularity than anything you have yet published of mine—being a regular romance, with a mysterious plot to it, & stirring passions at work, and withall, representing a new & elevated aspect of American life". Bentley had paid Melville £150 as an advance against the author's half-share in any profits earned by *The Whale*, but Melville offered to sell his new book "out-&-out" for £100. Bentley refused the offer; Harpers published *Pierre; or, The Ambiguities* in July and about four months later their English agents, having imported American sheets, issued the book in London. The publication of *Pierre* marked the turning point of Melville's career; during his lifetime, his popular reputation never recovered from the harm done it by this book, nor did he, except spasmodically, recover from the semi-paralysis of his talents induced by the mood in which the book was written.

With the steady growth of a Melville cult since the appearance of Raymond Weaver's biography thirty years ago, there have been numerous attempts to explain or to explain away *Pierre*. Since amongst its subject-matters are incest and the ambiguity of human motives, the book has been accounted a forerunner of Freudian psychology, or at least an anticipatory demonstration of its dogmas, and taken for one more proof of how far Melville was in advance of his age. "The greatest of Melville's books," Mr. Watson calls it. "It is the story of a conscious soul attempting to draw itself free from the psychic world-material in which most of mankind is unconsciously always wrapped and enfolded, as a foetus in the womb." [1] His age's failure to appreciate this advanced man also accounts for *Pierre*, it has been said; saddened and enraged by its misunderstanding of his gifts, he deliberately flung in its face an outrageous and nihilistic story. According to Mr. Braswell, "he intended *Pierre* to shock the readers of that day with its plot and theme, to irritate them with its characterization and style, and to bewilder them with its ambiguities".[2] Mr. Mumford is of the opinion that not only do the stupidity of the critics and the indifference of the public account for *Pierre* but also a maladjustment in Melville's life, perhaps sexual in character, that came to a crisis in 1851–1852.

All these deductions are drawn from some core of truth. However, the bad reception of Melville's books prior to *Pierre* has been exaggerated. It has been put forward by more than one writer that the praise given to the less ambitious stories as against the incomprehension with which *Mardi* and *Moby-Dick* were greeted especially hurt Melville's pride, at the same time making him hopeless of the success of the kind of book he really wished to write. Like any author who has to earn his living from his writings, he found the public demand on him irksome, complaining that though he wrote the Gospels in his century he would die in the gutter (overlooking that three authors of the Gospels died in worse places yet).

[1] "Melville's *Pierre*" by E. L. Grant Watson, *New England Quarterly*, April, 1930.
[2] "The Satirical Temper of Melville's *Pierre*" by William Braswell, *American Literature*, January, 1936.

For one who felt that he belonged to Shakespeare's company, in insight if not in accomplishment, the favorable notices that *Moby-Dick* received may have seemed rather too reserved, but nevertheless there *were* favorable notices and the most favorable of them—two in New York and one in London—were not unaware of the story's profounder meanings. Contemporary critics, to be sure, did not find in *Moby-Dick* the art and depths that have since been discovered there. Criticism of that kind is a cumulative growth, and one could hardly expect it to appear within a few months of the book's publication. Nor, again, could one expect Melville's work to engage his time as it has a later one: a great deal that we now see in the book is only to be seen down the vista of nearly a century. *Pierre* grew directly out of *Moby-Dick*, a sort of ponderous and ill-formed footnote to the earlier work rather than an answer to the public's reaction to that book, and much that is wrong with it follows on the impossible attempt to re-enact Ahab's tragedy with the protagonist as a youthful writer and the scene the world of every day.

Pierre is nineteen when the story opens. At this age, as we have seen, Melville was a short time back from his first voyage and was engaged in rural schoolteaching, while perhaps entertaining the literary ambitions shortly to be made evident by his contributions to the Lansingburgh paper; but Pierre Glendinning is the only heir of a patroon family whose estate, Saddle Meadows, stretches over two contiguous counties. His father has died in his son's thirteenth year, and Pierre lives with his mother, a proud lady who, though she is approaching fifty and her "grand climacteric", preserves her full beauty and whom he is in the habit of addressing as "sister Mary" in dialogues of such elephantine coyness that one wishes Mr. Braswell's explanation of them were correct. Pierre has everything to be wished for in this world: he is rich, he has position, he is healthy, he is handsome, he is contented in his situation, and he is engaged to Lucy Tartan, a lovely and devoted girl of seventeen. But when Lucy asks Pierre to swear that he will never keep any secret from her, he finds himself unable to do so, and his refusal is in some way connected with a face that has been haunting him ever since his seeing it at a village sewing bee to which he escorted his mother—a face "vaguely historic and prophetic; backward hinting of some irrevocable sin; forward, pointing to some inevitable ill. One of those faces, which now and then appear to man, and without one word of speech, still reveal glimpses of some fearful gospel truth." The face, it shortly turns out, is that of his half-sister, his father's bastard by a French émigrée. The girl, Isabel, has established her identity by a curious coacervation of circumstantial evidence, and Pierre is convinced of it because of a story concerning an early portrait of his father, because of the girl's resemblance to the portrait, and because in his last delirium his father cried out: "My daughter! my daughter!"

This knowledge of the existence of a half-sister overwhelms Pierre and opens up more problems for him than similar knowledge has perhaps ever opened up for a young man before—the usual reaction being, as Melville remarks, "a momentary feeling of surprise, and then a little curiosity to know more, and at last an entire unconcern". He is profoundly shocked by his father's misbehavior and feels that the issue of it, Isabel, must live with him and by the world be acknowledged as his equal. Since he knows from his mother's attitude toward a tenant's daughter who has got herself into "trouble" that she will never recognize Isabel, and since he does not wish to destroy his mother's image of his father, he decides to pretend he has married Isabel. The fictive marriage will enable him to take her under his roof, where he can force the world to accept her. Lucy of course must be sacrificed to this plan. He announces the marriage; his mother drives him from the house with blistering curses; and he sets off for New York with Isabel and Delly, the ruined farm-girl, hoping to support himself and his charges by writing, for which he has already evinced a certain talent.

But the world's refusal to accept Isabel is followed by its refusal to accept him now that he has lost his wealth and position. He becomes skeptical of all his former beliefs, and the book he undertakes to write, the story of an "author-hero" called Vivia, is an attack on accepted values and an exercise in nihilism. His publishers reject the book; in the meantime, he has used up what money they have advanced on it as well as what little money he managed to carry from Saddle Meadows, he has recognized his regard for Isabel as incestuous and her feelings toward him as the same, he has become physically ill, and, though Lucy (believing his marriage an actual one) has come to live in his odd ménage and help him as she can, he has lost his faith that anything will ever come out right in this world for one who tries to do the right. Calling himself "the fool of Truth, the fool of Virtue, the fool of Fate", he goes out and shoots his cousin Glendinning Stanly, who has several times insulted him and whom Mrs. Glendinning, before she too died mad, has made the heir of Saddle Meadows. In jail, where the two girls seek him, Lucy falls dead when she learns of the true relationship between Pierre and Isabel. Pierre cries out: "Girl! wife or sister, saint or fiend! in thy breasts, life for infants lodgeth not, but death-milk for thee and me!—The drug!" and takes from her bosom the poison which she has let him know she carries for herself should he ever leave her. As Lucy's brother and Pierre's one remaining friend rush into the cell and find the two corpses, Isabel takes the poison and quickly adds a third. ". . . She fell upon Pierre's heart, and her long hair ran over him, and arbored him in ebon vines."

Pierre, it is evident, is a tale of what Mr. Freeman has called "vast incredibilities". Curiously intertwined with these incredibilities are a number of things more or less equivalent to facts in Melville's own life and background. Saddle Meadows is Broadhall and its Berkshire landscape transported to the social circumstances of Dutch New York and there much blown up in size and grandeur. Pierre's military grandfather, whose namesake the young man is, is reminiscent of Peter Gansevoort in his initials and his great size. Maria Gansevoort and Mary Glendinning likewise share first names and initials. Herman's father, like Pierre's, "had died of a fever; and . . . at intervals lowly wandered in his mind", and though there is nothing to show that he ever had a French mistress, he had lived in France, so that a reader with this knowledge must wonder if Isabel is given a Frenchwoman for her mother only to supply her olive skin and raven hair. Allan Melville had had a portrait painted in 1810 that in some ways corresponded to the one that so fatefully influenced Pierre. The first of Pierre's literary productions, "The Tropical Summer: a Sonnet", is not implausibly a token for *Typee*. Pierre's sufferings with his eyes as he labors away at his book are certainly a reflection of Melville's own trouble during the composition of *Moby-Dick*. When Pierre's publishers, Steel, Flint & Asbestos, write to him that he has been receiving cash advances from them while passing through their press "the sheets of a blasphemous rhapsody, filched from the vile Atheists, Lucian and Voltaire", they do something that Harpers might not unreasonably have done about *Moby-Dick* and that it is surprising they did not do about *Pierre*.

These fragments of objective autobiography Melville may have introduced simply because in his previous writings he had always done something similar: his books had been compounded in varying degrees of his own adventures, his imaginings, and his reading. Pierre certainly is not offered as a faithful portrait of the young Herman, but there can be no doubt that he is a mask through which the Melville of thirty-two makes known his spiritual state. If, besides this, the external Pierre has a certain resemblance to the actual Melville, that is because by this time Melville was intimately involved in Ahab's experience and not merely imaginatively projecting it. Ahab's discovery of the contradiction at the center of being and his defiance of God for permitting it had been parts of an enormous fable, in constructing which the author enjoyed a kind of immunity from the evil consequences implicit in the story he had to tell. But Melville was not simply the artist, manipulating his materials for any aesthetic effects that might be obtained from them; he was also the Sage who sought after Truth, so capitalized. Having in *Moby-Dick* arrived at Truth, or at the truth that there was no Truth (the language that tries to express an entire negation is necessarily contradictory), he could not then abandon it as something which had been a convenient assumption for the writing of a tragedy, then was of no further use. Instead, it was Ahab's fabulous world that was abandoned, and the truth was retained to be demonstrated not with the huge symbols of the whale and the sea but with the unhappy situation of a young author come to grief in his effort to handle a number of practical problems.

Symbols are plentiful in *Pierre*, but the book attempts to observe the conventions of realism and presents us with people whom we are intended to take as real in the same way we take as real most of the characters in 19th-century novels. Despite this, the physical world is hardly present in the novel; the characters move, wraithlike and attenuated, against insubstantial backgrounds. Ahab, heroic in his proportions, is not one "of the same old crowd round the custom-house counter" but "is like a revolving Drummond light, raying away from itself all round it—everything is lit by it, everything starts up to it (mark how it is with Hamlet)", to use his author's own analysis of the "original" character in a later book. Melville's ambitions are obviously the same for Pierre, who is meant to be a kind of Hamlet, but the means of indicating his royal stature have not been found, so that we are steadily conscious of something disproportionate about him. Applying modern nomenclature to this disproportion, we can say that Pierre is neurotic. To call him neurotic still leaves him largely unexplained but does provide a convenient way of approaching him, for as the archetypal figure of other times was the hero or the saint so that of our times is the neurotic, the man whose contrary desires work their own frustrations, the man who has analyzed his motives and aspirations in all their aspects without ever coming to any satisfactory conclusion as to why he should entertain them. For Melville's heroes there was an intolerable contradiction at the heart of things; for the neurotic the contradiction is in his own heart. Perhaps the explanation of much personal unhappiness lies somewhere between these two extremes.

The subtitle of Melville's book is *The Ambiguities,* and the neurotic's attitude toward the things which trouble him is ambiguous. The neurotic's inability to come to a true practical decision, his doubts concerning the nature of his own feelings, the excess or deficiency of his responses—these follow on his values' being ambiguous or conflicting. The things his values seek to realize stand in opposition to one another—if one value is realized, it will cancel out the other; basically, the neurotic's position is "impossible". It is not only impossible subjectively taken but also impossible in the sense that his conception of the world and of himself in relation to it contains a false estimation of both. The proper estimation can only be determined with the help of metaphysics and, beyond them, of religion, though it is quite likely that there are psychiatrists who without the direct use of either can sufficiently restore a patient's use of common sense for him to avail himself of these further helps. However, the assistance of a psychiatrist was available neither to Pierre nor, so far as he was involved in the same kind of difficulties, to Melville. Pierre's was a metaphysical and religious problem. But since Pierre is given us as an entire individual, not merely as an embodiment of a number of general theses about life, we can inquire into just how his dilemma was peculiar to himself in our examination of its broader meaning.

What is immediately evident about Pierre is his egocentricity: his dedication to virtue is not so much from love of virtue as from the thought that nothing less high can be the goal of one like himself. When Isabel's letter reveals the flaw in the figure of his father which, "without blemish, unclouded, snow-white, and serene", long had been enshrined "in the fresh-foliaged heart of Pierre", his transports of anguish follow from the irreparable harm done to the ideal with which he identifies himself. The harm is irreparable because he will not accept any ideal other than the one he privately conceives. That is why he burns the offending portrait of his father, though a little charity, the recognition and forgiveness of his father's weakness, would have saved the portrait and encouraged a more mature form of the love for which it might then have stood. His deception of his mother and his fiancée (by which each is finally killed) is likewise prompted by his egocentricity; he elects for himself a lonely and heroic sacrifice rather than trusting to the power of love to render acceptable the revelations he should otherwise have to make. By concealing from Lucy the truth about his half-sister, it is *his* image of his father that he is preserving in her mind; and some admission to himself of just how selfish his mother was might have been the greater kindness to Mary Glendinning.

When the nature of his interest in Isabel becomes quite clear to him, Pierre is horrified that he should entertain such a passion, but he is not any the less unwilling to surrender what he esteems central to his personality and peculiarly his own. If his own "uttermost virtue, after all, prove but a betraying pander to the monstrousest vice", then the responsibility is not his: "For the rest, let the gods look after their own combustibles. If they have put powder-casks in me—let them look to it!" His entire self-dependence has brought him to the classic neurotic dilemma: he is tortured by guilt but he is not responsible for his own actions. In his loneliness, he experiences the full extent of human insufficiency:

. . . Pierre is quite conscious of much that is so anomalously hard and bitter in his lot, of much that is so black and terrific in his soul. Yet that knowing his fatal condition does not one whit enable him to change or better his condition. Conclusive proof that he has no power over his condition. For in tremendous extremities human souls are like drowning men; well enough they know they are in peril; well enough they know the causes of that peril;— nevertheless, the sea is the sea, and these drowning men do drown.

In his extremity, Pierre is not helped by either Lucy or Isabel. "On either hand clung to by a girl who would have laid down her life for him; Pierre, nevertheless, in his deepest, highest part, was utterly without sympathy from any thing divine, human, brute, or vegetable. One in a city of hundreds of thousands of human beings, Pierre was solitary as at the Pole." Though both Pierre and Melville have already glimpsed in Lucy "those high powers of immortal Love" that sustain the "weakest reed" against the "utmost tempest", at this point they have evidently arrived at the conclusion that love is a private affair, quite without efficacy to secure the good of its object (which unChristian conviction is one of the morals of the story). If, in a practical way, Lucy's love can find no sufficient access to Pierre, this is because of the deception he has practised on her, and the deception, as I have suggested, is a means by which he preserves his ideal picture himself, adhering to an isolated perfection that sets him off from the common humanity.

Romantic love is all a matter of ideals, but actual love is, among other things, a vehicle of knowledge, revealing a world in which at any one time the Ideal is only imperfectly embodied and, beyond this, indicating something more worthy and rewarding to be loved than the Ideal—the person. But no more than Ahab could can Pierre surrender the notion of his own perfection; as each facet of his revolving world shows that world in some new way short of what he asks it to be, he can only turn to himself for an example of all that is right and good. Turning thus inward, he cuts off all the avenues of love, and for him hate becomes the last possible emotion. When he crushes under foot the two insulting letters that impugn his integrity—the one from his publishers, the other from his cousin and Lucy's brother—he exclaims: "For now I am hate-shod! On these I will skate to my acquittal!" And when he shoots Glen Stanly, "spatterings of his own kindred blood" are on the pavement. Like Taji and like Ahab, his quarrel with things as they are demands his own blood.

From Pierre's relationship with Isabel there is of course no hope of any help for him; the relationship is, after all, the main exterior factor in his unhappiness. This anomalous business is the one instance in Melville's books in which love between the sexes is dealt with in any detail. The absence in Melville's works of sex as one of the chief of human concerns, with all its ennobling or degrading consequences, has often been remarked and, now and then, related to his own sexual experiences. Such a connection is wholly supposititious, since one of its terms is quite unknown, but Melville's general attitude toward sex is plainly enough set out where he addresses himself directly to the subject. Interpreting the zodiac, Stubb says in *Moby-Dick*: "Going from Virtue, Leo, a roaring lion, lies in the path —he gives a few fierce bites and surly dabs with his paw; we escape and hail Virgo, the Virgin; that's our first love; we marry and think to be happy for aye, when pop comes Libra or the Scales—happiness weighed and found wanting!"[3] and Melville seems to be speaking in his own person when in *Pierre* he reflects on "that nameless and infinitely delicate aroma of inexpressible tenderness and attentiveness which, in every refined and honorable attachment, is contemporary with the courtship, and precedes the final banns and the rite; but which, like the *bouquet* of the costliest German wines, too often evaporates upon pouring love out to drink, in the disenchanting glasses of the matrimonial days and nights".

Sexual love is one of the many worried ponderings of the hero of *Clarel*, and when he questions a saintly-looking monk about celibacy the monk, whose saintly looks evidently don't indicate wisdom, hands him a book of "old hermit-rhyme" in which Clarel reads "renouncings, yearnings, charges dread against our human nature dear". Clarel's worries are increased:

> Can be a bond
> (Thought he) as David sings in strain
> That dirges beauteous Jonathan,
> Passing the love of woman fond?

He reflects that "marrying none is in the heaven", then asks:

> But if Eve's charm be not supernal,
> Enduring not divine transplanting—
> Love kindled thence, is that eternal?
> Here, here's the hollow—here the haunting!

[3] Possibly Stubb here uses virtue and happiness with a general significance, but the context makes a sexual reference seem valid too.

The quotations from the novels seem to indicate some disillusion with love of the sort that comes when youthful expectations have much outrun what can be physically experienced, and the one from *Pierre* even extols courtship above fulfillment. Normally, human appetite establishes its own more feasible criterions, the satisfaction of which more than compensates for the loss of the illusion. But Clarel's difficulties are of a deeper kind, since they very plainly ask if love and sex are compatible and suggest that love between men, devoid of sex, is possibly loftier than that between man and woman. If we insist that all the satisfactions given to human nature are primarily sexual, we shall have to allow that sex is the genesis, in whatever remote fashion, of Clarel's reflections on masculine love; but if we give the priority to thought—which it must have in any ultimately meaningful analysis of the human circumstance—Clarel's inquiry is only in a negative sense sexually motivated. Clarel is plagued by Melville's own extremely dualistic conception of the universe; and all extreme dualisms look on sex with suspicion and repugnance, for in its mechanism sex is patently of the inferior order of things and its purpose is to perpetuate the evil of existence.

The mind's suspicions may deny to the body the pleasures of sex except on so low a level that for the whole man they cease to be pleasures at all, but the demand for love will remain, and so far as there seems a hope of meeting that demand in a human relationship, it will appear better for the relationship to be one free of all potentialities of sex. This, no doubt, is what Clarel has in mind. The same Manichaean type of thought may preserve the images of sexual delight but combine them with sterility. The heretical troubadours celebrated an endlessly unconsummated and sterile love, and the identical theme appears again in those Romantics who violently opposed flesh and spirit, then etherialized love between the sexes in a manner that has been a delight to later critics with an eye for the pathological.[4]

In a curious poem, included in the little book Melville privately issued in the last year of his life, the learned woman who speaks in it, having lost the opportunity for love by her devotion to study, asks of Nature in her tormented regret:

> Why hast thou made us but in halves—
> Co-relatives? . . .
> What Cosmic jest or Anarch blunder
> The human integral clove asunder
> And shied the fractions through life's gate?

Though we must allow for the dramatic situation that makes the occasion of the poem, this is a protest against the very nature of sexual love. Socrates' myth of the once-complete being now lost in the two sexes misses the essential fact of love, which is, after all, that the two sexes make it possible. The notion that sex is a means of recapturing a primal unity bears connotations, at once ridiculous and repellent, of an ideal solitude that is hardly the true circumstance of sex. The human integral, as it is conceived here, is really anti-sexual.

Isabel is Romantic in substance and accoutrement: her unbound black hair and dark eyes, the guitar from which she draws strange melodies by instinct and without musical training, the general dreaminess of her demeanor and behavior, the mystery about her origin and her life before her appearance at the sewing bee—all these are out of the gothic novel. What evidence we have of Melville's reading around this time does not show him especially devoted to contemporary fiction, but some of the

---

[4] The relation between Catharism and Romantic love is excellently traced out by Denis de Rougemont in *Passion and Society*, translated by Montgomery Belgion (London, 1940: Faber & Faber). The whole of the problem here incidentally touched on is dealt with by the Rev. M. C. D'Arcy, S. J., in his *The Heart and Mind of Love* (New York, 1947: Henry Holt, Inc.).

novels he is on record as reading (or at least either buying or borrowing) are of the broadest Romantic stripe, and it is quite possible that when he recommended *Pierre* to Bentley as "a regular romance", he thought he had sufficiently approximated the externals of certain of the books in Bentley's series of "Standard Novels" to make his description both attractive and exact for the Englishman's purposes. Yet he had been quite accurate when he said, before starting *Pierre*, that "write the *other* way" he could not. Isabel was surrounded with all the paraphernalia designed to give the gothic *frisson*, and though Melville made his book ludicrous by doggedly manipulating these to the very end, his mind once more dropped like a plummet to what the company of Isabels meant. Hindsight makes this meaning plainer than it can have been in the actual composition of the book, and there is no doubt that Isabel appeared to Melville's mind as a person rather than the illustration of a tendency and that as a human figure she fascinated him as much as he hoped she would fascinate his readers.

In recounting her early life to Pierre, Isabel raised an atmosphere of shifting uncertainties so that "all the world, and every misconceivedly common and prosaic thing in it, was steeped a million fathoms in a mysteriousness wholly hopeless of solution". Her childhood had been passed in places that she could not positively identify—a moldering building that might have been either a French château or one of the great houses built by French émigrés on the American frontier, on a ship that remained in her memory as a kind of land object, and in a madhouse where the sane visitors seemed the odder people —and when she at last came to distinguish herself as human and distinct in kind from her surroundings, she felt that "all good, harmless men and women were human things, placed at cross-purposes, in a world of snakes and lightnings, in a world of horrible and inscrutable inhumanities". In this antinomy, she experienced her humanity as a burden; it was anything but precious to her and she felt there could "be no perfect peace in individualness".

When Pierre was most bitterly engaged in the struggle to maintain his own unqualified individualness, she offered him peace in a renunciation that Dr. Henry A. Murray has called "the annihilation of the Ego".[5] "Then, my brother," she says to Pierre, "let us fancy ourselves in realms of everlasting twilight and peace, where no bright sun shall rise, because the black night is always its follower. Twilight and peace, my brother, twilight and peace!" The necessities of the story make Isabel propose twilit dimness instead of the blackness of night, but the figure she uses points toward the void. That her attendant mystery is the evil fascination of nothingness is indicated unmistakably when she, Pierre, and Lucy go for a boat-ride and, the swell of the waves evoking "her vague reminiscence of the teetering sea", she cries out: "Don't let us stop here. . . . Look, let us go through there! Bell must go out there! See! see! out there upon the blue! yonder, yonder! far away—out—out, out!—far, far away, and away, and away, out there where the two blues meet, and are nothing—Bell must go!"

Isabel's and Pierre's incestuous involvement has a variety of significances, but not the least of them relates to this aspect of her. After she has asked Pierre into her twilit realm and he becomes aware that he is entertaining inclinations toward "the monstrousest vice", he gets his first glimpse of the riddle that he will soon be self-destroyed in assailing. The riddle is the law, as he names it, "that a nothing should torment a nothing; for I am a nothing. It is all a dream—we dream that we dreamed we dream." If this is so, there is no reason why the pursuit of virtue should not terminate in vice and fraternal

[5] In his review of Lewis Mumford's *Herman Melville* in *The New England Quarterly*, July, 1929. Dr. Murray's reference is to *Mardi*.

loyalty hold the germs of sin. Though Melville notes that with Pierre "womanly beauty, and not womanly ugliness, invited him to champion the right", and that he could think of taking on a sister in the guise of a wife because he had played the rôle of his mother's suitor, only a modern prejudice will insist that his motive in taking up Isabel's cause was originally incestuous; it is implicit in the logic of his story that the best should develop into the worst on the plane where Pierre endeavors to carry out his actions.

Both Mr. Sedgwick and Mr. Braswell have identified Isabel as a symbol of the speculative intellect, in devotion to which Melville felt he had cut himself off from all normal human satisfactions. Whether or not Isabel was designed to stand for the agent of the inquiries to which Pierre committed himself, so that the incest is thus a symbol of his attachment to introspection, I think it can be argued without spinning too thin a thread of interpretation that Pierre's regard for her is intimately tied to his regard for himself and is indicative of how far gone is his allegiance to himself: intent on storming heaven and asserting his complete independence, he can give his love only to someone whose blood makes her an extension of himself. In the fantastic metaphysics of nothingness, where all things are equally true, there are no distinctions and no incest or, since there are no distinctions, perhaps all is an incest.[6]

About halfway in the story, Melville provides Pierre with advice that might have been the means of avoiding the ultimate tragedy. This advice is contained in a pamphlet that Pierre finds

---

[6] That Melville had a rather morbid curiosity about incest is plain. The story of the Cenci especially fascinated him, and in a note to *Journal up the Straights* Professor Weaver remarks: "There can be no doubt that the Cenci exerted upon Melville an almost obsessional fascination; first he goes shopping for a Cenci print, then to the Cenci palace (after thoughts of Shelley), and then to the Barberini Palace to see the painting."

in the coach in which he is riding to New York. Having read it in the coach, he cannot find it when he later wishes to consult it during his hard times in New York, not knowing that it has worked its way from his pocket into the lining of his greatcoat —a piece of symbolism too obvious to need explanation. The pamphlet is the only published work of Plotinus Plinlimmon, a "very fanciful and mystical, rather than philosophical lecture", in which Plinlimmon sets out a theory of two kinds of morality, analogous to the two kinds of time, chronometrical and horological. Chronometrical time is Greenwich time, the absolute standard of all time; horological time is the time in any given part of the world, relative to chronometrical time but of course not identical with it. There are then heavenly or chronometrical morals and earthly or horological morals. The first counsel perfection and the second undertake the degree of this perfection that is expedient. "In short, this Chronometrical and Horological conceit, in sum, seems to teach this:—that in things terrestrial (horological) a man must not be governed by ideas celestial (chronometrical); that certain minor self-renunciations in this life his own mere instinct for his own every-day general well-being will teach him to make, but he must by no means make a complete unconditional sacrifice of himself in behalf of any other being, or any cause, or any conceit."

This base philosophy of enlightened self-interest, Melville indicates quite plainly, sets out the only course alternative to the one on which Pierre is already launched; and Plinlimmon prophesies Pierre's fate when he says that "with inferior beings, the absolute effort in this world to live according to the strict letter of the chronometrical is, somehow, apt to involve those inferior beings eventually in strange, *unique* follies and sins, unimagined before". And it is of course fate rather than his will that brings Pierre to his follies and sins. Like Ahab, he is "gifted with the high perception" and lacks "the low, enjoying power"; in the malice of things, he has been given the chrono-metrical vision: he cannot escape its compulsion though to follow it in this world means disaster. Melville called the Sermon on the Mount "that greatest real miracle of all religions" from which flowed "an inexhaustible soul-melting stream of tenderness and loving-kindness", but he did not see what is truly the central miracle, the Incarnation, by which perfect love had come into the world that it might be concretely experienced by man.

To Pierre love was the abstraction; the rest was particular and experienced. Had Pierre been temperamentally fitted for it, he might have attained to Plinlimmon's entire abstraction (which, ironically enough, enabled the philosopher to be a practical man). When Pierre goes to live at the Apostles'—an abandoned church become a lamasery of Transcendentalist enthusiasts—he finds that Plinlimmon lives there too and occasionally sees him at the windows or in the hallways, but nothing passes between the two except the courtesy of smiles and tipped hats. The implication is surely that they can never come any closer. Plinlimmon is the "most miraculously self-possessed, non-benevolent man", wrapped in "a certain floating atmosphere" of "Inscrutableness". Plinlimmon is the man who having achieved a philosophy is willing to let the matter rest there: when one of his admirers sends him a collection of books on weighty matters, Plinlimmon returns them and, though an advocate of total abstinence, asks for "a few jugs of choice Curaçoa".

Plinlimmon uses his head, in all senses of the phrase, while Pierre has announced another allegiance: "Let me pursue the heart!" Though what Pierre finds in his heart he disguises "under the so conveniently adjustable drapery of all-stretchable Philosophy", he finds that "there is no faith, and no stoicism, and no philosophy that a mortal man can possibly evoke, which will stand the final test of a real impassioned onset of Life and Passion upon him. . . . Events are brass." A humanly insufficient faith and a humanly mistaken philosophy have led Pierre to a realm in which the last thing is the opposition of his heart to brazen fact. In a dream he sees the Titan Enceladus assailing the sky, seeking "to regain his paternal birthright even by fierce escalade", then sees that the Titan's face is his own. His may be the fault of angels, but for him the consequences are no less grievous.

Pierre, taken as a whole, is an artistic failure; it does not compel the reader to its sort of vision and it fails to create in the round. This is not the fault of the plot, despite all its absurdities, for on examination it proves to be a mechanism very well adapted to what Melville had to say. The "lesson" of the book is that truth is in its essence contradictory, that it reduces to two elements which stand in constant—and possibly eternal—opposition to each other, and that an insoluble ambiguity therefore plagues human existence. Though Melville is supposed to have expended all his creative energies in wrestling with the problems of metaphysics, his books, as Mr. Chase remarks, "are not philosophical in any strict sense of the word"; time and again Melville gave priority to the heart, and for him the heart was the register of immediate personal experience, the thing antecedent and superior to any general formulation. It is this irreducible kernel of the experienced thing to which Melville's mind, habituated by Calvinism to traveling along two discrete but simultaneous levels, returns after having propounded all its Platonic verities. "The heart, stirred to its depths, finds correlative sympathy in the head, which likewise is profoundly moved. Before miserable men, when intellectual, all the ages of the world pass as in a manacled procession, and all their myriad links rattle in the mournful mystery." Melville knew that this procession by itself did not make a proper book. Discussing Pierre's writings, he said: "For though the naked soul of man doth assuredly contain one latent element of intellectual productiveness; yet never was there a child born solely from one parent; the visible world of experience being the procreative thing which impregnates the muses."

The visible world of experience appears only intermittently in *Pierre* and nowhere with the fullness that it has in *Moby-Dick*. The Berkshire landscape—on which Melville must have looked as he wrote in his upstairs room—is not there and New York, the "vast triangular town", is only very dimly evoked. Nor do many of the characters have real substance. One gets the impression that Melville does not *see* Lucy, and though he is perhaps ironical when he says "her eyes some god brought down from heaven; her hair was Danae's, spangled with Jove's shower; her teeth were dived for in the Persian sea", she never becomes much more than the conventional figure the words suggest. Mrs. Glendinning, too, is largely a stock character— the woman "formed chiefly for the gilded prosperities of life" and "bred and expanded, in all developments, under the sole influence of hereditary forms and world-usages"—and if she has a little more substance than Lucy, it is only because she is the coarser type.

A good part of Melville's difficulties in this matter follow from the sort of dialogue he uses—a business of gothic Elizabethanism, full of hyperbole and thee's and thou's, which no character can utter without a great many hollow echoes. The sentimental novel of the first half of the 19th century abounded in such talk and possibly encouraged Melville in his extravagances; but Melville must have been his own model to some extent as well. When the characters in *Moby-Dick* use a Shakespearean mode of expression without losing credibility, it is because the world of the *Pequod* has its own laws, permitting the utmost eloquence to the simplest sailor. Pierre's world, on the other hand, is historically identifiable and the people in it, however lofty their thoughts or grand their emotions, are concerned with such things as surly cab-drivers, stovepipes, and sore eyes. There is no anachronism in Ahab's manner of speech because Ahab, almost a mythological creature, might really be less credible if he spoke colloquially, but a young woman, raised by tenant farmers in upper New York, no matter what mysteries she represents, cannot be made to say: "Thou art a visible token, Pierre, of the invisible angelhoods, which in our darker hours we do sometimes distrust. The gospel of thy acts goes very far, my brother. Were all men like to thee, then were there no men at all,—mankind extinct in seraphim!" And sometimes the dialogue is a mere arabesque of verbalism. Surely Melville did not have the suggested image in mind when he wrote: "Speak not to me yet awhile. . . . This thy clasping hand, my sister, *this* is now thy tongue to me."

Melville wrote thus badly because the task he had set himself moved away from the visible world of experience. He was intent on bringing forth the "invisible and eternally unembodied images in the soul" although, as he saw it, "better might one be pushed off into the material spaces beyond the uttermost orbit of our sun, than once feel himself fairly afloat in himself". He knew that in "the running stream of the outer world, there doubtless swim the golden perch and pickerel", but having already gone after the biggest of fish, he would not pursue these lesser inland creatures. He had thought to sail for the Kraken and the Kraken, as it turned out, was the void, into which in an impossible endeavor he threw his dart. *Pierre* is the description of that attempt and an object-lesson in the "certain downright infatuation, and no less, [that] is both unavoidable and indispensable in the composition of any great, deep book, or even any wholly unsuccessful attempt at any great, deep book".

As such it has its rewards for the patient reader, but Melville in his infatuation had turned his eyes away from the substantial world in which art must participate to exist. This inattention was something no novelist could afford.

XIII

MT. GREYLOCK AND
MT. AGONIA

IN THE MONTH OF "PIERRE'S" PUBLICATION, MELVILLE WENT to Nantucket, thus making, in what was probably a vacation after the labors on his book, his first visit to the island from which the *Pequod* had sailed. Either there or in New Bedford a lawyer of the latter place told him a story of a bigamous sailor, and shortly afterwards Melville sent the story on to Hawthorne with rather detailed suggestions of the way in which he thought Hawthorne might use it, saying that the stuff of the tale seemed better suited to the older man's talents than his own. A month later he visited Hawthorne in Concord, where they talked the story over further, though in the end, as Melville some thirty years later told Julian Hawthorne, Hawthorne did not seem to take to it. Shortly afterward, Melville considered using the story himself and wrote Hawthorne: "I invoke your blessing on my endeavors; and breathe a fair wind upon me." But his first attempt at short fiction [1] apparently came to nothing.

At Concord the friends presumably talked over a number of practical problems too, for around this time Hawthorne—who had written the campaign biography of Franklin Pierce, then the President—used what political influence he had in an effort to secure Melville a job in the consular service, besides giving Melville's name to Commodore Perry as someone who might

---

[1] The chapter in *Moby-Dick* called "The Town-Ho's Story" had been first published separately and may even have been written with separate publication in mind.

get together from the Commodore's notes an account of the opening of Japan. Hawthorne did better for himself than for Melville (there is no question of his not having urged Melville's case faithfully); he was made consul at Liverpool, where Melville, still a resident of Pittsfield and still attempting to earn a living by writing, would briefly call on him four years later.

For more than a year nothing of Melville's appeared in print. It may be that *Pierre* had left him with no more to say for the time being, although the letters he had written to Hawthorne were ones from a man still enthusiastic about what could be done in fiction. In the last novel he would publish, Melville remarked, rather ironically, that "so precious to man is the approbation of his kind, that to rest, though but under an imaginary censure applied to a work of imagination, is no easy thing". Still the quite real censure applied to *Pierre* can have discouraged him. The few notices it received were all unfavorable, and two essays, dealing with his work generally, that appeared in 1853 advised him to avoid any more performances like this one. Melville had already said: "All Fame is patronage. Let me be infamous: there is no patronage in *that*"; but, as his letter to Bentley suggests, he may have thought to combine dollar-earning melodrama with his own profoundest truths, so that he was overcome with a sense of personal inadequacy when he found he could not do it.

Around this time, as I have remarked earlier, Elizabeth said that all the family were worried about the strain on Herman's health; and it has been offered, on the authority of conversations with his daughters and granddaughters, that in the spring of 1853 his behavior was so difficult his family had him examined for his sanity by a number of doctors including Oliver Wendell Holmes. Much later he would write with signs of personal distaste about "the remunerated medical experts" with their "direct contradictions" and "perplexing strife" over questions of sanity. There is nothing implausible in supposing that a man who could not make his peace with God found peaceful relations with his family extremely difficult and that after his metaphysics had been given a species of ideal demonstration in *Pierre* they should, of their own power, work out to a practical, and less heroic, demonstration at Arrowhead. Neither is it implausible to suppose that a man who had found existence itself an irrational affair should seem, to those closest to him, deficient in the kind of surface consistency they at least were able to observe.

Certainly Melville in his early thirties had looked at madness and seen it plain, as he would do now and again to the end of his life, but what he saw we know from his own words—which means that he himself escaped it, however narrowly.[2] Madness assumes a world that does not exist. This world of endlessly "superinduced superficies", "appallingly vacant as vast" at its center, might attend the other world at Arrowhead and most make itself felt in the attic studio, but downstairs the other world's demands were quite unambiguously stated by the butcher, the baker, and the new baby, Elizabeth. By the end of 1854, Melville had in the attic studio made his response to these demands with seven pieces, one of considerable length, that were published in *Putnam's Monthly Magazine* and *Har-*

[2] In 1849 Melville had commented on the insanity of Charles Fenno Hoffman, who had been, among his many other literary activities, an editor of *The Literary World*: "This going mad of a friend or acquaintance comes straight home to every man who feels his soul in him,—which but few men do. For in all of us lodges the same fuel to light the same fire. And he who has never felt, momentarily, what madness is has but a mouthful of brains. What sort of sensation permanent madness is may be very well imagined—just as we may imagine how we felt when we were infants, tho' we cannot recall it. In both conditions we are irresponsible & riot like gods without fear of fate. —It is the climax of a mad night of revelry when the blood has been transmuted into brandy. —But if we prate much of this thing we shall be illustrating our own proposition." The madness Pierre had regarded was nothing so exhilarating.

per's New Monthly Magazine and a novel of more than 60,000 words, finished by the middle of June, 1854, and serialized in *Putnam's.*

The first two of the stories to appear, "Bartleby the Scrivener" and "Cock-a-doodle-doo! or, The Crowing of the Noble Cock Beneventano", are written by a hand in no manner uncertain of itself and "Bartleby" is as good as any shorter thing Melville wrote. If we look for autobiographical content in them, we are of course reduced to surmise, and especially in the case of "Bartleby" it is perhaps better to follow Isabel's advice and allow that "far sweeter are mysteries than surmises". "Bartleby" really invites to contemplation, not to interpretation, and when the critic says that Bartleby's answer to all the questions of his simple life, "I prefer not to", indicates Melville's response to the horrible complexities he himself had raised, Bartleby is no longer the completely independent creature in which all that is "given" in human nature appears like an object in a world of objects. Bartleby may well be the minus of which Ahab is the plus, and so a symbol of Melville's renunciation of impossible ambitions; and the rooster Beneventano, whose "triumphant thanksgiving of a cock-crow" dispels "the doleful dumps" and eases death itself, may represent what Melville then fell back on—that minimum of optimism which all of us carry with us and which will send even the gloomiest character into the village tavern for "a bottle of Philadelphia porter, and some Herkimer cheese, and a roll"; but when we insist on these things, both stories lose their fairy-tale charm. The charm of the fairy tale is to have no narrator, as children in their primitive clarity well appreciate: they know that a fairy tale is something that simply *is*, to be brought out each time exactly as it was before, with no nonsense about the evoking agent's weariness or boredom.

Mt. Greylock and Mt. Agonia

Melville's humor remains in the stories and essays of this period, but then it had not deserted him even in *Pierre*. Humor is no talisman against gloom and some of the darkest-minded men are, by intention, the funniest. Humor would appear to be, as Aristotle said of the gift for metaphor, something that is not acquired but a sort of disposition of the mind; as the man with a gift for metaphor sees resemblances where no logic indicates them, so the man with humor sees incongruities where other minds find a perfect decorum. Melville, in fact, rather violated the literary decorum of the *Hamlet* he attempted in *Pierre* by his burlesque account of American literary fame and by his fun with the Graham-cracker-munching advocates of "the Flesh-Brush philosophy" and "the Apple-Parings Dialectics" who were connoisseurs in the waters of the various city reservoirs. Yet Voltaire complained of the same fault in *Hamlet* itself. The conventions of 19th-century writing, with their allowance of discursive asides spoken by the author in his own person, of course made incidental humor an easier thing than it is today, and Melville was not the person to forgo these opportunities. There are, nevertheless, instances of humor in which the comic vision is fundamental. Among the best, is Turkey, the law-clerk in "Bartleby" who is a model of industry in the mornings and is in the afternoon, following a lunch we can deduce was beery, equally industrious, but now with a great deal of blotting of legal documents, splitting of pens, and boxing about of papers while the meridian or lunchtime glory of his red face gradually wanes toward six o'clock, along with the sun. Dickens has done better more times than one can recall, but Turkey, who has only a page or two to himself, has a surprising endurance in memory.

No general formulation that is very rewarding can be made about the sixteen shorter pieces Melville turned out in 1853–1856. Some, as I have mentioned, were concerned with poverty and its international contrasts. When Melville observed that "those peculiar social sensibilities nourished by our peculiar political principles, while they enhance the true dignity of a prosperous American, do but minister to the added wretchedness of the unfortunate . . . by furnishing them with the keenest appreciation of the smarting distinction between the ideal of universal equality and their grindstone experience of the practical misery and infamy of poverty", some personal reference was doubtless contained in what he said. After 1853, despite his magazine publications, his income from his writing was slight and, though there is no reason to think that he and his family suffered physical want, he—or, as it is in many cases, his wife—was under the necessity of watching every penny. In December, 1853, the Harper warehouse burnt down and the stocks of Melville's books were destroyed. While in due time they were reprinted, some damage to the sales of his books probably resulted from this accident. In the same month, Melville received an advance of $300 from his publishers, but the debt to which this was added was not cleared up until ten years later. These circumstances, it could be, gave some of the inspiration to the three stories Melville wrote of persons who in one way or another reconciled themselves to failure or bankruptcy.

The two longest and best of his stories came, as earlier things of his had, from his sea experiences and his reading. The first, "The Encantadas; or Enchanted Isles", was not properly a story but a series of ten sketches ascribed to Salvator R. Tarnmoor, dealing with the Galapagos, on only the tip of one of which, according to Victor Wolfgang von Hagen,[3] Melville can have landed during the voyage of the *Acushnet*. Melville supplemented what he himself had seen with accounts of earlier

[3] See his edition of *The Encantadas or, Enchanted Isles* (Burlingame, Calif., 1940: William P. Wreden).

travelers and from the two sources created something that has, on its smaller scale, the evocative grandeur and bony reality of *Moby-Dick*. The sketches of "The Encantadas" perhaps have no central theme other than the islands they describe—"a group rather of extinct volcanoes than of isles; looking much as the world at large might, after a penal conflagration"—but in reading these last of Melville's descriptions in prose of Pacific islands, one remembers that his first were of luxuriant Typee, where in the happy valley the clear stream ran between the coconut palms. He recalls a night in the Encantadas, spent aboard ship in his hammock, while overhead he "heard the slow weary draggings of the three ponderous strangers along the encumbered deck"—captured tortoises.

Listening to these draggings and concussions, I thought me of the haunt from which they came; an isle full of metallic ravines and gulches, sunk bottomlessly into the hearts of splintered mountains, and covered for many miles with inextricable thickets. I then pictured these three straightforward monsters, century after century, writhing through the shades, grim as blacksmiths; crawling so slowly and ponderously, that not only did toad-stools and all fungus things grow beneath their feet, but a sooty moss sprouted upon their backs. With them I lost myself in volcanic mazes; brushed away endless boughs of rotting thickets; till finally in a dream I found myself sitting crosslegged upon the foremost, a Brahmin similarly mounted upon either side, forming a tripod of foreheads which upheld the universal cope.

The second tale, "Benito Cereno", appeared in *Putnam's* nearly two years later. The scenario for this piece Melville took from the *Voyages* of Captain Amasa Delano, which had been published in Boston in 1817, a work so obscure that, although Melville called Captain Delano by name in his story, it was not identified until over seventy years later and Melville was meanwhile credited with the entire invention of "Benito Cereno's" plot. The story is, in a way, an epitome of Melville's talents, even to its faults, which are serious. Melville's genius resides peculiarly in his language and, as we know he said of Shakespeare, in "those short, quick probings at the very axis of reality" which are made almost incidentally to the task in hand. These probings are not outshoots of close-reasoned thought, and the premeditated craftsmanship and form realized by balance of part against part that go with such thought Melville does not have, but there is time and again some fire in him that forges a new edge for the word and in whose light the reader is able to see creation with a new immediacy. This especial power is manifested throughout the first part of the long story. We are affected by it on the initial page, where Captain Amasa Delano, in the year 1799 commanding "a large sealer and general trader" that has touched for water "in the Harbor of St. Maria—a small, desert, uninhabited island toward the southern extremity of the long coast of Chili", comes on deck to see a strange sail approaching:

The morning was one peculiar to that coast. Everything was mute and calm; everything gray. The sea, though undulated into long roods of swells, seemed fixed, and was sleeked at the surface like waved lead that has cooled and set in the smelter's mould. The sky seemed a gray surtout. Flights of troubled gray fowl, kith and kin with flights of troubled gray vapors among which they were mixed, skimmed low and fitfully over the waters, as swallows over meadows before storms. Shadows present, foreshadowing deeper shadows to come.

Captain Delano gets into his whaleboat to meet the incoming vessel:

Upon gaining a less remote view, the ship, when made signally visible on the verge of the leaden-hued swells, with the shreds of fog here and there raggedly furring her, appeared like a white-washed monastery after a thunder-storm, seen perched upon some

dun cliff among the Pyrenees. But it was no purely fanciful resemblance which now, for a moment, almost led Captain Delano to
think that nothing less than a ship-load of monks was before him.
Peering over the bulwarks were what really seemed, in the hazy
distance, throngs of dark cowls; while, fitfully revealed through
the open port-holes, other dark moving figures were dimly described, as of Black Friars pacing the cloisters.

Upon a still nigher approach, this appearance was modified, and
the true character of the vessel was plain—a Spanish merchantman
of the first class, carrying negro slaves, amongst other valuable
freight, from one colonial port to another. A very large, and, in
its time, a very fine vessel, such as in those days were at intervals
encountered along that main; sometimes superseded Acapulco
treasure-ships, or retired frigates of the Spanish king's navy, which,
like superannuated Italian palaces, still, under a decline of masters,
preserved signs of former state.

As the whale-boat drew more and more nigh, the cause of the
peculiar pipe-clayed aspect of the stranger was seen in the slovenly
neglect pervading her. The spars, ropes, and great part of the
bulwarks, looked woolly, from long unacquaintance with the
scraper, tar, and the brush. Her keel seemed laid, her ribs put
together, and she launched, from Ezekiel's Valley of Dry Bones.

The *San Dominick's* appearance is accounted for when Captain Delano boards her and is told by her captain, Don Benito
Cereno, that she has been more than six months out of Buenos
Aires for Lima, delayed by a storm at the Cape, then calms,
next scurvy, and now need of water. The true explanation of
her voyage is not made, however, until there has been raised in
a good many pages an atmosphere of suspicious strangeness and
otherwise inexplicable oddities in the behavior of crew and captain have been noted; then, with the leap of the elegantly
dressed and sickly Benito Cereno into the departing American's
whaleboat, we learn that the slaves aboard the ship have re-
volted and are in command of it and that Babo, apparently

Cereno's faithful bodyservant, is the leader of the revolt and Don Benito has been his puppet during the day-long presence of Captain Delano on the *San Dominick*. At this point Melville unhappily resorts to the legal documents with which the historical Captain Delano in part told his tale, and the vivid writing that has gone before is disadvantageously pointed up by a great lawyer's sentence of semi-colons and "and that's", coiling along like a wounded snake. This serious technical fault was noted by George William Curtis,[4] who, as an editor of *Putnam's*, was one of the first readers of the story; the documents, he told the magazine's publisher, "should have made part of the substance of the story". Energy, taste, or technical resources here failed Melville in writing the story that otherwise might in all senses have been what James O'Brien, a later and lesser Curtis, called "the noblest short story in American literature".

The solution of a mystery must always be in some way disappointing: the solution, after all, does away with the fascinating mystery. The most effective of Poe's tales of mystery are those in which the mystery is simply presented, not those in which it is cleared up with the busy rattling of syllogisms that Poe was so fond of. Quite possibly Melville's reactions during the writing of "Benito Cereno" were those of the average reader, and the explanation seemed a merely conventional necessity. One can ask—as, of course, it has been asked—if Melville did not conceal some autobiographical vein in "Benito Cereno" or postulate metaphysical entities as informing its characters, placing in it a deeper layer of mystery. Why Melville should find attractive on more than one level the story of a sailor over-

---

[4] Curtis, a writer of pleasant but definitely minor talent, was a prominent New York man-of-letters and civic reformer until his death, a year after Melville's own. He was an admirer of Melville's writings, more particularly the earlier books and the short stories, and mentioned them, with autobiographical reference, in his works; but Melville next to a passage in Matthew Arnold remarking that anyone could express trite ideas well put down the initials "G.W.C."

come by the dark agents supposedly under his control needs at this stage of his own story no explanation. Too much explaining may destroy the mystery by which "Benito Cereno" exists, and we may understand a great deal more simply through observing the way in which it ends. After the *San Dominick* with Captain Delano's help has been brought to Lima, and the rebel slaves there tried and condemned, Don Benito continues in his melancholy, so puzzling when first encountered. "You are saved," Captain Delano tells him, "you are saved: what has cast such a shadow upon you?" "The negro." Don Benito retires to a monastery on Mount Agonia, where shortly afterwards he dies.

In May of 1856 "Benito Cereno", "The Encantadas", and "Bartleby" were published along with three lesser pieces as *The Piazza Tales* by Dix & Edwards, apparently more for the firm's prestige than its profit. Melville received no advance (since Dix & Edwards were the publishers of *Putnam's Monthly Magazine*, the sums paid for the appearance of the stories there can have taken the place of an advance) and was to have a royalty of 12½ per cent after expenses were met. About a year before he had published his novel, *Israel Potter: His Fifty Years of Exile*, through G. P. Putnam & Company on a similar basis and it too had been serialized in *Putnam's*. While *The Piazza Tales* were rather widely noticed and on the whole favorably, *Israel Potter*, with a great deal of the stuff of popularity and not a single difficult passage in it, seems to have engaged hardly any attention at all, so that ten years later a Philadelphia publisher who had bought the plates from Putnam thought it safe to bring out an unauthorized edition, changing the title to *The Refugee* but using Melville's name.

Like "Benito Cereno", *Israel Potter* borrowed heavily from a written source and freely used the names found there. Melville acknowledged this in his dedication, to "His Highness the Bunker Hill Monument", and said his novel preserved, "almost as in a reprint, Israel Potter's autobiographical story", which had been published in Providence in 1824 as *The Life and Remarkable Adventures of Israel R. Potter*. Melville's additions to the earlier pamphlet were actually many but he said his account was "a dilapidated old tombstone retouched" and modestly signed his dedication and preface "The Editor". Since Melville had thought of writing about Israel Potter as early as 1849, when he mentioned "the Revolutionary narrative of the beggar" in his travel diary, the book obviously was not a pot-boiler hastily contrived to meet the needs of the moment. Israel is no Drummond light, and Melville's aspirations for the book in which he placed him were certainly not those of the books, one a success and one a failure, that had held Ahab and Pierre; but Melville's continued interest in the original story shows that his concern with the lonely and defeated figure antedated the period when he might have considered himself as such. Israel is the Melville hero whose high dedication (in Israel's case, the service of his country) all circumstance denies its proper rewards.

Israel starts out as a farmer's son in the Berkshires who, thwarted by his father in a marriage he intends, runs away to become in turn a farm hand, a hunter, a farmer, a peddler amongst the Indians of Canada, a merchant sailor, and a whaleman. He is again a farm hand and still unmarried when the Revolution begins and he goes off to Bunker Hill with the minutemen. Next he is aboard a brigantine as a Continental sailor and before long he is in a prison hulk in Portsmouth as a British captive. Escaping, he makes his way toward London and, after a variety of adventures which includes his working as a gardener for the King, he becomes acquainted with a group of American sympathizers, who send him, with messages in the heels of his boots, to Franklin in Paris, where he also meets John Paul Jones. Chance and mischance bring him to Jones's ship, on which he serves during Jones's raids in English waters. He is returning to America when in a curious manner he is dropped aboard an English vessel [5] that carries him back to England, where he remains in great poverty and hardship until, fifty years after leaving Boston as a prisoner, he goes home for the last few months of "a long life still rotting in early mishap".

Despite the liberties he takes with the original text, Melville sometimes follows it in a pedestrian manner, simply making this or that statement of fact, plainly using the motive power of the original where his own interest fails. Yet these very passages by their contrast with those written on a higher level raise the question of what he might have done had he been willing to carry on in later years merely as a professional writer, content to turn out his daily stint of words without waiting on inspiration. Feeling, as Matthew Arnold had said of Maurice de Guérin in a sentence that he later marked, that "to a sensitive man . . . to silence his genius is more tolerable than to hackney it", Melville after 1856 expressed himself in verse, for which his talent was not suited and which did in effect silence it. Perhaps if his talent had appeared to him something not quite so irrefrangible, it would have found in just such endeavors as *Israel Potter* more expression than he supposed possible. Corinth cannot be burned every day and some ores of great value are uncovered only with the patient and drudging pickaxe.

The story of Israel did lead to several veins of considerable

---

[5] Once more Melville anticipated a real event. In the diary he kept when in 1860 he was sailing on his brother Tom's ship to California, he recorded on June 11: "This afternoon had a collision with an English brig from Pernambuco bound for Liverpool. She blundered down across our bows and was locked with us for a time; ripping & tearing her sails. We also were damaged in fore-yard & main. At the moment of collision the Steward of the brig being in jeopardy, leaped aboard of us, and the vessels separating remained aboard, till taken off by a boat sent from the brig."

wealth. The portrait of Franklin is an amusing one, in which the old man appears in the character of Poor Richard in exactly the kind of room Melville had had in Paris, there bestowing on poor Israel a great wealth of sound advice but not so much as the means for a drink of brandy from the tempting bottle on the mantel. In contrast to this 18th-century Plinlimmon, Jones is a figure more in Melville's sympathy and he is summed up as "combining the vengeful indignation and bitter ambition of an outraged hero, with the uncompunctious desperation of a renegade. In one view, the Coriolanus of the sea; in another, a cross between the gentleman and the wolf." Jones is apprized by Melville as a distinctly American product, for "intrepid, unprincipled, reckless, predatory, with boundless ambition, civilized in externals but a savage at heart, America is, or may yet be, the Paul Jones of nations". Ethan Allen, who appears during his English captivity, "scornful and ferocious in the last degree", is similarly estimated: "Though born in New England, he exhibited no trace of her character. He was frank, bluff, companionable as a Pagan, convivial, a Roman, hearty as a harvest. His spirit was essentially Western; and herein is his peculiar Americanism; for the Western spirit is, or will yet be (for no other is, or can be), the true American one."

This amalgam of cynicism and heartiness appears a little later in *The Confidence-Man* in a philosophical misanthrope "somewhat ursine in aspect; sporting a shaggy spencer of the cloth called bear's-skin; a high-peaked cap of raccoon-skin, the long bushy tail switching over behind; raw-hide leggings; grim stubble chin; and to end, a double-barreled gun in hand,— a Missouri bachelor, a Hoosier gentleman, of Spartan leisure and fortune, and equally Spartan manners and sentiments; and, as the sequel may show, not less acquainted, in a Spartan way of his own, with philosophy and books, than with woodcraft and rifles." Natty Bumppo may give him his clothes but otherwise is no true ancestor to the Missouri bachelor. In their especial sort, this back-woodsman, the Scotch adventurer, and the Vermont Deist appear for the first time in American fiction and are progenitors—not through any direct influence but in the attitude they uncover—of the tough guy who figures so large in our current writing and who made his first entrance in modern dress at the beginning of the century in the novels of the Westerner Frank Norris. Melville's tough guy is of course more eloquent and given to grander gestures than the modern one, whose romantic philosophy is expressed in a convention of understatement in speech and direct violence in action.

Jones has only a small part in the account of the historical Israel R. Potter, but he provides Melville with opportunities to describe the raid on Whitehaven and the fight between the *Bonhomme Richard* and the *Serapis*. In both descriptions Melville combines in his best manner what is given to an eye sharpened by seafaring and what this evokes in a space- and time-roaming imagination. He presents the harbor of the coal-mining town of Whitehaven:

About three hundred of these vessels [colliers that carried coal to London] now lay, all crowded together, in one dense mob, at Whitehaven. The tide was out. They lay completely helpless, clear of water, and grounded. They were sooty in hue. Their black yards were deeply canted, like spears, to avoid collision. The three hundred grimy hulls lay wallowing in the mud, like a herd of hippopotami asleep in the alluvium of the Nile. Their sailless, raking masts, and canted yards, resembled a forest of fish-spears thrust into those same hippopotamus hides. Partly flanking one side of the fleet was a fort, whose batteries were raised from the beach. On a little strip of this beach, at the base of the fort, lay a number of small rusty guns, dismounted, heaped together in disorder, as a litter of dogs.

The battle-piece does not lend itself to detached quotation.

The fight is seen from two aspects—the one from Flamborough Head and the other from the decks of the *Bonhomme Richard* —so that the reader is at once right on the scene of the struggle and sufficiently distant to take in the two ships maneuvering about each other on the sea. Again Melville draws his figures from the American scene: the gunners of the *Serapis* tend "those rows of guns, as Lowell girls the rows of looms in a cotton factory" and the *Bonhomme Richard's* eighteen-pounders peer "just above the water-line, like a parcel of dirty mulattoes from a cellar-way". For Israel's miserable forty years in London, Melville drew on his own acquaintance with the city, perhaps recalling it in his later mood, as we have seen in his description of London Bridge, as more sooty and begrimed than it had first appeared to him. The brickyard in which Israel works for a time before going to London, his Egypt before his entry into the city of Dis, might be one of Piranesi's "Prisons" etchings translated into a colder and smokier climate. "The yard was encamped, with all its endless rows of tented sheds, and kilns, and mills, upon a wild waste moor, belted round by bogs and fens. The blank horizon, like a rope, coiled round the whole."

On October 1st, 1856, Melville was in New York, preparing to take the "glorious Eastern jaunt" that he had thought of seven years before. In the five years between his discharge from the U. S. Frigate *United States* and his sailing for England in the *Southampton*, he had written five books. In the seven years before his next voyage, he had written another five books and scattered pieces enough to make up a small volume when they were gathered together in the 1920's in the second burgeoning of his fame. As a public figure, he was still chiefly "the man who lived among cannibals", "H. M. author of 'Peedee' 'Hullabaloo' & 'Pog-Dog' ", but to himself he was no longer the person who had taken off in the cutter on Guy Fawkes Day with the cousin of Bayard Taylor and the young professor of German. Since our own lives grow around us like a coral accretion, none of us is ever the same person seven years later; we carry with us the always-widening territory of our personalities on whose external edges accumulate all that voluntarily we have done or left undone and a great deal in which we never thought our wills involved. In 1849 Melville had *Redburn* and *White-Jacket*, however much he despised them, between him and the conclusion of *Mardi*, but in 1856 *Moby-Dick*, *Pierre*, and the last of his novels, still in manuscript, were there to mark the stages of an inward journey from whose barren termination this new crossing of the ocean was undertaken to help him escape. He now had as well the added years of marriage, in which he had "perceived that in all cases man must eventually lower, or at least shift, his conceit of attainable felicity"; he had his responsibilities multiplied by four children (the last of them, his daughter Frances, born in 1855); and he had a sense of obligation that cannot have been entirely pleasing to a man who had written of Israel Potter "that however desperately reduced at times, even to the sewers, Israel, the American, never sunk below the mud, to actual beggary", for Justice Shaw had provided the money for the trip.

"This time Melville did not go away on his own," says Mr. Olson; "he was—though guardedly—sent away." In any case, it was an openly troubled man, and one for whom his family was troubled, who went off. When Melville saw Hawthorne in Liverpool, "he said [Hawthorne noted in his journal] that he already felt better than in America; but observed that he did not anticipate much pleasure in his rambles, for the spirit of adventure is gone out of him. He certainly is much overshadowed since I saw him last. . . ." And after his return, his cousin Henry Gansevoort wrote to his father that "Herman

Melville seems considerably improved in health and spirits by his interspersing the spice of variety with the reality of life"—which must mean that before his sailing the family had seen a necessity for such improvement. To his friend Evert Duyckinck, however, none of this was evident, and Melville passed at least one good evening in conforming to Duyckinck's image of him, for not the least pleasant part of our lives is lived out in our friends' opinions of us. Duyckinck wrote in his diary:

. . . Herman Melville passed the evening with me—fresh from his mountain charged to the muzzle with his sailor metaphysics and jargon of things unknowable. But a good stirring evening— ploughing deep and bringing to the surface some rich fruit of thought and experience—Melville instanced Burton as atheistical —in the exquisite irony of his passages on some sacred matters; cited a good story from the Decameron the *Enchantment* of the husband in the tree; a story from Judge Edmonds [6] of a prayer meeting of female convicts at Sing Sing which the Judge was invited to witness and agreed to, provided that he was introduced where he could not be seen. It was an orgie of indecency and blasphemy. Said of Bayard Taylor that as some augur predicted the misfortunes of Charles I from the infelicity of his countenance so Taylor's prosperity "borne up by the Gods" was written in his face.

If on this occasion the circumstances came closer than ever before to making Melville an Ishmael driven into the desert with no maternal Hagar to comfort him, part of the parallel lay in the mockery he had left with his publishers. *The Confidence-Man: His Masquerade* was not published by Dix & Edwards until shortly before he set sail on his return voyage to America, and it appeared in England, under Longmans' im-

---

[6] John Worth Edmonds (1799–1874), a prison reformer who, in later life, was convinced that he was in touch with departed spirits.

print, around the same time. American criticism dealt with the difficulties of the book by ignoring it and the English critics simply ignored the difficulties, taking pleasure, as Mr. Thorp says, in the thought "that here was an *exposé* of Yankee shams and hypocrisies". But it is likely that for Melville's time the book was less difficult than for ours, which allows for much profundity in its author and is therefore hard put to find just what he is trying to say in a work that in any age must seem repetitive and dull.[7] Its dullness, however, need not be too great an obstacle for an age that can read with close attention Kafka's *The Trial* and *The Castle,* for like these novels *The Confidence-Man* is a fictional demonstration by a series of incidents all coming out to an invariable result of a single dominating idea. Kafka's dominating idea is the inscrutability of the powers greater than himself which, in one way or another, intervene in a man's life; Melville's is that, given what one can observe of man's heart, charity will not work.

The Mississippi steamer *Fidèle* is at the dock in St. Louis "at sunrise on a first of April", preparing to leave for New Orleans (and the name of the steamer and the date both carry obvious enough meanings). There appears amongst the boarding passengers a man dressed in cream colors and "in the extremest sense of the word, a stranger". He moves into a crowd of persons reading a placard "offering a reward for the capture of a mysterious impostor, supposed to have recently arrived from the East" and, apparently a mute, takes from his pocket a slate on which he writes "Charity thinketh no evil" and so on till he has written all of I Corinthians 13, when the boat's barber hangs over his shop the sign: "No Trust". The stranger goes aboard the *Fidèle*, where "merchants on 'change seem the passengers that buzz on her decks, while, from quar-

[7] When, in the autumn of 1947, I read Peter Gansevoort's copy of *The Confidence-Man* in the New York Public Library the last pages were uncut.

ters unseen, comes a murmur as of bees in the comb. Fine promenades, domed saloons, long galleries, sunny balconies, confidential passages, bridal chambers, state-rooms plenty as pigeonholes, and out-of-the-way retreats like secret drawers in an escritoire, present like facilities for publicity or privacy." The man falls asleep on the deck; the steamer starts downstream; and after several stops the crowd begins "to break up from a concourse into various clusters or squads".

As among Chaucer's Canterbury pilgrims, or those Oriental ones crossing the Red Sea towards Mecca in the festival month, there was no lack of variety. Natives of all sorts, and foreigners; parlor men and backwoodsmen; farm-hunters and fame-hunters; heiress-hunters, gold-hunters, buffalo-hunters, bee-hunters, happiness-hunters, truth-hunters, and still keener hunters after all these hunters. Fine ladies in slippers and moccasined squaws; Northern speculators and Eastern philosophers; English, Irish, German, Scotch, Danes; Santa Fé traders in striped blankets, and Broadway bucks in cravats of cloth of gold; fine-looking Kentucky boatmen, and Japanese-looking Mississippi cotton-planters; Quakers in full drab, and United States soldiers in full regimentals; slaves, black, mulatto, quadroon; modish young Spanish creoles, and old-fashioned French Jews; Mormons and Papists; Dives and Lazarus; jesters and mourners, teetotalers and convivialists, deacons and blacklegs; hard-shell Baptists and clay-eaters; grinning negroes, and Sioux chieftans solemn as high-priests. In short, a piebald parliament, an Anacharsis Cloots congress of all kinds of that multiform pilgrim species, man. . . .

Here reigned the dashing and all-fusing spirit of the West, whose type is the Mississippi itself, which, uniting the streams of the most distant and opposite zones, pours them along, helter-skelter, in one cosmopolitan and confident tide.

This is an auspicious-seeming beginning, and one might expect that the *Fidèle* with her variety of passengers is starting out on a trip that will in some ways resemble that of the *Pequod* with her oddly assorted crew. Early in the *Pequod's* voyage Ishmael announced: ". . . I have swum through libraries and sailed through oceans; I have had to do with whales with these visible hands; I am in earnest; and I will try." But when Melville wrote of the *Fidèle's* journey, he had not seen the Mississippi since his boyhood and, though many an author is mentioned in the book's pages, it cannot be said to be derived from his reading; he was in earnest, no doubt, but the book has no core of observation or fact and is spun out into a great involution of sophistry never once troubled by any breath of life, mortal or fabulous. He might be referring to his own difficulties when toward the end of the book he remarks that for a fiction the author's imagination alone is not enough—"it being as true in literature as in zoology, that life is from the egg".

Had Melville known the West of his time and had it moved him imaginatively, there is no reason to think that he would have given us any detailed observation of its social anatomy, anticipating Mark Twain, but there is yet the possibility that he might have written an allegory or symbolic tale with solid Western flesh on its bones. This voyage in a Mississippi steamboat might as well have been one in a rocket into outer space with all the passengers committed to play in turn a round of solitaire while the other passengers watched over their shoulders. When the questions of interest and subject-matter are put aside, the technical performance of the book is as good as one could ask for and every device in it is efficiently pointed toward a single conclusion: man's want of confidence in man. The writing, too, remains always under control; it is anything but the "drunken and reeling" prose of which Fitz-James O'Brien complained in *Pierre*, yet to see this fine instrument so well used toward such an end is like watching a clever fencer scoring points on a feather pillow. O'Brien had warned Melville in 1853 in *Putnam's Monthly Magazine* that he tottered on the edge of a precipice, and four years later, in the same publication, he cautioned him once more against speculation. In *The Confidence-Man* Melville had fallen over the precipice, if not exactly the one O'Brien had in mind; he was in an element too thin to sustain the body of a novel.

So soon as the voyage of the *Fidèle* is well begun, there appears a crippled negro begging in the fore part of the boat. His honesty and the reality of his condition are called into question by "it may be some discharged custom-house officer, who suddenly stripped of convenient means of support, had concluded to be avenged on government and humanity by making himself miserable for life, either by hating or suspecting everything and everybody". The negro mentions a number of persons aboard the boat, all of whom can vouch for him; and these persons in due time turn up through the story—being, of course, the white-habited confidence man in the various rôles of his masquerade. A young Methodist clergyman comes to the negro's defense and is finally exasperated into clouting the custom-house official for his lack of charity. This so affects a bystander that he gives the negro a half-dollar, in doing which he unwittingly drops his card. A short time later, the merchant is accosted by name by a man in mourning (one of the persons the negro said would vouch for him) and the story's pattern is established.

The pattern is this: the confidence man, having in one disguise hinted at his next one or gained information to be used in his next one, appears with the single message that is a pun on his name—have confidence in humanity—and attempts to gull one of the passengers, each of whom to some extent lacks this confidence, and a few he succeeds in cheating, for the pleasure of the thing itself rather than for the money—"How much money did the devil make by gulling Eve?" asks the customs-house man. His operations are followed through the day, and at midnight, as the lights go out and he is leading off to bed an old man who has a well-stuffed moneybelt, he speaks out one last time for confidence: ". . . I believe in a Committee of Safety, holding silent sessions over all, in an invisible patrol, most alert when we soundest sleep, and whose beat lies as much through forests as towns, along rivers as streets. In short, I never forget that passage of Scripture which says, 'Jehovah shall be thy confidence.' " With this he gives to his charge—who has become increasingly less the trusting old farmer and more the querulous and suspicious gaffer and has asked for a life preserver—what is presumably a chamber pot. The last lamp expires, and Melville concludes: "Something further may follow of this Masquerade."

Nothing more did follow; *The Confidence-Man* was the last of Melville's prose fiction to be published. Since the work is unfinished, a strictly literary judgment on it would have to be in some measure conditional. Taking it in its largest reference, we seem justified in saying that its being incomplete shows it never held the potentialities of any but a chance conclusion. Although its characters are rarefied to embodiments of a single trait, the book is not further advanced along the route of speculation on which *Moby-Dick* and *Pierre* are signposts. All general conclusions in it are foregone, and it merely seeks to demonstrate from the facts of human behavior what, in a speculative way, had been arrived at so early as *Mardi*. It shows that in the real order, as well as in the ideal, metaphysics precede experience.

The opinions entertained about the Creator in the earlier books are in *The Confidence-Man* logically developed as they concern the creature, and the result is misanthropy. Misanthropy sometimes drives men into a morbidly curious examination of their kind, as we see in persons so different as Swift and Flaubert, and what they report has a kind of scientific verity, not because they are in any way detached but because only they have the inverted enthusiasm thoroughly to search their fields. Melville's misanthropy, to judge by *The Confidence-Man,* was not anything felt so immediately, and though he detailed particular instance after particular instance it was a general proposition that he had in mind. He was too detached from the creatures he dealt with. Had he, in a sort of collected fury, set out to adduce examples of man's lack of charity, he might have piled up enough to make it seem to anyone who did not look away for the moment that there was no charity in the world. Instead he tried to show in a book which was one vast ironical trope that charity simply would not work and that even those who hypocritically preached it for reasons of their own could not count on it. In this he was single-minded to the point of obsession, and no amount of skill could make up for his appalling narrowness. One feels that Melville himself must have been aware of how the point he sought to demonstrate never carried in his demonstrations the conviction with which he held it: he stated it again and again, manipulating language and characters with a skill intensified by each failure. Only strong and bitter feelings will secure a man's perseverance in such a task. That Melville entertained these feelings privately, in connection with other things than the work in hand, there is more than enough evidence, but by abandoning the task when it was half-finished he gave the indication of having come to some kind of victory over himself, the precise nature of which is still left to surmise.

GHASTLY THEOLOGY, MYSTERIOUS CHEER

SOME TIME IN 1841 MELVILLE HAD SAILED INTO THE PACIFIC Ocean. ". . . Now," Ishmael later said, certainly speaking for his author, "the long supplication of my youth was answered; that serene ocean rolled eastwards [1] from me a thousand leagues of blue." How powerfully his encounter with the great ocean affected his imagination all his best writings testify, for not even Dante or Milton better conveys the sense of immensity.

There is, one knows not what sweet mystery about this sea, whose gently awful stirrings seem to speak of some hidden soul beneath; like those fabled undulations of the Ephesian sod over the buried Evangelist St. John. And meet it is, that over these sea-pastures, wide-rolling watery prairies and Potters' Fields of all four continents, the waves should rise and fall, and ebb and flow unceasingly; for here, millions of mixed shades and shadows, drowned dreams, somnambulisms, reveries; all that we call lives and souls, lie dreaming, dreaming, still; tossing like slumberers in their beds; the ever-rolling waves but made so by their restlessness.

To any meditative Magian rover, this serene Pacific, once beheld, must ever after be the sea of his adoption. It rolls the midmost waters of the world, the Indian ocean and Atlantic being but its arms. The same waves wash the moles of the new-built Californian towns, but yesterday planted by the recentest race of men, and lave the faded but still gorgeous skirts of Asiatic lands, older

[1] Ishmael, it will be remembered, rounded the Cape of Good Hope, entering the Pacific from the Indian Ocean, while Melville on the *Acushnet* had come to it around Cape Horn, so that for him it rolled westward.

than Abraham; while all between float milky-ways of coral isles,
and low-lying, endless, unknown Archipelagoes, and impenetrable
Japans. Thus this mysterious divine Pacific zones the world's whole
bulk about; makes all coasts one bay to it; seems the tide-beating
heart of earth. Lifted by those eternal swells, you needs must own
the seductive god, bowing your head to Pan.

This of course was written ten years after the event. The
fullness of any experience is known only in retrospect, and
when on November 23rd, 1856, Melville's ship passed Cape
St. Vincent on its way toward the Straits of Gilbraltar, the
most important notation he made in his brief entry in his journal was "The whole Atlantic breaks here." The next day at
four in the afternoon the ship entered the Straits; the sun was
setting and all was in shade except the Rock—"England throwing the rest of the world in shade". Having passed through
the portals of the ancient world, this voyager from what were
once the unpeopled lands beyond the sun jotted down in his
diary the word "Pacific". He was upon the midmost sea around
whose waters the civilization of the West had arisen and at
whose furthest end had appeared the religion that held depths
for which the Pacific was at best an inadequate symbol. These
depths he had attempted to sound with no more help than
came in the thought that he was one of "the whole corps of
thought-divers, that have been diving & coming up again with
blood-shot eyes since the world began". Much of what he
would write in the next thirty-five years would refer in one
way or another to what he had seen and thought in the Mediterranean world and would exceed in plain prose wisdom what
he had written before, but if some poetic fire had gone out of
his writing, that was because the seductive god dies not only
with the world's youth but also with man's. The birth that
makes the recurrent death of Pan untragic Melville could not
grasp as a fact, because he believed that of its nature the world

could not be redeemed. Evil, he said in his old age, was "like good . . . an irremovable element. Bale out your individual boat, if you can, but the sea abides."

In the particular vessel he had been in, on the anniversary of the birth that as a simple matter of fact disproved this statement, "the Captain mildly celebrated the day with a glass of Champagne", and when after spending Christmas in the harbor at Syra they sailed out the next day, Melville wrote in his journal: "Contrast between the Greek Isles & those of the Polynesian archipelago. The former have lost their virginity. The latter are fresh as at their first creation. The former look worn, and are meagre, like life after enthusiasm is gone. The aspect of them all is sterile & dry. Even Delos whose flowers rose by miracle in the sea, is now a barren moor, & to look upon the bleak yellow of Patmos, who would think that a God had been there?" In a poem he may have composed not so long afterward but did not publish until 1891, he spoke of these "isles of absentees—Gone whither?":

> 'Tis Polynesia reft of palms,
> Seaward no valley breathes her balms—
> Not such as musk thy rings of calms,
>   Marquesas!

The tone of Melville's journal is, to put it mildly, only intermittently cheerful and then mainly when he is engaged in recording his observations, not in reflecting upon them. He had sailed from New York in the steamer *Glasgow* for Glasgow on October 11th, "right hearty" on "yet another of the series of Extraordinary fine days; sunny, mellow, quiescent", quite different from the weather at his departure in 1849—as we know from Duyckinck's diary, for Melville did not begin his own until his arrival in Liverpool and after he had seen Glasgow, where, he then recalled, "all looked like a picture of the old masters smoked by Time". Of his visit with Hawthorne his diary says little; it is Hawthorne's journal that tells how they walked along the seashore at Southport "and sat down in a hollow among the sand hills (sheltering ourselves from the high, cool wind) and smoked a cigar. Melville, as he always does, began to reason of Providence and futurity, and of everything that lies beyond human ken, and informed me that he had 'pretty much made up his mind to be annihilated' . . ." By this last Melville meant neither that he was thinking of suicide nor of his own end as a writer, as it has been interpreted, but that he had given up hope of immortality, which Hawthorne noted he was better worth than most of us. After being shown about Liverpool by Henry Bright and about Chester by Hawthorne, he sailed on November 18th with Jerusalem as his eventual destination, "leaving a trunk behind him, and taking only a carpet-bag to hold all his travelling-gear".

The first stop at Syra was not on Christmas but around two weeks earlier. Here Melville had his first strong impression of foreignness: "Take all the actors of opera in a night from theatres of London, & set them to work in their fancy dresses, weighing bales, counting codfish, sitting at tables on the dock, smoking, talking, sauntering,—sitting in boats &c—picking up rags, carrying water casks, lemonade &c—will give some notion of Greek port." He remarked too "some old men [who] looked like Pericles reduced to a chiffonier" (apparently meaning either a rag or a ragpicker). On his second visit, he "was again struck by the appearance of the town on the hill. The houses seem clinging round its top, as if desperate for security, like shipwrecked men about a rock beaten by billows." Going ashore again, he was once more impressed by the fancy dress here assumed for everyday life. "The Greek, of any class, seems a natural dandy. His dress, though a laborer, is that of a gentleman of leisure. This flowing, & graceful costume, with so much of pure ornament about it & so little fitted for labor, must needs have been devised in some Golden Age. But surviving in the present, is most picturesquely out of keeping with the utilities." And on the quay he observed "what you would call rows of dead goats, but which prove to be goat skins, filled not with the flesh of goats, but the blood of the grape". When he later put the scene in verse—"A Transmitted Reminiscence", in most aspects less vivid than the hasty entries in his journal—his preposterous (but usual) Northerner's sense of superiority was canceled by a feeling of something fundamental lost, far more serious than aptitude for "serious work" loading codfish:

> Such chatterers all! like children gay
> Who make believe to work, but play.
>
>   I saw, and how help musing too.
> Here traffic's immature as yet:
> Forever this juvenile fun hold out
> And these light hearts? Their garb, their glee,
> Alike profuse in flowing measure,
> Alike inapt for serious work,
> Blab of grandfather's Saturn's prime
> When trade was not, nor toil, nor stress,
> But life was leisure, merriment, peace,
> And lucre none and love was righteousness.

After the first departure from Syra, at daybreak on the 6th Melville was roused by the captain to come on deck and see Mt. Olympus, "covered with snow at the summit, & looking most majestic in the dawn". They lay over at Salonika, where the filthy and rotted bazaar reminded him of Five Points—the ugliest of the slums in New York at that time and notorious for crime and vice—and where he noted that all the women he

saw about were old. "In the evening Captain told a story about
the heat of arms affecting the compass." Whether this story was
a sailor's yarn or had to do with the arms that were the next
day "all taken down into the cabin after being discharged"
is not clear, but it made a deep impression on Melville, for he
three times put into verse the tale of a ship sunk because her
compass was made false by arms (in two of the poems trophies
of war and in the other poisoned sword-blades hidden in a
passenger's baggage).

On the last day in Salonika, he remained aboard "observing
the arrival of deck passengers for Constantinople. . . . Among
others 'two beys effendi' in long furred robes of yellow, looking like Tom cats." The beys set up their harems in tents on
the deck, and as a change from the female population of Salonika Melville was able to remark "some very pretty women of
the harem", though they were covered in the Moslem style
with "ashmacks". When three days later they were lying off
Constantinople because of the fog, which lifted only enough
to show "the base & wall of St. Sophia but not the dome", he
thought again of the women of the harem: "It was a coy dis-
closure, a kind of coquetting, leaving room for imagination
and heightening the scene. Constantinople, like her Sultanas,
was thus seen veiled in her 'ashmack'."

Lodged at the Hôtel du Globe, where he had a "5th story
room without a carpet" for ten francs, Melville spent almost
a week going about the city and its environs, with which he
already had a sort of remote acquaintance from the copy of
Thomas Hope's *Anastasius; or, Memoirs of a Greek* that he
had bought during his 1849 trip. The confused and teeming
life of what had once been one of the world's twin capitals fascinated him, but amongst its multi-national crowds, in all their
fantastic variety of garb, he wandered rather forlornly, his eye
appreciative enough though in other ways he was almost as

remote as any less sensitive tourist. In the streets he feared for his safety and his purse and to protect both at night he remained at his hotel.

With an English acquaintance he went in a steamer up the Bosporus. "Europe & Asia here show their best," he wrote after the exclamation "Magnificent!" "A challenge of continents, whereby the successively alternate sweeps of the shores both sides seem to retire from every new proffer of beauty, again in some grand prudery to advance with a bolder bid, and thereupon again & again retiring, neither willing to retreat from the contest of beauty." Back in Constantinople, he "stood on the First Bridge", then set down in general terms his own loneliness: "Curious to stand amid these millions of fellow beings, some of whom seem not unwilling to accept our civilization, but with one consent rejecting much of our morality & all of our religion." His dark mood was recollected in a poem which, so far as any felicity of expression is concerned, he wisely left unpublished:

> From bright Stamboul Death crosses o'er;
> Beneath the cypress evermore
> His camp he pitches by the shore
>   Of Asia old.
>
> Requiting this unsocial mood
> Stamboul's inmyrtled multitude
> Bless Allah and the sherbert good
>   And Europe hold.
>
> Even so the cleaving Bosphorous parts
> Life and Death.—Dissembling hearts!
> Over the gulf the yearning starts
>   To meet—infold!

He proceeded on for Alexandria by way of Smyrna, around which he was conducted by "a grave ceremonious man with frogged coat carrying a silver mounted sword in a velvet scabbard in one hand, and a heavy silver mounted cowhide in the other". Here he apparently saw his first camel, "a most ungainly creature".

From his long curved and crane-like neck, (which he carries stiffly like a clergyman in a stiff cravat) his feathery-looking forelegs, & his long lank hind ones, he seems a cross between an ostrich & a gigantic grasshopper. His hoof is spongy, & covered with hair to the ground, so that walking through these muddy lanes, he seems stilting along on four mops. —Carries his neck out like a tortoise. Tail like a long eel, driver holds it & steers him. Has a way of turning his head so that his face & tail face you together.

On the last day of the year, he was outside of Cairo looking on the pyramids. The immense, which had always so fascinated him, here proved quite overwhelming, and in writing of his terror he made plain that the huge was the symbol of what he had feared and sought for a long time now:

It was in these pyramids that was conceived the idea of Jehovah. Terrible mixture of the cunning and awful. Moses learned in all the lore of the Egyptians. The idea of Jehovah born there. . . . Nought but earthquake or geological revolution can obliterate them. Only people who made their mark, both in their masonry and their religion (through Moses). These the steps Jacob lay at. . . . *No vestige of moss upon them. Not the least. Other ruins ivied. No speck of green.* . . . Pyramids still loom before me—something vast, indefinite, incomprehensible, and awful. Line of desert & verdure, plain as line between good and evil. An instant collision of alien elements. A long billow of desert forever hovers as in act of breaking, upon the verdure of Egypt. Grass near the pyramids but will not touch them—as if in fear or awe of them. Desert more fearful than ocean.

And a little later he wrote:

After seeing the pyramid, all other architecture seems but pastry. Though I had but so short a time to view the pyramid, yet I doubt whether any time spent upon it, would tend to a more precise impression of it. As with the ocean, you learn as much of its vastness by the first five minutes glance as you would in a month, so with the pyramid. Its simplicity confounds you . . . It refuses to be studied or adequately comprehended. . . . When the pyramid presented a smooth plane, it must have lost as much in impressiveness as the ocean does when unfurrowed. A dead calm of masonry. But now the ridges majestically diversify. It has been said in panegyric of some extraordinary works of man, that they affect the imagination like the works of Nature. But the pyramid affects one in neither way exactly. Man seems to have had as little to do with it as Nature. It was that supernatural creature, the priest. They must needs have been terrible inventors, those Egyptian wise men. And one seems to see that as out of the crude forms of the natural earth they could evoke by art the transcendent mass & symetry & [illegible] of the pyramid so out of the rude elements of the insignificant thoughts that are in all men, they could rear the transcendent conception of a God. But for no holy purpose was the pyramid founded. Casts no shadow great part of the day.

Reversing Jonah's course, he fled to Jaffa, whence he went on directly to Jerusalem. Here he roamed about the city and made excursions to Jordan and the Dead Sea. Despondency weighed on him heavily, and shortly after his visit to the Dead Sea he wrote of it: "foam on beach & pebbles like slaver of mad dog—smarting bitter of the water,—carried the bitter in my mouth all day—bitterness of life—thought of all bitter things —Bitter is it to be poor & bitter to be reviled, & Oh bitter are these waters of Death, thought I." Two weeks after arriving in Jerusalem, he left in the company of a Frederick Cunningham of Boston, went to Ramleh, "the sail-white town", thence to Lydda, then across the Plain of Sharon to Jaffa, where he awaited the steamer. "I have such a feeling in this lonely old

Jaffa," he wrote after remarking that the town was too ancient to have any antiquities, "with the prospect of a prolonged detention here, owing to the surf—that it is only by stern self-control & grim defiance that I contrive to keep cool & patient." Till the arrival of the steamer on January 26th, he spent his time in reading Dumas's *The Queen's Necklace* and, presumably, in writing down his general impressions of Jerusalem:

In pursuance of my object, the saturation of my mind with the atmosphere of Jerusalem, offering myself up a passive subject, and no unwilling one, to its weird impressions, I always rose at dawn and walked without the walls. Nor so far as escaping the pent-up air within, was concerned was I singular here.

For daily I could not but be struck with the clusters of the townspeople reposing along the arches near the Jaffa Gate where it looks down into the Vale of Gihon, and the groups always haunting the neighboring fountains, vales & hills. They too seemed to feel the insalubriousness of so small a city pent in by lofty walls obstructing ventilation, postponing the morning and hastening the unwholesome twilight. And they too seemed to share my impatience were it only at this arbitrary limitation & prescription of things.—I would stroll to Mount Zion, along the terraced walks, & survey the tomb stones of the hostile Armenians, Latins, Greeks, all sleeping together.—I looked along the hill side of Gihon over against me, & watched the precipitation of the solemn shadows of the city towers flung far down to the bottom of the pool of Gihon, and higher up the haunted darkened valley my eye rested on the cliff-girt basin, haggard with riven old olives, where the angel of the Lord smote the army of Sennacherib. (Hill of Evil Counsel) And smote by the morning I saw the reddish soil of Aceldama, confessing its inexpiable guilt by deeper dyes. On the Hill of Evil Counsel, I saw the ruined villa of the High Priest where tradition says the death of Christ was plotted, and the field where when all was over the traitor Judas hung himself.

And in the afternoon I would stand out by St. Stephen's Gate,

Nigh the pool likewise named after him, occupying the spot where he was stoned, and watch the shadows slowly sliding (sledlike) down the hills of Berotha & Zion into the valley of Jehosophat, then after resting a while in the bottom of the ravine, slowly begin creeping up the opposite side of Olivet, entering tomb after tomb & cave after cave. . . .

Had Jerusalem no peculiar historic associations, still would it, by its physical aspect evoke peculiar emotion in the traveller. [As the sight of haunted Haddon Hall suggested to Mrs. Radcliffe her curdling romances, so I have little doubt, the diabolical landscape of Judea must have suggested to the Jewish prophets their ghastly theology. . . .

The color of the whole city is grey & looks at you like a cold grey eye in a cold old man.—its strange aspect in the pale olive light of the morning. . . .

Is the desolation of the land the result of the fatal embrace of the Deity? Hapless are the favorites of heaven.

In the emptiness of the lifeless antiquity of Jerusalem the emigrant Jews are like flies that have taken up their abode in a skull.

He went on for Piraeus by way of Beirut and Smyrna, suffering from the "affliction of bugs & fleas & moschitos [which] counterbalances to me all the satisfaction of Eastern travel". As the ship passed by moonlight through the Sporades and toward Samos and Patmos, he "was here again afflicted with the great curse of modern travel—skepticism" and wished the higher critics, Niebuhr and Strauss, to the dogs for having taken the bloom off things. But though skepticism had affected his view of religious history, he was not particularly skeptical of a story told by the Captain about the sale in Jerusalem of tickets—as for reserved seats in the theater—to Heaven, bought by pilgrims. On the evening of February 8th he landed at Piraeus and had his first glimpse of the Acropolis by moonlight. In each of the four entries in which he noted something about the Acropolis, he compared its stones to ice, and perhaps the most vivid of his phrases was "Ruins of Parthenon like North River breaking up", but in none of the four brief poems he called "The Parthenon" does this figure recur.

Ten days later he was in Naples, the "gayest city in the world", where he bought himself a good coat for nine dollars. Driving through "the older & less elegant part of town" after a visit to the cathedral of St. Januarius, his carriage was halted by some acrobats in the street. When the crowd had cleared to let him through, he rose in the carriage and gave his most graceful bow, much to the good-natured amusement of the Neapolitans. This little piece of merriment was incorporated by Major Jack Gentian of the Burgundian Club in a rambling series of verses called "Naples in the Time of Bomba", which though it looked forward to the time when an amazing combination of high-minded liberals, fanatic nationalists, and organized criminals would force out the last of the Bourbon kings, is mainly concerned with the gaiety that accompanies the Italian genius for externality, the sunlit and reasonable behavior that to Northern prejudice, with its inclination toward the dark and hidden, often seems operatic because at least as much is assumed to be on view in the world as in the theater. The persistent idealism of the Northern and Protestant mind makes it ascribe a higher degree of reality to the intangible, and the "realities" to which Jack Gentian refers in the following lines cannot have been Ferdinand II's troops alone, for the happy crowds in the street were just as "real" as they:

> Ah, could one but realities rout
> A holiday-world it were, no doubt.
> But Naples, sure she lacks not cheer,
> Religion, it is jubilee here—
> Feast follows festa thro' the year;
> And then such Nature all about!

No surly moor of forge and mill,
She charms us glum barbarians still,
Fleeing from frost, bad bread, or duns,
Despotic *Biz*, and devils blue. . . .

Though Melville had puritanical misgivings about the "little shrines of Virgin & child, lit" he saw in the lottery shops and thought them a "religious inducement to wickedness", the sympathetic attitude toward Catholicism that he later showed in *Clarel* had its beginnings in what he saw of the popular manifestations of religion in Italy. If he did suffer it, he quickly recovered from

> . . . that shock of novelty
> Which makes some Protestants unglad
> First viewing the mysterious cheer
> In Peter's fane.

Jack Gentian's account of his carriage ride comes to a close when he describes, with entire respect, a priest bearing the Viaticum through the streets, then turns to the rose given him by a flower-girl and finds its "last petals falling, and its soul of musk dissolved in empty air!" The contrast implied here the poet does not pursue, nor perhaps could he, since for him the evanescence of the rose was the dominant fact. The rose was not only emblematical of a few cheerful hours in the Neapolitan streets; what was elusive in it stood also for that sinuous discontent that had made Melville unable to credit the stony reality of Patmos.

Visiting Pausilippo, the ancient resort town on the eastern side of the Bay of Naples whose name derives from the Greek for "easing pain", he noted its entangled "snarls of beauty" but of himself put down: "At Posilipo found not the cessation which the name expresses." When he wrote a poem about Pausilippo, the theme was the same: the exterior and interior facts could not be reconciled and the pity with which "the bland untroubled heaven" looked down on this conflict was humanly of no avail. It is not surprising that he found the cathedral in Milan more to his taste than St. Peter's; the Gothic church, aspiring upward "like multitudinous forks of fire" and defiant of the restrictions of physics, was more significant of his cloven world than the great Roman basilica that contains its ecstatic baroque detail with a calm and almost mathematically ordered coherence. Fire was a religious token for Melville but one that always carried with it the suggestion of it negativing darkness, and it was here of course that he stood at his furthest remove from the spirit of Catholicism, whose image of the final mysteries is not darkness but the utmost intensity of light. In any case, no Catholic—however infrequent a voyager in this depth-sounding instrument—could entertain Melville's reflection on a confessional seen in a church of Padua:

> Dread diving-bell! In thee inurned
> What hollows the priest must sound,
> Descending into consciences
> Where more is hid than found.

Traveling by diligence, Melville arrived in Rome on the morning of January 25th, presumably entering the Porta San Giovanni near the site of the ancient Porta Asinaria. He had announced his departure for the city by writing the word ROME in his journal with a great flourish. Exactly what he had expected we do not know—probably not the late Renaissance city with Imperial outcroppings and rococo embellishments that Rome must have been in 1857. He was disappointed: ". . . Rome fell flat on me. Oppressively flat. . . . Tiber a ditch, yellow as saffron. The whole landscape nothing independent of associations." However, his enthusiasm was soon aroused and he began to do the sights vigorously. The record of his stay in Rome is sparse in comment, being pretty much a list of things and persons seen—perhaps the fact that his eyes were again troubling him badly prevented his writing more fully.

On his return to America, he would lecture on the statuary of Rome, and we may suppose what he then said closely approached his first impressions. His young cousin Henry Gansevoort, who had heard Herman's talk in Boston early in December, 1857, wrote about the lecture in considerable detail to his father, Peter Gansevoort, preceding his account with some undergraduate reflections on his relative's character and his inaptitude at "captious criticism":

. . . He spoke of the gigantic figures which surmounted like storks the pediment of St. John Lantern as a meet company to welcome one to the eternal city—These with their thousand companions in other places in the city abide & mock the human census, the true and abiding population of Rome. The statues at first startle our preconceived opinions. Seneca presents the appearance of a disappointed pawnbroker. Socrates of a comic musique. Caesar of a practical business man. Nero of a fast young man. Plato the aristocratic transcendentalist of a Venetian exquisite. On closer examination however we perceive our former ideas to be correct. The component parts of character are the same now as then. Although the arch dissembler Tiberius wears a sad intellectual countenance still deep attention recalls its sinister lines. . . .

When he stood in the Colliseum its mountain hights of ruins waving foliage & girdling him around as some vast green hollow in the Appenine range, the solitude was that of savage nature, but restoring its shattered terraces and arches he repeopled them with the statues from the Vatican and in the arenas turfy glen he fancy free confronted the fighting Gladiator from the Louvre with the dying one from the Capitol. Again he heard the ruffian huzzah for the first mingle with the pitiless hiss for the last and felt that more than one in the host around, shared not in the passions of the hour but some hearts felt the horror then as keenly we would now. . . . He compared the elements of Roman greatness wh. are incorporated into our system of Government and present civilization. The Locomotive and the Laocoon. Our printing press circulating thoughts which they begot and their example which is the basis of our *idea*. The Roman arch entering into and sustaining our architecture and the Roman spirit still animating & supporting Societies and states. The Colliseum and the Crystal Palace as exponents of our respective characters. Will the glass of the former equal in durability the travertine of the other [?]

Peter Gansevoort replied to his son's letter, agreeing that Herman "would be more at home in Narrative than in Criticism". He supposed that his nephew might put "a narrative of his recent tour on the borders of the Mediterranean & Constantinople &c &c" "into a Book, which would be not only instructive to others, but very profitable to himself—Such a work would not make a requisition on his imagination." He asked Henry to suggest this to Herman when he saw him again, little foreseeing that Herman would weave this same tour into a two-volume poem as much critical as narrative for the publication of which he (Uncle Peter) would advance twelve hundred dollars.

In Rome Melville called on some members of the American colony. Perhaps the most noted of the persons he saw was the sculptor Thomas Crawford, the husband of Julia Ward Howe's sister and the father of F. Marion Crawford. After briefly seeing his brother-in-law Samuel Shaw, who gave him news of home, he left for Leghorn on March 21st. From Leghorn he went to Pisa, whose tower he afterward called "hovering, shivering on the verge, a would-be suicide". He then went down the valley of the Arno to Florence, where again his notes tell little and where his sightseeing must have been cursory, for none of his later versified references to art touch on anything Florentine. In Florence he called on another American sculptor, Hiram Powers, whose statue "The Greek Slave" had by its not exactly austere nudity aroused much discussion in New York a few years before, in which Evert Duyckinck had joined on the approving side. The most celebrated of the foreign residents in Florence, Robert Browning, Melville did not see, though he had borrowed Elizabeth Barrett's poems from Duyckinck's library in 1850. It is probably quite idle but certainly amusing to conjecture what might have happened had he met one of Mrs. Browning's American friends then in Florence—the medium Dougald Home, who had the gift of floating in and out of windows.

By April 1st he was in Venice, having stopped on the way at Bologna, Ferrara, and Padua; and in Venice he remained for six days, a short-enough visit for one who would "rather be in Venice on a rainy day, than in other capital on fine one", especially considering how miserable a rainy day in Venice can be. In Venice he remarked the singular beauty of the women and their "rich brown complexions" which Titian had put into his paintings. As he rode in a gondola along a side canal amongst the "reefs of palaces", apparently one of these Venetian beauties beckoned to, or at least rolled her eyes at, him from a window, whereupon he told the gondolier to make off in a hurry, reflecting (when he came to put the incident in verse) that he had fled one of the Sirens exactly as had Ulysses, "brave, wise, and Venus' son". Without doubting that he had acted quite wisely, we may join Mr. Mumford in wondering why more than thirty years later Melville should publish the verse telling of this in "Fruits of Travel Long Ago". Did he, for all those years, nourish a regret for an opportunity missed (though, as such opportunities usually are, sweeter for being missed); or did he feel self-righteous that he had resisted sexual temptation, something for a man of his temperament not to be lightly acceded to?

From Venice Melville returned northward and westward, arriving in Switzerland after having stopped at Milan, Turin, and Genoa. He spent several days in Switzerland, then passed through Germany to Holland, whence he sailed for England on April 25th, his last visit to the Continent trailing off in a shadowy way so far as the written record goes, rather like certain paintings of the Dutch school that he had admired in Amsterdam. As in Rome he had gone to see the graves of Keats and Shelley, so in England he made an act of literary homage by a visit to Stratford-on-Avon. He went also to Oxford, where he for the first time felt strongly America's English origins— though these had been so evident in all that he had written. He appears not to have called on any of his English acquaintances.

On May 4th he was in Liverpool and saw Hawthorne again, but what passed between them neither his nor Hawthorne's journal says. The following day he sailed on the *City of Manhattan* for New York. It must have been after he had ceased making regular entries in his journal that he separately noted in it: "Seeing is believing." What he had seen was there to be seen, and below he set down the subjective fact that fell between the seeing and the believing: "The pains lie among the pleasures like sand in rice, not only bad in themselves but spoiling the good."

GOLDEN MOTTOES

THOUGH THE WRITTEN FRUITS OF MELVILLE'S TRAVELS IN
1856–1857 were to be a long time in appearing, he did, as I
have said, shortly begin to lecture on what he had seen abroad.
The business of lecturing he undertook without any personal
enthusiasm. So far as writing went, he was determined to have
nothing to do "with palterers of the mart" who abandoned
Truth "mid loud gregarious lies", but he wrote to George
Duyckinck at the end of 1858, "if they will pay expenses, and
give a reasonable fee, I am ready to lecture in Labrador or on
the Isle of Desolation off Patagonia". In four years of lecturing
on Roman sculpture, the South Seas, and traveling in general
he made a little more than a thousand dollars and went as far
north as Montreal and as far south as Clarksville, Tennessee.

His manner of speaking seems not to have been well suited
to lecturing: newspaper accounts of his talks frequently complained that he could not be heard, and the reporter for the
Yonkers, New York, *Examiner,* with the personal viciousness
and uncertain grammar that characterized so much newspaper
reviewing of the period, complained that "the close of his sen-
tences have a descending and rising cadence, which can be
likened to nothing on earth but the graceful twist in a porcine
afterpart". However, earlier in the same year a Cincinnati
paper had mentioned him more favorably and given one of
the few records of his personal appearance, remarking his small
eyes, as Sophia Hawthorne had, and speaking of him as

rather an attractive person, though not what anybody would describe good looking. He is a well built, muscular, gentleman, with

a frame capable of great physical exertion and endurance. His manner is gentle and persuasive, while a certain indefinable sharpness of features, with small twinkling blue eyes under arched brows, and a rather contracted and rugged forehead, indicates the spirit of adventure which sent him roving a sailor's sturdy life. . . . His voice is as soft and almost as sweet . . . as the warbling of the winds in the cocoa groves.

Just when Melville began writing verse is not known. In August, 1857, he signified his willingness to be a contributor to *The Atlantic Monthly,* the first number of which appeared the following November, and perhaps he had poetry in mind when he did this. *The Atlantic* never printed anything of his, but in May, 1859, he was offering two of his poems to the editors of some unidentified magazine with all the modest hopefulness of a young and quite unknown poet. "Here are two Pieces," he wrote, "which, if you find them suited to your magazine I should be happy to see them appear there.—In case of publication, you may, if you please, send me what you think they are worth." Around the same time his wife wrote to her stepmother that Herman had "taken to writing poetry. You need not tell any one, for you know how such things get around." Elizabeth's warning was doubtless meant not to guard Herman's literary reputation but to fend off criticism in the family circle, for financial matters were none of the best in Pittsfield and the writing of verse was hardly the way to improve them. But while there is no doubt that the Melvilles had a hard time making both ends meet, there is not any reason to think that their poverty was so great as to be their main concern. In July of the same year Melville wrote an entirely gay-minded invitation to Daniel Shepherd, a Wall Street lawyer who was the author of two novels, and wrote it in verse. He said he could offer Shepherd neither claret nor cognac, but

Golden Mottoes

—Of Bourbon that is rather new
I brag a fat black bottle or two.—
Shepherd, is this such Mountain-Dew
As one might fitly offer you?

A little less than a year later, as he was preparing to set out for what he thought would be a voyage around the world in his brother Tom's ship, he had ready a volume of verse, to secure the publication of which he had enlisted the services of his wife, his brother Allan, and the two Duyckincks. For Allan he left a list of twelve memoranda, telling him that he wished the volume's title-page to read simply "Poems by Herman Melville" without reference to any of his previous works, that he expected no advance from the publisher, and that "of all human events, perhaps the publication of a first volume of verses is the most insignificant; but though a matter of no moment to the world, it is still of some concern to the author— as these *Mem.* show". In writing to Evert Duyckinck, he dissembled rather less concern: "As my wife has interested herself a good deal in this matter, and seems to know more about it than I do—at least about the *merits* of the performance—I must therefore refer you to her, in case of any exigency requiring information further than you are now in possession of." Elizabeth was, in fact, as enthusiastic as her husband for the publication of the book that had, as she wrote to Duyckinck, "been such a profound secret between Herman and myself for so long".

No publisher was found for the volume, and it became a lost book—though the poems comprising it have probably really survived, incorporated as lyrical interludes into *Clarel*, included in *Timoleon*, or left in manuscript at their author's death. After his return from his voyage, Melville wrote to Tom recalling "the romantic moonlight night" on which he had repeated "about three cables' length of his verses" and saying that Tom would be glad to learn that "a trunk-maker took the whole lot off my hands at ten cents the pound. . . . If you were not such a devil of a ways off, I would send you a trunk, by way of a presentation-copy."

Melville sailed from Boston on the *Meteor* on the last day of May, 1860, and four and a half months later landed in San Francisco. Apparently the only interruption of the voyage was when the *Meteor* came in sight of a whaler and Melville was rowed over for an hour's "gam" with her captain. Aside from an irregularly kept journal and two letters sent to his children, nothing remains that he committed to writing about his last trip around the Horn. The reasons for which the journey was undertaken are obscure: perhaps for his health, though a long ocean voyage in a clipper ship does not seem the best treatment for the rheumatic complaint—with such symptoms as severe "crick in the back" and inability to use his hands—from which he intermittently suffered during the latter half of his life; perhaps for what the Orient promised in the way of literary material. He had the humiliation for an old sailor of suffering from seasickness for nearly two weeks, but even when his stomach improved the tone of his journal did not: the first glimpse of shore, Staten Land and Tierra del Fuego, was a "Hell-landscape" and the sight of Cape Horn was "horrid". As they were rounding the Cape, there occurred an accident that provoked the longest entry in his journal and led him to reflect that death was indeed "the King of Terrors, not to the dying or the dead" but to those who survived. To his eleven-year-old son he wrote an account of the mishap as gloomy as anything in *Goody Two-Shoes* and without a moral to point to the hope of something better:

Whilst the sailors were aloft on one of the yards, the ship rolled and plunged terribly; and it blew with sleet and hail, and was very cold & biting. Well, all at once, Uncle Tom saw something falling through the air, and then heard a thump, and then,—looking before him, saw a poor sailor lying dead on the deck. He had fallen from the yard, and was killed instantly.—His shipmates picked him up, and carried him under cover. By and by, when time could be spared, the sailmakers sewed up the body in a piece of sail-cloth, putting some iron balls—cannon balls—at the foot of it. And, when all was ready, the body was put on a plank, and carried to the ship's side in the presence of all hands. Then Uncle Tom, as Captain, read a prayer out of the prayer-book, and at a given word, the sailors who held the plank tipped it up, and immediately the body slipped into the stormy ocean, and we saw it no more.—Such is the way a poor sailor is buried at sea. This sailor's name was Ray.—He had a friend among the crew; and they were both going to California, and thought of living there; but you see what happened.

He remained in San Francisco for a little more than a week, but we do not know what he thought of the city that his friend Dana had found so European in character when he visited it the year previous, twenty-four years after the young Bostonian had first "floated into the vast solitude of the Bay of San Francisco". Herman, as Lizzie wrote in her diary, "returned in the *Carter* October 20th to Panama—crossed the Isthmus & sailed for New York on the *North Star*". Back home, he was faced once more with the necessity of adding to his income. Shortly before he had sailed, his father-in-law had discharged all his debts, in return for which he had transferred the title of Arrowhead to his wife's name, but this of course bettered Melville's financial standing only on paper. Abraham Lincoln had just been elected President, and Melville had hopes of getting from the new administration the consular appointment he had failed to get from Pierce's. In the middle of March, 1861, he wrote to his Uncle Peter, who had influence in Republican circles, asking his aid in procuring "some foreign appointment under the new Administration—the consulship at Florence, for example. In many respects such an appointment would be desirable for me, altho' the emoluments are not very considerable." He also enlisted Dana's help for the same post, and Dana wrote to Charles Sumner, describing the applicant as "a capital good fellow, good manners & feelings".

Melville went to New York in an unsuccessful attempt to see Thurlow Weed, whom he had found equally inaccessible when, in 1846, he had presented the political boss with a copy of *Typee* in the hope of his good offices in obtaining a job in the Treasury. A few days later, he was in Washington, "boarding in a plain home—plain fare plain people—in fact all plain but the road to Florence". He called at Sumner's and found the Secretary out, then went on with another office-seeker to a dinner at which he met the Vice-President; he sat sunning himself on a bench opposite the White House and twice looked on at the sessions of the Senate; and he attended a public reception at the White House, where Lincoln "shook hands like a good fellow—working hard at it like a man sawing wood at so much per cord". Perhaps Melville was called away from his unpromising suit by the death, on March 30th, of Judge Shaw.

Elizabeth's share of her father's estate was rather less than $20,000. On the income from this and whatever, if anything, his books continued to bring in, Melville and his family of five lived. He made no attempt to earn anything by writing, and it is not unlikely that when in 1862 he received $900 as a legacy from his Aunt Priscilla, he reflected wrily that here was more than any new book of his could win him. Perhaps he had equally ironical musings when, the same year, he attended the semi-centennial celebration of the Albany Academy as one of its most celebrated alumni. The following year it was decided to exchange Arrowhead, along with a considerable piece of

Elizabeth's legacy, for a house in New York owned by Allan, and the motive, according to a chronicler of the Pittsfield region who knew Melville, was Melville's health. In the autumn of 1863 the Melvilles moved to 104 East 26th Street, a brick house with brownstone trim and an iron balcony, like most city houses of the period generally crepuscular but not lacking some ante-bellum grace, and from there on the "Last Day of 1863" Melville wrote to Duyckinck, returning a book he had been asked to review and explaining: "I have read it with great interest. As for scribbling anything about it, tho' I would like to please you, I have not spirit enough."

Yet it will not do to suppose that Melville's spirits had quite gone from him during this period. He always carried with him what he called "mine infirmity of jocularity", and gloom seen in a proper light has something absurd about it. It is the attitude of the human creature that introduces gloom into the universal scheme, where the same attitude, viewed with sufficient detachment, is seen to be ridiculous. Such detachment is considerably short of a sufficient wisdom. Sorrow, which is not gloom, is not alien to wisdom, since wisdom sees things in the double light of love that reveals things both as they are and as they might be. In the disparity there is room enough for sorrow and, for the same reason, no room for despair. But if we do not have the full vision of reality—in which its present being is qualified by its potentialities—we can only say "What is, is" or, as Melville wrote to his sister Kate, "But don't let us become too earnest. A very bad habit." A few months before, writing to his brother-in-law Sam to let him know that he was recovering from the injuries received when he had been thrown from a wagon, he had said:

I begin to indulge in the pleasing idea that my life must needs be of some value. Probably I consume a certain amount of oxygen, which unconsumed might create some subtle disturbance in Nature. Be that as it may, I am going to try and stick to the conviction named above. . . . I once, like other spoonies, cherished a loose sort of notion that I did not care to live very long. But I will frankly own that I have no serious, no insuperable objections to a respectable longevity. I don't like the idea of being left out night after night in a cold church-yard. —In warm and genial climes death is much less of a bugbear than in our frozen latitudes. A native of Hindostan takes easily and kindly to his latter end. It is but as a stepping round the corner to him. He knows he will sleep warm.

This was of course intended to be only so much "trifling", but it must at the same time have seemed the expression of a mood that would at least carry him through each day of the situation in which he found himself. Not steadily but enough for the practical business of living, he sustained the mood, though at the end of fifteen years it seemed to point in a quite different direction, and he wrote to another brother-in-law, John C. Hoadley: "You are young; but I am verging on three-score, and at times a certain lassitude steals over one—in fact, a disinclination for doing anything but the indispensable. At such moments the problem of the universe seems a humbug, and epistolary obligations mere moonshine, and the—well, nepenthe seems all-in-all."

In the period with which we are immediately concerned, it may well be that Melville also took vigor from a more public mood—the one attending the Civil War. "There is no doubt that the prosecution of the war quickened Melville," says Mr. Mumford, "and made him feel a purpose instead of the dull, fearful hollow of an empty and respectable life." The war indeed quickened every versifying talent in America, and 1861–1865 saw more occasional poetry than any other period in the nation's history. Though the young Edmund Clarence Stedman was hopeful that the war would save not only the nation but also the future of poetry, such was hardly the case: a great deal of metrical rhetoric was released, but only Walt Whitman, in *Drum-Taps,* produced any verse readable by present-day standards and Stedman himself became one of the "squires of poesy" who pretty much ruled the grey landscape of American poetry for the next forty years.

Melville's own contribution to this soon-withered efflorescence of verse appeared in 1866, and most of the poems in *Battle-Pieces and Aspects of the War* were composed, according to the preface, after the fall of Richmond (April 3rd, 1865). Thus, though the poems form a kind of selected history of the war from the hanging of John Brown to Lee's appearance before the Reconstruction Committee in Washington, they were not all written contemporaneously with the events they describe. They are versified journalism, but at one remove, and for his historical data Melville relied chiefly on Frank Moore's *The Rebellion Record,* one of those many-volumed publishing ventures of which the Civil War and the decade following it were so prolific.

Malcolm, his eldest son, was of course too young to serve in the Union forces, and Melville himself felt too old, though he was only forty-two when the war began, or perhaps he was too ill. The first of the great modern wars of its nature intruded to some extent into every American's life, but the closest Melville came to its actual field was when, in the spring of 1864, he visited with his cousin Colonel Henry Gansevoort the camp of General Robert O. Tyler at Fairfax, Virginia, in the region where John S. Mosby, the Confederate ranger or guerrilla, carried on his romantic operations.[1] His rôle during

---

[1] Colonel Gansevoort later took Mosby's camp (though not Mosby). The longest poem in *Battle-Pieces* is a ballad about Mosby's border warfare.

the conflict was that of the meditative bystander, much interested, in both senses of the word, but able to see things in
proportions not given to those more actively engaged:

> I muse upon my country's ills—
> The tempest bursting from the waste of Time
> On the world's fairest hope linked with man's foulest crime.

"Senior wisdom suits not now," he reflected, for "all wars are
boyish, and are fought by boys". These it was, "Moloch's
uninitiate", who

> > Went from the North and came from the South,
> > With golden mottoes in the mouth,
> >   To lie down midway on a bloody bed.

Melville had no doubts of the justice of the Northern cause,
though for him that cause was less concerned with any *mystique*
of the Union than with the abolition of slavery. Twelve years
before the war he had foreseen, in *Mardi*, that slavery might
lead to it. While he looked on slavery as a foul crime that
sought to breed the souls out of men "as the instinct of scent
is killed in pointers", he at that time wondered if, faced with
war as the alternative to negro slavery, one hadn't better
choose "present woes for some, than future woes for all". The
solution would have to be left to "Time—all-healing Time—
Time, great Philanthropist"; but it was from the waste of Time
that the tempest finally burst. The war was inevitable, and he
wrote of a Northern naval maneuvre, "in geometric beauty
curved", in which

> > The rebel at Port Royal felt
> >   The Unity overawe,
> > And rued the spell. A type was here,
> >   And victory of Law.

If Melville in the poem just quoted ("Dupont's Round Fight") and in a number of others where the Lord is pictured as active on the Northern side (though there is nothing amiss in being thankful to God for a victory of what one considers the right) numbered himself amongst the "bards of Progress and Humanity", he was hardly of the temperament to see everywhere the victory of Law in a humanly viable way. "Abolitionism . . . but expresses the fellow-feeling of slave for slave," said the Missourian in *The Confidence-Man,* and Melville perceived that since slaveries were various, in the abolition of one the way might be opened for another. The South's argument on these lines he stated in "The Conflict of Convictions" with what must have been a good measure of agreement:

> Power unanointed may come—
> Dominion (unsought by the free)
>   And the Iron Dome,[2]
> Stronger for stress and strain
> Fling her huge shadow athwart the main;
> But the Founders' dream shall flee.

Ten years later, in *Clarel,* the Southern refugee Ungar would further urge the same argument, protesting against "an Anglo-Saxon China" where all was a "dead level of rank commonplace", and once more we may suppose that Melville agreed. The only other poem of immediate political implication in the volume—and the one essay in blank verse—deals with the New York draft riots and is written as though Melville had been a witness of them. Taking the poem by itself, its conclusion is sufficiently ambiguous, so far as the author's own judgment on the matter is concerned, to meet even Mr. Empson's test of poetry, but biography is a vain exercise if we cannot

[2] The dome of the Capitol.

decide that Melville reluctantly gave his assent to wise Draco's action:

> Wise Draco comes, deep in the midnight roll
> Of black artillery; he comes, though late;
> In code corroborating Calvin's creed
> And cynic tyrannies of honest kings;
> He comes, nor parlies; and the Town, redeemed,
> Gives thanks devout; nor, being thankful, heeds
> The grimy slur on the Republic's faith implied,
> Which holds that Man is naturally good,
> And—more—is Nature's Roman, never to be scourged.

However this was, *Battle-Pieces* was partly offered as a warning against any Draconian treatment of the South. Melville made his dedication to "the Three Hundred Thousand who in the war for the maintenance of the Union fell devotedly under the flag of their fathers", but he added a prose supplement to his book, in violation of its symmetry as he said, in which he spoke eloquently against the temptation "to pervert the national victory into oppression for the vanquished". The North, having made the great effort of winning the war, would have to make the still greater effort of not playing the live dog to the dead lion; and in pleading for this Melville was aware that he went against the tone of some of his own verses celebrating Northern victories. Most of all his appeal for generosity contradicted his poem on the assassination of Lincoln, "The Martyr, Indicative of the Passion of the People on the 15th Day of April, 1865", with its refrain,

> Beware the People weeping
> When they bare the iron hand.

If the occasion called from Melville this rather hackneyed piece of public rage and from his shallower-minded contemporary Whitman the lovely "When Lilacs Last in the Dooryard

Bloomed", the explanation lies in his misconception of the nature of poetry. In the reading of poetry that Melville did after 1857, he frequently marked the more ingenious rhymes and the archaic "poetic" words—which makes it appear that poetry for him was a way of saying things rather than of seeing them. The result of this attitude, generally speaking, is that the content of a poem is something which might be stated in prose but, because rhyme and meter become objects in themselves, is even less well realized in verse. And, in the end, the manner dictates the matter. Something of this kind surely explains "A Canticle: Significant of the National Exaltation of Enthusiasm at the Close of the War", whose sub-title seems to reflect a doubt Melville had when he read what he had written. The final verses are:

> The Generations pouring
>   From times of endless date,
> In their going, in their flowing
> Ever form the steadfast State;
>   And Humanity is growing
>   Toward the fullness of her fate.
>
> Thou Lord of hosts victorious,
>   Fulfill the end designed;
> By a wondrous way and glorious
>   A passage Thou dost find—
>   A passage Thou dost find:
> Hosanna to the Lord of Hosts,
>   The hosts of human kind.

In those poems dealing with naval warfare, Melville was at his best and furthest remove from such verbalism, for where the sea was concerned he was, as might be expected, able to draw on his own direct perceptions to give his verse an inde-

pendent body. "A Requiem, For Soldiers Lost in Ocean Transports" is written in a convention of poetic diction looked on
with disfavor now (when a convention of labored originality
prevails) but, the convention allowed, speaks with singular
economy and force:

> When, after storms that woodlands rue,
>   To valleys comes atoning dawn,
> The robins blithe their orchard-sports renew;
>   And meadow-larks, no more withdrawn,
> Caroling fly in the languid blue;
> The while, from many a hid recess,
> Alert to partake the blessedness,
> The pouring mites their airy dance pursue.
>   So, after ocean's ghastly gales,
> When laughing light of hoyden morning breaks,
>   Every finny hider wakes—
>   From vaults profound swims up with glittering scales;
>   Through the delightsome sea he sails,
> With shoals of shining tiny things
> Frolic on every wave that flings
>   Against the prow its showery spray;
> All creatures joying in the morn,
> Save them forever from joyance torn,
>   Whose bark was lost where now the dolphins play;
> Save them that by the fabled shore,
>   Down the pale streams are washed away,
> Far to the reef of bones are borne;
>   And never revisits them the light,
> Nor sight of long-sought land and pilot more;
>   Nor heed they now the lone bird's flight
> Round the lone spar where mid-sea surges pour.

And again the sea yielded up to him an adequate symbol in
"Commemorative of a Naval Victory":

But seldom the laurel wreath is seen
   Unmixed with pensive pansies dark;
There's a light and a shadow on every man
   Who at last attains his lifted mark—
   Nursing through night the ethereal spark.
Elate he never can be;
He feels that spirit which glad had hailed his worth,
   Sleep in oblivion.—The shark
Glides white through the phosphorous sea.

The worst that can be said about Melville's verse has been said by William Plomer: "Much of his verse is flat and tedious, or sprightly in a heavy way; it is full of the faults of the period—trite poeticisms and mythological formulae, rhetorical questions and so on; it conveys the sense of strain produced by a moralist's yearnings after hedonism; above all, it is technically weak, monotonous and unresourceful." [3] No doubt Dr. Johnson's hard judgment on Donne may be reversed for Melville: he should have been hanged for keeping meter. But if *Battle-Pieces* is taken as a commonplace book in which Melville made versified entries, it is not less interesting than any other volume of verse contemporary with it and more interesting than most. To us of today, for whom the only acceptable war poetry is one that shows the utter futility of war in the human heroism wasted by it, certain of Melville's poems will appear to celebrate with civilian ease "that scorn of death which is life's crown". An example is the often-praised but embarrassingly inferior "Lyon", the subject of which eagerly seeks out "a field to die on" (and some of the faults of which are no doubt owing to a rhyme scheme involving the repetition of Lyon's name in each quatrain). Still it must be remembered that, in Melville's view, the war was being fought for the

[3] *Selected Poems of Herman Melville*, edited by William Plomer (London, 1943: The Hogarth Press).

Right, so of those who had died for the Right—dangerously abstract concept that it is—he could say, perhaps with some loss of "realism" but certainly without essential falsification:

> Forever they slumber young and fair,
> The smile upon them as they died;
> Their end attained, that end a height:
> Life was to these a dream fulfilled,
> And death a starry night.

In terms of the individual experience, he knew "what like a bullet can undeceive!" and he saw the impersonal hugeness of modern war made "the garniture, emblazonment, and heraldry all decay". In *White-Jacket* he had made it plain that battles between the wooden seventy-fours were less romantic for the sailor on the blood-soaked gun-deck than for the landsman looking at a painting of a naval engagement all wind, water, and gun-smoke, but the fight of the *Monitor* and *Merrimac* stirred some regrets for "the carved and castled navies" now that "all went on by crank, pivot, and screw, and calculations of caloric".

> . . . War-paint shows the streaks of weather;
> War yet shall be, but warriors
> Are now but operatives; War's made
> Less grand than Peace,
> And a singe runs through lace and feather.

Collectively men will subscribe to things that they cannot accept as individuals. This is probably less a result of mass emotionalism than of the fact that a man's private beliefs are the ones on whose universal validity he most insists: what he feels most intimately is what is finally and inevitably true. He assents to the public dogma that neither his personal reasoning nor experience establishes precisely because as a member of the collective he feels somehow less "involved"; what he commits himself to as a member of the group he commits himself to as less than a whole person, for something of his own identity is lost in his identity with the group. Patriotism may not only move a man to acts—heroic or barbarous—he would not undertake singly but it may also demand of him thoughts impossible as products of his private mental economy. Melville answered such a demand in the last lines of "Lee in the Capitol":

> Catching the light in the future's skies,
> Instinct disowns each darkening prophecy:
> Faith in America never dies;
> Heaven shall the end ordained fulfill.
> We march with Providence cheery still.

As the lines show, on this level of optimism the re-invigoration of his talent was not to be found. We can all be patriots but we cannot all be artists, and the artist's first obligation is to be himself. The nature of the self that obligation implies was a question with which Melville was still wrestling.

UNDER THE VAULT OF
HOLLOW HEAVEN

AS MELVILLE HAD ANTICIPATED, THE PUBLICATION OF
Battle-Pieces was not a matter of much moment to the world.
About eighteen months after publication Harpers were able to
report the sales of only 486 copies, but Melville did not wait for
this proof of his wife's contention that *"poetry* is a compara-
tively uncalled for article in the market": before even the first
reviews had appeared, he took a job in the Customs House at
470 West Street. Neither in emoluments nor dignity was inspecting cargoes equal to the consulship at Florence. The
former were about four dollars a four-hour day,[1] not exactly
a handsome salary even in 1866 but probably enough to double
the family's income. Around this time, too, Malcolm secured
a job with the Atlantic and Great Western Insurance Company, whose president Richard Lathers had married Allan
Melville's sister-in-law. Neither of Melville's sons went to
college and both began to support themselves at an early age.
In this their situation was not so different from what their
father's had been, and the little that is known of the short
lives of both boys leads one to think they also had their sad
disappointments which made them think much and bitterly before their time. As for the dignity of Melville's office as customs inspector, Mr. Mumford remarks that it was "one of the

---

[1] According to William Charvat's "Melville's Income", *American Literature*,
November, 1943. Mr. Charvat shows that the Melvilles were not so poor as has
been assumed, thanks largely to legacies. On her death in 1906, Mrs. Melville left
an estate valued at $170,000—a good deal of which was, of course, the natural
increment to be expected in those happy days of the small capitalist.

lowest political positions open to patronage" and of the kind that went to "impecunious bankers, broken-down sports, bankrupt merchants, political nondescripts". Indeed, Melville did not even have the bourgeois felicity of sitting all his working day at 470 West Street and scrawling his name and title on papers handed to him by subordinates; an outdoor officer, presumably he had to board in foul weather or fair the ships whose cargoes he inspected.

That a man of Melville's singular genius should have to spend twenty years on the West Street waterfront earning a meager living is not the sort of thing that would happen in an ideal world (at least of the kind envisaged by authors); but the entire blame does not fall on 19th-century American society for ignoring Melville and his gifts. Melville's retreat into the Customs House was to a good extent a voluntary one. To be sure, had he had the means he would have led a life of "superabundant leisure". Money and leisure were equivalent and both convertible into a third term whose worth was immediately evident, for, as he told his cousin Kate, "whoever is not in the possession of leisure can hardly be said to possess independence". Lacking the means, he hoped for a better job than the one he eventually got. He had determined not to make in his writing any attempt after "the triumph of the insincere unanimous Mediocrity", and in his particular case the alternative to this was the customs inspectorship. Some failure of the creative energies may have been involved here, since more than one author has insisted on having his say despite all public indifference. Then there is the fact that as a man grows older what he has to say appears to him to have less of necessity about it: the young turn out the baldest imitations of their betters with a feeling of absolute originality, because what they repeat is original in their own experience, but the mature writer produces less from inspiration than from habit.

Melville, in taking his customs-house job, escaped any practical compulsion to write, so that during the last twenty-five years of his life whatever free time he had was left to attend on inspiration. Inspiration, when it came, was of a various quality; it probably led to nothing either better or worse than would have the simple determination to write; but it was not infrequent. The legend that after 1857 Melville remained in a sort of artistic doldrums is curiously persistent though the evidence that refutes it has frequently been pointed to. As we have seen, he lectured whenever the opportunity offered; in 1860 he had a volume of poems ready for publication; and at the end of the Civil War he addressed himself to the public on a subject that he conceived to be in the national interest. Ten years later he published the 20,000 lines of *Clarel*. And during this period of his obscurity he also produced two privately published little books of verse, a collection of poems addressed to his wife, enough miscellaneous verses to make a volume by present-day standards, and a story of more than 30,000 words.

Except for the lost book of poems and *Battle-Pieces*, all this writing was mainly a private exercise. Melville did not despair of his ability to write but he did despair of public acceptance of what he wrote. *Clarel* he only issued under his own name "on the *very strong* representations of the publishers", and Mrs. Melville said that some time afterward he withdrew the book from circulation. The two privately published volumes, *John Marr and Other Sailors* and *Timoleon*, were brought out in editions of twenty-five copies each—probably not enough to supply the personal acquaintances who would have read them sympathetically but a matter of delight to later book-collectors. The bulk of the unpublished poems Melville was wise in not committing to print; worked over though many of them were, they remained fugitive and private efforts. The short novel, on the other hand, he certainly intended for publication, and only his death delayed its appearance for more than thirty years. Some element of bitterness was involved in this relative secrecy.

Authorship presupposes an audience of some kind, and the limitation of his own—which he obviously estimated at twenty-five persons—Melville never accepted with entire indifference. No more than Milton could he be blind to the attractions of fame, however much he might tell himself or others that he had rejected fame's patronage, and in his reading he marked numerous passages touching on the question of renown: it was certainly with self-concern that in Arnold's "Stanzas from the Grand Chatreuse" he marked "Silent,—the best are silent now". A shame at not having attained the ataraxia he asked of himself must have caused him to withhold from print one of his most moving poems, "Immolated", in which he spoke to his earlier works:

> Children of my happier prime,
> When One yet lived with me, and threw
> Her rainbow over life and time,
> Even Hope, my bride, and mother to you!
> O, nurtured in sweet pastoral air,
> And fed on flowers and light, and dew
> Of morning meadows—spare, Ah, spare
> Reproach; spare, and upbraid me not
> That, yielding scarce to reckless mood
> But jealous of your future lot,
> I sealed you in a fate subdued.
> Have I not saved you from the drear
> Theft and ignoring which need be
> The triumph of the insincere
> Unanimous Mediocrity?
> Rest, therefore, free from all despite,
> Snugged in the arms of comfortable night.

(Actually, we have seen, there was not much dew of morning meadows on what Melville considered the better works of his happier prime. What he meant to convey was the notion of his youthful energy, but apparently the poeticism obscured from his sight that energy as it had in fact been. In the last six lines of this poem, incidentally, is found one of the few occasions in Melville's verse when rhythm escapes the bondage of meter.)

That Melville was embittered and cankered in his personal relationships more than most men who have missed their worldly mark there is no reason to suppose. The literary-cum-social life of the period he avoided, nor did he join that peculiarly masculine society of the last decades of the 19th century centered in clubs to which married men went even to celebrate their Christmases. His withdrawal here may have been, as he said in a poem of an old mirror put away in a garret, to "escape from the anguish of the Real and the Seeming in life" or, what is just as likely, it may have been motivated equally by individual preference and lack of sufficient cash. At any rate, he continued to see the best of his old friends and, we may suppose, to drink whisky punch now and then with the Duyckincks; at the same time he made a number of new friends—notably the Stedmans and Stoddards—and in his last years corresponded at some length with two English admirers, W. Clark Russell and James Billson.

The death of Malcolm on September 11th, 1867, attended as it was with painful publicity, certainly further prompted Melville's retirement. Whether or not Malcolm committed suicide, it was first announced in the New York papers that he had, and the denial had to be entered by his friends, who wrote protesting that such an act was not in keeping with the boy's character and explaining that he was in the youthfully romantic habit of sleeping with a pistol under his pillow. On the night of the 10th, Malcolm had come home at three in the morning and, greeted with his mother's reproaches, promised to mend his ways. When his father returned from work the next day, Malcolm, who had not yet appeared, was discovered dead in his room with a pistol wound in his right temple. According to a letter of Samuel Shaw's, Melville had taken away his son's latchkey. Whatever can be said about Malcolm's death beyond the barest facts is, after these many years, necessarily conjectural and, as far as I can see, gives us no rewarding light on the relationship of father and son. No written mention of Malcolm seems ever to have been made after his tragic end either by Melville or his wife, but Elizabeth, presumably after her husband's death, went through the European journal Herman had kept in 1849 and wherever there was an obscure reference to Malcolm added a pitiful explanatory footnote—"Macky" or *"Baby boy"*.

Clarel: A Poem and Pilgrimage in the Holy Land—whose subtitle Melville later in a letter expanded to "a metrical affair, a pilgrimage or what not, of several thousand lines, eminently adapted for unpopularity"—was published by G. P. Putnam's Sons in 1876, bearing a dedication to Peter Gansevoort, who shortly before his death had "provided for the publication of this poem, known to him by report, as existing in manuscript", and prefaced with a brief and weary note: "If during the period in which this work has remained unpublished, though not indivulged, any of its properties have by a natural process exhaled; it yet retains, I trust, enough of original life to redeem it at least from vapidity. Be that as it may, I here dismiss the book—content beforehand with whatever future awaits it." Because of this note, it has been supposed that Melville finished the book some years before his uncle gave him the means to put it into print. But Walter Everett Bezanson has recently shown [2] that in all likelihood the second half of *Clarel* was not begun until 1870, in April of which year Melville acquired the copy of Dean Arthur Penrhyn Stanley's *Sinai and Palestine*, which he used extensively to supplement his own knowledge of the scene of the poem. Alternatively, it is possible that he revised the book again and again after having completed it in one form long before 1876 and feared that he had in this manner rubbed out its first vitality.

In either case, the poem would accurately reflect his frame of mind and his opinions as he approached sixty and be a depository of all the matured reflections he had had since seeing the Holy Land twenty years before. Over its 150 cantos we may picture him working in the evenings and holidays when he was freed from the Customs House, seated at his mahogany desk in the brown-papered second-story bedroom and study whose darkness and austerity would later impress his little granddaughter almost as much as the bag of figs he kept on his book-littered table. With what intensity he applied himself to his book right up to the moment of its appearance (apparently incurring a charge of an extra $100 for last-minute revisions of the proofs) we may gather from a letter that Elizabeth wrote to Catherine Gansevoort, who had proposed visiting Twenty-sixth Street from Albany:

I have written you a note that Herman could see, as he wished, but want you to know how painful it is for me to write it, and also to have to give the real cause—The fact is, that Herman, poor fellow, is in such a frightfully nervous state, & particularly now with such an added strain on his mind, that I am actually *afraid* to have any one here for fear he will be upset entirely, & not be able

[2] In his unpublished doctoral dissertation, *Herman Melville's Clarel* (New Haven, Conn., 1943: Yale University). Mr. Bezanson is announced as the editor of *Clarel* for the collected edition of Melville's works that is being published serially by Hendricks House, Farrar Straus of New York.

to go on with the printing—He was not willing to have even his own sisters here, and I had to write Augusta before she left Albany to that effect—that was the reason she changed her plans and went to Tom's—If ever this dreadful *incubus* of a *book* (I call it so because it has undermined all our happiness) gets off Herman's shoulders I do hope he may be in better mental health—but at present I have reason to feel the gravest concern & anxiety about it—to put it in mild phrase. . . .

The incubus of a book that had compelled poor Lizzie to this duplicity is one of the curiosities of American literature. Like *The Book of Mormon* and *Science and Health*,[3] *Clarel* is long beyond any internal necessity and the length is made harder to bear with by a curious style—in the case of Melville's work, caused by the use of an irregularly rhyming tetrametric line that, as I have said Mr. Brooks suggests, may have been inspired by the Hudibrastic couplet. Given a detailed account of travel in the Holy Land, undertaken by a group of characters prone to reflection on most of the problems of Christian belief, incorporating many elliptical references to Biblical history and the author's varied reading and some very harsh judgments on latitudinarian Christianity and democratic optimism, all of which is set forth in verse, it is not hard to see why Peter Gansevoort had to subsidize the publication of the book and why, in the seventy years since its publication, *Clarel* has been reprinted only once, in an expensive limited edition. The tortured syntax, the rhythmic monotony, the rhymes superfluous to sense, and the failure of the metaphor to flow out into its full analogical

[3] Those who collect coincidences might be interested to observe that two of the religious classics of post-bellum America—one a best-seller and the other barely known to its age—were both what is now called "vanity" publications and were composed over roughly the same period. With his customs job probably began Melville's most serious application to *Clarel*; and in 1866 Mrs. Eddy took the fall on the ice—on her way to a temperance meeting, strangely—to which she ascribed the revelation of the message contained in *Science and Health*, a book published less than a year before Melville's.

implication make *Clarel* a second-rate piece of work, in the kindest judgment. Yet, just because of the tedious lack of selection it shows and its failure often to bring off the high points it itself indicates, one must be careful not to underestimate it; second-rate though it is, almost every page shows the evidences of a first-rate mind; the insights are undoubtedly there, even though they are not fully realized in the terms of poetry.

Once the concession is made that this, after all, is a narrative poem of travel and as such is not open to the criticism that would apply to dramatic or tragic poetry, the defects of *Clarel* are not extraordinary. As C. S. Lewis notes in *A Preface to Paradise Lost*, we no longer have the faculty of reading long poems; we think of them as a series of lyrics with a certain amount of connective tissue. *Clarel* has its "good lines"—and they would make a respectable little anthology—but it is not to be condemned because, sharing a similarity of mood, it does not sustain the poetic tension of "Dover Beach" or *In Memoriam*.

The poem's story is a fairly simple one. Clarel, a young divinity student troubled by doubt, arrives in Jerusalem on the Vigil of Epiphany, seeking to escape in Palestine his "cultivated narrowness" and, by walking where Christ walked, to restore his lost faith. Stopping by the Jaffa Gate, whence the road goes to Emmaus, he wishes that he also might encounter "some stranger of a lore replete" who would answer his questions— and he is hailed by "a flitting tract-dispensing man", Nehemiah, a mildly cracked old American who has long lived in Jerusalem in expectation of the imminent Second Coming. He accepts the company of this kindly old man and through him comes to make the acquaintance of Ruth, the daughter of an American who has been converted to Judaism through his love for a Jewess, after losing his Christian faith by reading Tom Paine.

With Ruth Clarel falls in love with romantic promptness, but when her father Nathan—perhaps one of the first Zionists in literature—is slain on his farm by Arab raiders, the young man's courtship is interrupted by the period of mourning prescribed by Jewish law, and he joins a group of tourists on a visit to the Dead Sea and Bethlehem, taking Nehemiah with him and setting out on the Feast of the Purification. Returning from this minutely described journey, "brief term of days, but a profound remove", with his religious difficulties still unsettled but full of eagerness for his fiancée, we have seen he meets the funeral procession of Ruth and her mother outside the walls of Jerusalem (three other characters in the poem die with equal suddenness). This is on the night of Shrove Tuesday. Clarel remains in Jerusalem through Lent and Easter, while "sluggish, life's wonted stream flows on" without answer to his questions, and we last see him walking down the Via Crucis on Pentecost:

> Dusked Olivet he leaves behind,
> And, taking now a slender wynd,
> Vanishes in the obscurer town.

Poor Clarel is apparently fated to live an eternal Ash Wednesday.

Mr. Mumford hazards that Ruth, the Yankee Jewess, may represent Melville's own infatuation with "ancient Jewish thought", and Mr. Bezanson interprets five different characters in the poem as being personifications of as many stages of the author's religious development. That one character, Rolfe, is meant to be Melville himself there can be no doubt. Rolfe,

> Though given to study, as might seem,
> Was no scholastic partisan
> Or euphonist of Academe,
> But supplemented Plato's theme
> With daedal life in boats and tents,
> A messmate of the elements;

> And yet, more bronzed in face than mind,
> Sensitive still and frankly kind—
> Too frank, too unreserved, may be,
> And indiscreet in honesty.

He has Melville's infirmity of jocularity, so that the pale, and rather pale-minded, Clarel finds it hard to

> . . . reconcile Rolfe's wizard chord
> And forks of esoteric fire
> With commonplace of laxer mien.

It is he who recalls Eden in old Medanna's sea, and in his blue eyes Vine (or Hawthorne) first thinks to catch a glimpse of "an ocean-waste of earnestness without a buoy". But no key as to real persons drawn on or symbolism employed is necessary to understand *Clarel*; whatever the obscurity of many of its allusions, it presents none of the difficulties of interpretation that are found in *Moby-Dick*, *Pierre*, and *The Confidence-Man*, and Melville in verse here states his general meaning far less equivocally than he elsewhere does in prose. Indeed, the characters of the poem go to some pains to elucidate their opinions, and their author must have gone to greater pains still.

How far Melville was in agreement with their opinions is less easy to say, though the opinions he states most eloquently are, we may suppose, closest to those he held on any matter discussed. A book devoted to the sympathetic exposition of doubt is not likely to conclude in a set of affirmations (though, as we shall see, Melville attempted a positive announcement of sorts in the end). Doubt is not entire denial: it is a state of precarious and usually painful balance between two contradictory tenets. This is the state of most of the characters in *Clarel*, but for only one of the contradictory tenets, the religious one, do they advance the arguments; the half-persuasion of its opposite has brought them to their present tension—ranging from Vine's aloof sadness to the bitterness that actually kills Mortmain, the Swedish revolutionary—but all they say about that opposite is in illustration of its inadequacy. Except for an apostate Jew, Margoth, who has found the explanation of everything in geology, these people do not question the value in itself of religious faith; dogmatic atheism they greet with horror because they see it undermines the moral values which they feel persist beyond any choice of their own:

> Bonds sympathetic bind these three—
> Faith, Reverence, and Charity.
> If Faith once fail, the faltering mood
> Affects—needs must—the sisterhood.

Science and the examination of the historical evidence for Christianity have destroyed their faith, and the implication is that their difficulties are in the strictest sense intellectual. The two characters who are entire in their religious faith—Nathan, the convert to Judaism who has traveled back through time, and Nehemiah, the eccentric "Bible" Christian—are, as Clarel reflects, "mindless". But all this doubt, it soon becomes evident, has very little to do with any apparent defects in the rationality of Christianity: doubt, really, is interchangeable with the reluctance to make the full surrender asked by faith—and faith, as Melville observed in another place of God's demand on Abraham, is an "exacting behest". Clarel cries out to Derwent, the blandly cheerful Anglican priest whose faith is "an over-easy glove":

> Own, own with me, and spare to feign;
> Doubt bleeds, nor Faith is free from pain!

This is the problem that is central to *Clarel*, and Melville's resolute grappling with it makes his book humanly more profound than anything that Clough, Howells, and Henry Adams —to choose three men very different in mind and temperament—wrote when they considered their own and their contemporaries' disbelief. Much of the agonized skepticism to which science led the Victorians strikes one as the result of the loss of a world-picture comfortable and familiar; in their doubts that God ran the world, they did not suffer so much from the loss of a person as from the loss of the assurance that existence was benevolently disposed toward them. Twisting one of Paley's figures, one might say that the world for them was a watch, with God for its mainspring, on the face of which the moral law was proclaimed with unvarying certainty. With the American gift for abstraction, persons like Emerson and Thoreau were able to discern the moral law operating quite by itself, an abstract time fully there whether there was any watch to tell it or not; but Melville, the man who was supposed to have lost himself and his talent in the wastes of metaphysics, would assent to no ideal he could not test by concrete and experienced fact. No psychological study of hidden motives and unrecognized influences will explain the ultimate mystery of the human heart; it is beyond communication between men, and in his own heart each man can catch a fructifying glimpse of the mystery only with God's aid. In all systems that pretend to absolute clarity, the human person disappears; our assurance that we or others exist is in the shadow our own or their existence casts. The biographer's task forces on him the arrogant assumption that he can see in his subject's life things to which the subject was too close to see, but no perspective of time or place will allow him to see into the center of the shadow, out of which his subject could at least speak. Precisely what obstacle lay between Melville and faith on this plane we cannot hope to discover, but what he said of the situation is surely valid in its own claims and, as experience, needs no explanation in other terms.

Early in the poem there appears a character whose failure in faith is archetypal of the failures of the others. He is Celio, a young hunch-backed Roman staying at the Franciscan monastery in Jerusalem, to which city he also has come "to pluck the talisman from fold". Celio and Clarel never make acquaintance but, briefly passing each other outside the walls, recognize a bond of sympathy. After this wordless meeting, Celio goes on into the city, and there, before the arch from which Pilate is said to have shown Christ to the mob, he in his later time becomes one of the mob and, as any of us might and as most of us have, upbraids the Son of God for the offer of salvation:

> Upbraider! we upbraid again;
> *Thee* we upbraid; our pangs constrain
> Pathos itself to cruelty.
> Ere yet thy day no pledge was given
> Of homes and mansions in the heaven . . .
> The natural law men let prevail;
> Then reason disallowed the state
> Of instinct's variance with fate.
> But Thou—ah, see, in rack how pale
> Who did the world with throes convulse;
> Behold Him—yea—behold the Man
> Who warranted if not began
> The dream that drags out its repulse.

Celio then asks a question more likely to occur to a disillusioned Protestant than to a lapsed Catholic—how Christ's love can have led to sectarian strife—and concludes:

> Anew, anew,
> For this Thou bleedest, Anguished Face;
> Yea, Thou through ages to accrue,
> Shalt the Medusa shield replace:
> In beauty and in terror too
> Shalt paralyze the nobler race—
> Smite or suspend, perplex, deter—
> Tortured, shalt prove a torturer.

> Whatever ribald Future be,
> Thee shalt these heed, amaze their heart with Thee—
> Thy white, Thy red, Thy fairness and Thy tragedy.

For some, surely, so much pain would prove the existence of Him Whose denial caused it, for many, though by no means all, men will accept the reality of the spear that has wounded their own sides. Celio, however, visiting with a procession of monks the tomb of Lazarus, exclaims:

> Raiser and raised divide one doom;
> Both vanished now.

"Batter my heart, Three-Person'd God!" pleaded John Donne. Celio demands the same assault and, "a sovereign nature (in himself) amid the powers of heaven, hell, and earth", at the same time cannot allow God's right to make the siege.

Although Celio's is the model of the others' griefs, these pilgrims are not entirely without the characteristics of their age: they attest to the intellectual currents of the time by their resistance to them. As they approach the Dead Sea, they meet a Syrian monk, another doubter who is roaming in the wilderness, where the Fiend has put to him a question for which he can find no answer:

> Goodness is justice. See,
> Through all the pirate-spider's snare
> Of silken arcs of gossamer,
> 'Tis delicate geometry:
> Adorest the artificer?

The Syrian goes up again to the "Quarantanian height" where he has meditated for forty days, and as he climbs the exceeding high mountain Margoth comes down from it—he has been collecting geological specimens toward "a monograph he would indite—the theme, that crag". When the pilgrims reach the margin of the Dead Sea, inscribed upon a rock there by Mortmain, who has gone on before them, they find:

Under the Vault of Hollow Heaven

>   Emblazoned bleak in austral skies—
> A heaven remote, whose starry swarm
> Like Science lights but cannot warm—
> Translated Cross, hast thou withdrawn,
> Dim paling too at every dawn,
> With symbols vain once counted wise,
> And gods declined to heraldries?
> Estranged, estranged: can friend prove so?
> Aloft, aloof, a frigid sign:
> How far removed, thou Tree divine,
> Whose tender fruit did reach so low—
> Love apples of New Paradise!
> About the wide Australian sea
> The planted nations yet to be—
> When, ages hence, they lift their eyes,
> Tell, what shall they retain of thee?
> But class thee with Orion's sword?
> In constellations unadored,
> Christ and the Giant equal prize?
> The atheist cycles—*must* they be?
> Fomenters as forefathers we?

Under this Margoth chalks:

> *I, Science, I whose gain's thy loss,*
> *I slanted thee, thou Slanting Cross.*

The Dead Sea is, geographically and spiritually, the extreme low point of their journey. As they sleep by its shore, the New Jerusalem appears in a dream to Nehemiah, and the next morning he is found upon the beach dead. There he is buried with the Bible that he has always carried with him. The import of this is too plain to need comment. The pilgrims continue on their way, also continuing, except for the generally silent Vine, their "weary length of arguing" under "the clear vault of hollow heaven". Must the bright expectations of the age, they ask

> . . . ere long be cowed
> Before the march in league avowed
> Of Mammon and Democracy?
> In one result whereto we tend
> Shall Science disappoint the hope,
> Yea, to confound us in the end,
> New doors to superstition ope?
> As years, as years and annals grow,
> And action and reaction vie,
> And never men attain, but know
> How waves on waves forever die;
> Does all more enigmatic show?

The one person who is willing to turn away from the enigma is Derwent, who sees

> The object clear: belief revised,
> Men liberated—equalized
> In happiness. No mystery,
> Just none at all; plain sailing.

If Mortmain carries with him "grief's intolerant fire unwearied and unweariable", Derwent is the indefatigable advocate of cheerfulness. "To avoid the deep saves not from storm" Clarel had been told, but Derwent's determined superficiality seems disproof of this. All the 19th century's optimism is incorporated in Derwent, who is out "to cheerfulize Christ's moan" and overlook everything that may be wrong today for whatever may be better tomorrow. The others heap their coals of fire upon his head, but Derwent's is always the soft answer; a thoroughgoing pragmatist, he can even temper his self-esteem to each occasion. Yet when he speaks with Clarel about the young man's difficulties, Derwent reveals that he lacks faith as much as does any of the rest and that his cheerfulness is a homage demanded by his self-regard. The green sunny surface, he says, is "for man appointed, man's true home", and if probing shows that the verities, posited for "nature's active scene", do not exist, why, it is better to carry on as though they did: any fuss over their absence is both obsolete and indecorous. Derwent assumes that everything will be for the best in the end because to do so fosters a pleasant state of mind. But faith, as Clarel sees, is not free from pain; faith is not a pleasant state of mind, a vague eudaemonical something, but is just what his theological textbooks must have called it—the acceptance by the mind, heart, and will of the fact that God has extended his favor to man through Christ. From dwelling on whether this is fact or not the poem never moves very far.

Derwent, the optimist whose optimism is thus seen to be as negative as the others' pessimism, is alone amongst the pilgrims in hostility toward Catholicism, which he finds an impediment to progress. Derwent objects to the forms and formalities of Catholicism because, for him, their elaboration is false to their historical origins: he has that laborious regard for "fact" in the minuscule so often found in men for whom the true is the convenient. That Melville had any acquaintance with Catholic apologetics seems most unlikely; the list of his reading painstakingly compiled by Mr. Sealts, so far as it has been published, does not reveal any such literature.[4] His trip to the Mediterranean, that "tideless sea eternal in fresh delight", gave him, his journal shows, a pleasure in the externals of Catholicism, for, despite his objections to shrines in lottery shops,[5] he certainly did not have the exaggerated Protestant sensibilities of the "solid stolid Elder" in *Clarel*, at whom he poked fun and of whom he said:

[4] See "Melville's Reading: A Check-List of Books Owned and Borrowed" by Merton M. Sealts, Jr. in *Harvard Library Bulletin*, Spring, 1948, Autumn, 1948, Winter, 1949, ff.

[5] But in *Clarel* he found commendable the Italian bandits' practice of pausing on business to say a prayer at wayside shrines.

> Traditions beautiful and old
> Which with maternal arms enfold
> Millions, else orphaned and made poor,
> No plea could lure him to endure.

The "legends of the Old Faith", he wrote to his brother-in-law John C. Hoadley on Easter Saturday in 1877, he thought "really wonderful both from their multiplicity and their poetry. They far surpass the stories in the Greek mythologies." And some years later he marked in one of Arnold's volumes of essays a passage which said that the future of Christianity lay with Catholicism (as understood by Arnold, to be sure). Seven years before the American publication of Arnold's book, Melville had said much the same thing, putting the arguments for it into the mouths of three of his characters. Toward the beginning of the poem, Rolfe tells how, after the first earthquake in Lima, "the prelate with intrepid train" went forth to mark out new boundaries for the fallen churches, and says the priest will continue to do so after each terrestrial upset. "That is not my mind," replies Clarel uneasily. "Rome's priest forever rule the world?" "The priest, I said," answers Rolfe, his eyes altering to that "eerie hue, like Tyrrhene seas when overcast" which disturbs Vine, and he cites them Rome when "the gods were gone".

> Tully scarce dreamed they could be won
> Back into credence; less that earth
> Ever could know yet mightier birth
> Of deity. He died. Christ came.
> And, in due hour, that impious Rome,
> Emerging from vast wreck and shame,
> Held the forefront of Christendom.
> The inference? the lesson?—come!
> Let fools count on faith's closing knell—
> Time, God, are inexhaustible.

The Christian of course holds that time is anything but inexhaustible, and Rolfe's argument for the Church is a "natural" one, soon open to perversion. Even the Dominican whom the travelers later meet by the River Jordan does not so much stress the Roman Church's uniqueness (in virtue of which men's allegiance is owing to her, forsaking all others) as her endurance in time and her answer to what is constant in human nature. Against the modern fraction of belief—in which, Clarel elsewhere notes, "the very pews are each a sect"—says the Dominican,

> . . . stands Rome's array:
> Rome is the Protestant to-day:
> The Red Republic slinging flame
> In Europe—she's your Scarlet Dame.
> Rome stands; but who may tell the end?
> Relapse barbaric may impend,
> Dismission into ages blind—
> Moral dispersion of mankind. . . .
> Be not so mad, unblest, and blind
> As, in such days as these, to try
> To pull down Rome. If Rome could fall
> 'Twould not be Rome alone, but all
> Religion. All with Rome have tie,
> Even the railers which deny,
> All but the downright Anarchist,
> Christ-hater, Red, and Vitriolist. . . .
> Weigh well the Pope. Though he should be
> Despoiled of Charlemagne's great fee—
> Cast forth, and made a begging friar,
> That would not quell him. No, the higher
> Rome's *In excelsis* would extol
> Her God—her *De profundis* roll
> The deeper. Let destructives mind
> The reserves upon reserves behind.

Certainly nothing doctrinal is involved here, and agreement with this does not make one a Catholic. That Melville in all likelihood accepted it is indicated by Derwent's interruption of the Dominican's talk to ask the monk if his companions aren't calling him to continue his journey. After the Dominican has left, Derwent remarks that *"doubt* late was an aristocrat" but now, when even barbers' clerks are skeptics, the distinction is to him who believes the most. Not trying to refute this, Rolfe says he applauds the "Bayard knight ecclesiastic" and, repeating the Dominican's argument, asks "Who's gained by all the sacrifice of Europe's revolutions?"

> The Protestant? The Liberal?
> I do not think it—not at all:
> Rome and the Atheist have gained:
> These two shall fight it out—these two;
> Protestantism being retained
> For base of operations sly
> By Atheism.

This theme and its implications are considerably enlarged upon with the appearance of one of the most interesting characters in the poem—Ungar. Ungar is reminiscent of that American Southerner with whom in his youth Joseph Conrad ran guns to the Spanish Carlists and who used proudly to say that he lived by his sword; and he has some intellectual affinities with the Southern hero of Henry James's *The Bostonians*. He is a former Confederate soldier of Maryland Catholic and Indian ancestry (the last explaining his name), a voluntary exile from America now in the military service of the Turkish sultan. Rolfe has his hesitations about democracy and particularly about the godless man it breeds, who "hopes no heaven, but fears no fall"; Ungar is an unequivocal reactionary, without "elected creed or rite" himself but unabashedly maintaining the necessity of one for the health of the body politic as well as for the individual person. Let men openly confess God, he says, as they did

> in those days that come
> No more to misnamed Christendom!
> Religion then was the good guest,
> First served, and last, in every gate . . .
> She every human venture shared. . . .
> Men were not lettered, but had sense
> Beyond the mean intelligence
> That knows to read, and but to read—
> Not think. 'Twas harder to mislead
> The people then, whose smattering now
> Does but the more their ignorance show—
> Nay, them to peril more expose—
> Is as the ring in the bull's nose
> Whereby a pert boy turns and winds
> This monster of a million minds.
> Men owned true masters; kings owned God—
> *Their* master; Louis plied the rod
> Upon himself. . . .
> The coronation was a prayer
> Which yet in ceremonial clings.
> The church was like a bonfire warm:
> All ranks were gathered round the charm.

But these, Derwent interrupts, were the "Dark Middle Ages, time's midnight!" At least "it was not starless one," replies Ungar. The advance of science and industry is no assurance of improvement, for

> How many Hughs of Lincoln, say,
> Does Mammon in his mills, to-day,
> Crook, if he does not crucify?

The arts are tools, which are to the strong, and Satan is not weak:

> Your arts advance in Faith's decay:
> You are but drilling the new Hun
> Whose growl even now can some dismay;
> Vindictive in his heart of hearts,
> He schools him in your mines and marts—
> A skilled destroyer.

America's wealth and untried opportunities, diverting men's energies into their exploitation, may for a time put off the awful reckoning entailed by "the impieties of Progress", but that reckoning is equally foreboded in her other circumstances:

> If a people be which began
> Without impediment, or let
> From any ruling which foreran;
> Even striving all things to forget
> But this—the excellence of man
> Left to himself, his natural bent,
> His own devices and intent;
> And if, in satire of the heaven,
> A world, a new world have been given
> For stage whereon to deploy the event;
> If such a people be—well, well,
> One hears the kettledrums of hell!

And, above all, it is idle to think of democracy as the preventative of any of this:

> The future, what is that to her
> Who vaunts she's no inheritor?
> 'Tis in her mouth, not in her heart.
> The Past she spurns, though 'tis the Past
> From which she gets her saving part—
> That Good which lets her Evil last.

Behold her whom the panders crown,
Harlot on horseback, riding down
The very Ephesians who acclaim
This great Diana of ill fame!

But here Ungar's prophetic faculty deserts him and he does not foresee the extent of this democracy's triumph:

Arch-strumpet of an impious age,
Upstart from ranker villanage,
'Tis well she must restriction taste,
Nor lay the world's broad manor waste:
Asia shall stop her at the least,
That old inertness of the East.

Mr. Thorp cautions against taking these opinions for Melville's own. They are, he explains, those of "an expatriate Southerner, whom the war has ruined in spirit and estate"; and it is true that Ungar's listeners in *Clarel* allow his bitterness may have been caused by defeat. Yet, as I have suggested, there is probably an equation of Melville's sympathy with his eloquence, and Ungar's eloquence is considerable. Rolfe is assuredly speaking his author's mind when he calls Ungar an Ethan Allen—whose appearance in *Israel Potter* is first in a chapter called "Samson Among the Philistines"—and a "Herbert lord of Cherbury, dusked over".[6] The character to whom Ungar stands in entire opposition is, of course, Derwent, and to which of these poles of thought Melville felt the magnetic pull there can be no doubt.

But Melville brings in another character, whose introduction in the tale is pointless (even allowing that persons drift in and out of the pilgrim group for no more evident reason than Melville's interest in them as human specimens) unless it is to pro-

[6] The allusion is apparently to thinking soldiers rather than to Deistic-minded ones, though Herbert is considered the first of the English Deists and Allen plagiarized and published a book advocating Deism.

vide a contrast with Ungar and to show the Southerner's opinions do not issue only from grief and defeat. He is Don Hannibal Rohon del Aquaviva,[7] a veteran of some Mexican war in which he had lost an arm and a leg. Don Hannibal is fleeing into Asia from "this cursed *Progress*", he is in thorough agreement with what Ungar says, and he is the very epitome of good cheer and Spanish reaction. While Ungar, carrying his grief and the sword that, as a young Franciscan monk has told him, has the shape of a cross, wanders "an armed man in the Druid grove", Don Hannibal, presumably a believing Catholic, spends a pleasant hour's conversation in the workshop of a coffin-making monk, resting his two limbs in a coffin "almost as in a barber's chair".

When Clarel returns to Jerusalem, his journey lost "in waste of words, that waste of all", his friends stop a while to comfort him for Ruth's death, then go their ways out of his life. There is no dramatic impact of character in the poem: each person moves his plotted course, undeflected by the influence of the others, casting his appropriate light or shadow. The spokesmen of kinds and degrees of doubt or faith, the persons of the poem do not need to supplement their spoken rôles with any action beyond their journey (the description of most of which the reader could, without any loss, forgo, despite the extent to which their dialogue is determined by its background). Clarel's love story is, considering the impact of the whole book, an appendage or two appendages—a prologue and epilogue—not alone because Ruth is hidden behind a sort of Hebrew purdah (conveniently enough, considering Melville's difficulties in picturing women) but also because Clarel is no more than the audience to the dialogues of which the book is largely made.

[7] This name should provide a spring of meanings for Melville's more subtle exegetes, but none of them, so far as I know, has yet dipped into it.

Nevertheless, lacking though it is in human conviction, the story has its formal uses: as the symbol of Clarel's hope and that hope's disappointment, it provides the book with its termini. Judged entirely according to the standards of realism, it would not even serve this function, for in the life outside of books sexual love answers no final question and the moral problems of marriage could only have aggravated Clarel's other ones. But technical criticism of *Clarel* is superfluous: no great discernment is required to see the poem's faults or to appreciate that it cannot be read like Lowell's or Holmes's didactic verse, on the one hand, or, to seek something equally ambitious in its scope on the other, Longfellow's *Christus: A Mystery*—its rewards are different and, if we close our ears as we read it, I think the rewards will be found to be greater.

Melville was one of the considerable company of 19th-century thinkers—as different in their various kinds as Joseph de Maistre and Walter Bagehot—who foresaw tyranny in an ever-broadening democracy and an ever-narrowing realm of religious influence and who expected "in glut of all material arts" a relapse into "civic barbarism". That company was, however, largely a European one, for in America of the Gilded Age the promises and facts of material accomplishment and increasing wealth seemed to most minds empirical disproof of the gloomier critics and the general mood was opposite to that of *Clarel's* pilgrims, who

> felt how beyond the scope
> Of elder Europe's saddest thought
> Might be the New World sudden brought
> In youth to share old age's pains—
> To feel the arrest of hope's advance,
> And squandered last inheritance;
> And cry—"To Terminus build fanes!
> Columbus ended earth's romance:
> No New World to mankind remains!"

It was Whitman who had cheerfully prophesied the American mood of the decades his disciples would excoriate. In his last years, as muddled in his thought and as optimistic as ever, the old man sat in his little house on Mickle Street in Camden, the world beating a path to his door. There he received the homage of the many visitors, American, English, and European, who came on pilgrimage to the poet who had written the "bible of democracy" and there he told them fibs about his youth. One of these pilgrims, the Englishman Robert Buchanan, sought also to call on Melville but later reported that no one in New York knew the whereabouts of "the one great imaginative writer fit to stand shoulder to shoulder with Whitman on this continent". While it seems probable that Buchanan cannot have inquired very strenuously after Melville, the incident and its implied contrast with Whitman's circumstances are symbolic of Melville's turning away from the age. The contrast between the two men in this matter can be seen, too, in the way the Philadelphia Centennial Exposition of 1876 struck them. Whitman saw in its huge array of scientific and industrial exhibits the sure augury of the "orbic" fraternity for which he longed. Melville paid it one brief visit and found it "a sort of tremendous Vanity Fair".

Yet, despite their differences in these matters and in ones more important still (Whitman had said "No array of terms can say how much I am at peace about God and about death"), at the end of *Clarel* Melville takes up an attitude in essence not different from Whitman's. This is the position that the final justification of life is found on the subrational level in what might be called our mere animal persistence. There is no doubt that the simple and immediate appetite for experience, disciplined by a proper teleology, makes possible man's profoundest happinesses, but that in itself it guarantees no happiness the whole enormous effort of *Clarel* testifies. The very nature of all thought not directed to practical ends is to question the adequacy of what Mr. Mumford calls the "dim, plasmal sense that bottoms all of us". This sense, Melville concluded, gave the promise of the thing all his reasoning could not establish, and his final advice to Clarel might almost have come from Derwent:

> Then keep thy heart, though yet but ill-resigned—
> Clarel, thy heart, the issues there but mind;
> That like the crocus budding through the snow—
> That like a swimmer rising from the deep—
> That like a burning secret which doth go
> Even from the bosom that would hoard and keep;
> Emerge thou mayst from the last whelming sea,
> And prove that death but routs life into victory.

The same theme Melville developed rather more effectively in "Pontoosuce", a poem he did not publish. Standing in a pine wood near the lake that gives the poem its title, the poet reflects that "all dies"

> And present nature as a moss doth show
> On the ruins of the Nature of the aeons of long ago,

when he is greeted by a garlanded nymph who sings that everywhere everything dies and begins again, "over and over and over", and bids him "Let go, let go!"

> With that, her warm lips thrilled me through,
> She kissed me, while her chaplet cold
> Its rootlets brushed against my brow,
> With all their humid clinging mould.
> She vanished, leaving fragrant breath
> And warmth and chill of wedded life and death.

There is no assurance of man's rebirth in nature's renewal, where the individual's disappearance continues the species. The claim that man can triumph over death must always appear on the natural plane the greatest stumbling-stone and rock of offense. "Science," decided all those who spoke in *Clarel* to Melville's sympathies, "the feud can only aggravate"; but they too nurtured that feud so long as they hesitated at the affirmation demanded by St. Paul's question: "Hath not the potter power over the clay, of the same lump to make one vessel unto honor, and another unto dishonor?"

THE BEING OF THE MATTER

THE U. S. BRIG "SOMERS", CAPTAIN ALEXANDER MACKENZIE
commanding, was on her way from the coast of Africa to the
island of St. Thomas when, on the night of November 25th,
1842, Midshipman Philip Spencer, an eighteen-year-old boy of
a good New York family, invited the purser's steward to climb
into the booms with him and there, according to this man's later
testimony, suggested that he join in a mutiny for which Spencer
had already laid all the plans and which would be followed by
a voyage of piracy. The next morning the steward reported this
to the purser, from whom the news was carried through the first
lieutenant to the captain. Captain Mackenzie had Spencer placed
in irons and the next day, when part of the mainmast was damaged, as he thought by design, had two more of the crew put in
chains. With the discovery in Spencer's razor-case of a list of
names written in Greek characters, the captain had four other
members of the crew arrested. Thinking that signs of revolt
still persisted amongst the seamen, Captain Mackenzie consulted with his officers and, apparently without any proper trial,
decided to hang young Spencer and the two seamen first
arrested. The three were hanged from the yardarms on December 1st; there were no further incidents; and the vessel
arrived in New York two weeks later.

Philip Spencer was the son of the Secretary of War, John
Canfield Spencer, and the affair of the *Somers* excited national
interest. James Fenimore Cooper wrote a pamphlet denounc-
ing Mackenzie and later a review of the naval court martial that
had found Mackenzie innocent of any crime. During the trial,

Mackenzie issued a pamphlet in his own defense. That Spencer had intended more than a youthful prank seems very doubtful and that none of the hanged men had committed any overt act of mutiny is certain. Cooper's publications appeared in the year Melville was discharged from the U. S. Frigate *United States*, but probably the young ex-sailor did not have to turn to them for information about the affair, for the *Somers's* first lieutenant had been his cousin Guert Gansevoort. Whether Guert ever told his younger cousin more about what had happened on the *Somers* than was revealed in the court martial there is no way of telling. The portrait of Guert that Melville gave under the name of Tom Tight in some ramblingly reminiscent verses in *John Marr* hardly makes it seem so:

> Tom was a lieutenant in the brig-o'-war famed
> When an officer was hung for an arch-mutineer,
> But a mystery cleaved, and the captain was blamed,
> And a rumpus too raised, though his honor it was clear.
> And Tom he would say, when the mousers would try him,
> And with cup after cup o' Burgundy ply him:
> "Gentlemen, in vain with your wassail you beset,
> For the more I tipple, the tighter do I get."
> No blabber, no, not even with the can—
> True to himself and loyal to his clan.

But it is also possible that whatever Cousin Guert had to say privately showed him in an even less favorable aspect than he shows in the printed records, so that it was Herman who was being tight out of loyalty to the Gansevoort clan. In any case, when in 1888 (the same year *John Marr* was published) *The American Magazine* published an article by a Lieutenant H. D. Smith called "The Mutiny on the *Somers*" Melville must have read it and with considerable interest. On November 16th, 1888, six months after the appearance of the *American Maga-*

zine piece, Melville started writing the story of a young seaman falsely accused of plotting mutiny and hanged at sea, and for two and a half years he continued to work on the story, revising and expanding it into a short novel that tells us in what frame of mind he himself faced the King of Terrors.[1]

By the time Melville addressed himself once more to writing prose fiction, he had been retired from the Customs House for almost three years. His resolve to resign the inspectorship may have been strengthened by the fact that his wife had recently received a bequest of some size through the will of her brother Lemuel, though reasons of health were given as the main ones for his resignation in a letter his wife wrote to Cousin Kate. "—For a year or so past he has found the duties too onerous for a man of his years," explained Elizabeth, "and at times of exhaustion, both mental and physical, he has been on the point of giving it up, but recovering a little, has held on, very naturally anxious to do so, for many reasons—" Elizabeth went on to say that there was enough unfinished work on his desk, together with his love of books, to "prevent time from hanging heavy on his hands". ". . . I hope," she concluded, "he will get into a more quiet frame of mind, exempt from the daily invitation of over work—" Six months earlier, when there had been one of the periodical sweepings-out of the sinecures in the Customs House, and Elizabeth had feared that Herman might be unjustly discharged, she had asked Kate to have her husband

[1] The connection of Guert Gansevoort with the *Somers* affair and Melville's probable inspiration by the *American Magazine* article (along with the possible influence of another piece on the same subject that appeared just a year later in *The Cosmopolitan Magazine*) have been pointed out by Charles R. Anderson and F. Barron Freeman—respectively in "The Genesis of *Billy Budd*", *American Literature*, November, 1940, and *Melville's Billy Budd* (Cambridge, Mass., 1948: Harvard University Press). Mr. Freeman's edition is the first accurate transcription of Melville's manuscript and includes all the variant readings. My quotations from *Billy Budd* follow Mr. Freeman's text, except that I have introduced a certain number of commas in the interest of clarity.

Abraham Lansing say something in Herman's favor, since
"apart from everything else the *occupation* is a great thing for
him".

In the course of the ten years between the publication of
Clarel and the coming "into possession of unobstructed leisure,
but only just as, in the course of nature, my vigor sensibly de-
clines", Melville appears not to have even projected any work
of much ambition. Perhaps the one exception to this is the manuscript fragment called "Rammon"—which, taking its name
from an apocryphal "unrobust child of Solomon's old age", was
an intended confrontation of Jewish religious thought with
Oriental, probably mainly in verse. "To Rammon . . . cessation of being was the desirable event", and to this Melville
evidently intended to bring him, for in *John Marr* there is a
poem, noted as coming "from '*Rammon*'", about "The En-
viable Isles"

> Where, strown in flocks, what cheek-flushed myriads lie
> Dimpling in dream—unconscious slumberers mere,
> While billows endless round the beaches die.

One supposes that "Rammon" was conceived before Melville's retirement because "cessation of being" seems no likely
objective for a man who spent the last five years of his life
writing as busily as he did. However, there is not any warrant
to suppose an entire difference of mood between the last ten
years in the Customs House and the six years that remained to
Melville after them. To the ten years certainly belong a good
number of his attempts at lighter verse, and though, as I have
earlier said, the dedication to *Weeds and Wildings with a Rose
or Two*—the collection of verses, mostly referring to the days
at Arrowhead, that he gathered together for his wife—must
have been written in 1890, some of the poems in this fair-sized

unpublished volume can of their character have been in the unfinished work on his desk of which Elizabeth spoke. In the
closing poem he mentions the "arid years that filed before" and
says that "wiser in relish . . . come gray-beards to their roses
late", but what he called the arid years had, from what little
we know of them, their good moments and the rosy years still
brought forth their protest.

Clarel, according to Mr. Bezanson, received but one review
of any length and it was not exactly a favorable one. Perhaps
Melville was as indifferent to this as he had said in his prefa-
tory note he would be; perhaps, again, his reaction was the same
as on some unexplained occasion, a few months later, when
Elizabeth wrote that "he is *morbidly* sensitive, poor fellow, and
I always try (though I can't succeed to my sorrow) to smooth
the fancied rough edges to him wherever I can". But three
months later she was able to rejoice that he had had a moment's
relief from the mental suffering he underwent "(and oh how
all unnecessary)". Shortly after this Melville went off to join
his family on a vacation in the White Mountains and described
a stop he made at Saratoga Springs in a letter whose triviality
certainly reflects what he later called "the most precious things
I know of in this world—Health and Content":

I staid over about three hours or so at the Springs. I lunched at a
neat little restaurant I found there, and visited the hotels, presenting no doubt a distinguished appearance in my duster, and
finally took up a commanding position on the piazza of the Grand
Union, and surveyed at my leisure the moving spectacle of fashion
and in some instances—folly. A New York paper also of the day
helped to occupy the time.

In the first year of his retirement his son Stanwix died.
Stanny, who suffered from "catarrhal weakness", had gone
West fifteen years before, wandering about in search of jobs
and seeing, his mother had said, "some very hard times" and

deserving "much credit for his pluck and patience under difficulties and disappointments". Eventually he went to California, where he died of tuberculosis at San Rafael. Once more, there are no records of Melville's reactions. But the signs are that around this time his eyes turned away from the physical present.

Nothing like dotage need be assumed in this. The limitations of the human organism are such that in his old age the imaginative writer must increasingly draw on the sensory perceptions of his youth, and Melville turned once more to the sea, for it was with him as it was in a quotation that many years before he had written into a gift-copy of *Moby-Dick*: " 'All life' says Oken 'is from the sea; none from the continent. Man also is a child of the warm and shallow parts of the sea in the neighborhood of the land.' " *John Marr and Other Sailors* was an entirely nautical volume: it was dedicated to W. Clark Russell, the English writer of sea stories who had dedicated one of his novels to Melville, and its nineteen pieces all dealt with the sea.

The John Marr of the title-poem was a former sailor who had settled down in a frontier community, for whose occupants, "hereditary tillers of the soil . . . the ocean, but a hearsay to their fathers, had now through yet deeper inland removal become to themselves little more than a rumor traditional and vague"; and when John Marr sought to speak of his ocean adventures, a neighbor said to him: "Friend, we know nothing of that here." The twenty-five friends to whom Melville presented his little book would know more of these things, the hope must have been, and those who knew him best would recognize that he had placed in a quatrain the theme he had expanded in a great book nearly forty years before:

> Curled in the comb of yon billow Andean,
>   Is it the Dragon's heaven-challenging crest?
> Elemental mad ramping of ravening waters—
>   Yet Christ on the Mount, and the dove in her nest!

For the same initiate ones he ended the volume with a verse of quite unusual personal directness:

> Healed of my hurt, I laud the inhuman Sea—
> Yea, bless the Angels Four that there convene;
> For healed I am even by their pitiless breath
> Distilled in wholesome dew named rosmarine.

Timoleon, the title figure of the volume Melville published three years later, was as lonely as John Marr, if for other reasons. Timoleon, having for the public good slain his brother Timophanes, the tyrant of Corinth, was troubled both by "the whispering-gallery of the world" and the uncertainties of a conscience that had come "to doubt the irrevocable doom herself had authorized when undismayed"—uncertainties fostered by the wavering beliefs of the age. He left Corinth to live in solitude, "estranged through one transcendent deed from common membership in mart". In his self-imposed exile Timoleon repeated (and there is no anachronism here) Pierre's complaint:

> To you, Arch Principals, I rear
> My quarrel, for this quarrel is with gods. . . .
> Are earnest natures staggering here
> But fatherless shadows from no substance cast?

Did the gods answer Timoleon's question? We cannot say; but Corinth called him from exile to defend her in battle and, when he had triumphed in Sicily, acclaimed him no fratricide but "savior of the state, Jove's soldier, man divine". He remained in Sicily and, ignoring his city's invitations, "never for Corinth left the adopted shore". We cannot say whether the gods answered Timoleon's question, but I think we can say that Melville's was in some manner answered. That at the same time he was posing Timoleon's question his own was being answered shows the answer he received was neither what he demanded nor expected. The answer to "Why hast thou made me thus?" can never be what man expects or demands. Incompatible though the answer was with pride's requisites, there can have been no doubt in Melville's mind that it was given, for he had been laboring on its statement in the years between the issuance of his books of verse. However faulty his critical faculties were when his verse was concerned, he must have known that this other work in prose was something altogether different from what lay in the manuscripts from which he had culled *John Marr* and *Timoleon*. He knew it because more than half a lifetime earlier he had known the same sense of accomplishment as he wrote in his second-story room at Arrowhead, damned by dollars. Now he wrote at his leisure—so far as that word would have meaning to a man of seventy with such a task in hand—and in a different mood, but he wrote with the compulsion of the writer who feels that his theme is quick within him and has the prerogative of delivery at any cost to himself. They cannot have been placid hours in the brown-papered room at 104 East 26th Street, but the better kind they were Melville described in *Timoleon*:

> In placid hours well-pleased we dream
> Of many a brave unbodied scheme
> But form to lend, pulsed life create,
> What unlike things must meet and mate:
> A flame to melt—a wind to freeze;
> Sad patience—joyous energies;
> Humility—yet pride and scorn;
> Instinct and study; love and hate;
> Audacity—reverence. These must mate,
> And fuse with Jacob's mystic heart,
> To wrestle with the angel—Art.

When, slightly more than five months before his death, Melville lay down his pencil on the manuscript of *Billy Budd*, ready for Elizabeth's copying and his final corrections, he knew that for the first time in many years the messenger had been there. He did not date his poems but he carefully set down the first and last day he had worked on his story.

An old man's youth must often seem to him to have belonged to a more distant age than the calendar will allow, and when Melville began his second story about life on a man-of-war he placed it in the time of Nelson, though in his mind's eye the image of the ship was obviously the U. S. Frigate *United States.* The scene in *Billy Budd* does not, as it does in *Moby-Dick,* rank in importance with the human drama, but it is nevertheless essential to Melville's story, in which the human relationships are determined by the circumstances of time and place. In one point of view, the story is simple enough: Billy Budd, the "Handsome Sailor" and paragon of natural virtues, is impressed aboard H. M. S. *Indomitable,* where Claggart, the master-at-arms and an example of "natural depravity", conceives a violent hatred of him and accuses him of being ringleader in plans for a mutiny; Billy, hampered by a stutter, cannot when accused answer the master-at-arms, strikes him, and kills him; Captain Vere, convinced of Billy's innocence but fearing for the consequences amongst the crew if his act goes unpunished, agrees that he should be hanged; Billy's last words are "God bless Captain Vere!", he is hanged, and his name becomes legendary among the common sailors. Regarded thus, there is a mythical quality about *Billy Budd*; it puts into the simplest (not necessarily the least ambiguous) forms of action certain things that are constantly recurrent in the human situation. In another point of view, there is nothing so simple about the story: it is a short historical novel whose characters are acted upon by the various forces of their age; the characters' actions, to the extent that they are free, involve a number of psychological inferences and metaphysical implications; and the author is simultaneously

307

viewing events on a British seventy-four in the Mediterranean in 1797 and the constant "mystery of iniquity".

Melville did not turn to the year 1797 merely to make external the long perspective in which he saw his own youth; the year in which it was placed gave part of the mechanism of his story. 1797 was the year of the two fleet-wide mutinies in the British Navy at Spithead and at the Nore, and these two uprisings had to loom large in the immediate background to decide Captain Vere, a thoroughly just man, upon the execution of Billy. Further, the year, as Melville says in his preface, "belongs to a period which as every thinker now feels, involved a crisis for Christendom not exceeded in its undetermined momentousness at the time by any other era whereof there is record", and Captain Vere was strongly opposed to the ideas of the Revolution "because they seemed to him incapable of embodiment in lasting institutions [and] at war with the peace of the world and the true welfare of mankind". Billy was thus not only executed in obedience to the Mutiny Act and to preserve naval discipline but also, in the exigencies of history, for the true welfare of mankind. (We shall see later that Billy's execution had to appear just, not alone to make its occurrence plausible but for a deeper reason as well.)

Billy and Claggart are both figures of a very simple cast though vast complexities open out from their relationship; Captain Vere, who has the task of adjudication, is necessarily a more involved personality. Billy was of unknown beginnings, found, he told the officer who mustered him into the service on the *Indomitable*, "in a pretty silk-lined basket hanging one morning from the knocker of a good man's door in Bristol". "A presumable bye-blow, and, evidently, no ignoble one", he was, according to a brief and unfinished outline for the story, "in person . . . goodly to behold; his features, ear, foot, and in a less degree even his sailor hands, but more strikingly his frame and natural carriage indicating a lineage contradicting his lot". Though illiterate and "with little or no sharpness of faculty or any trace of the wisdom of the serpent, nor yet quite a dove, he possessed that kind and degree of intelligence going along with the unconventional rectitude of a sound human creature". "His original constitution aided by the cooperating influences of his lot," Billy was "a sort of upright barbarian, much such perhaps as Adam presumably might have been ere the urbane Serpent wriggled himself into his company". Yet the Serpent's touch was manifested in him in a curious way and, as we have seen, he had "in fact more or less of a stutter or even worse. In this particular Billy was a striking instance that the arch interferer, the envious marplot of Eden, still has more or less to do with every human consignment to this planet of earth."

With Claggart the interference had been far more extensive, if not indeed essential, though in appearance he was not too strikingly Billy's inferior. "Of no ill figure upon the whole", he had "features, all except the chin, cleanly cut as those on a Greek medallion". The effluvium of good birth hung about him, too, and he looked "like a man of high quality, social or moral, who for reasons of his own was keeping *incog.*" Behind this aristocratic exterior—incongruous in a man who prowled below decks in the office of a minor Vidocq—there was "the mania of an evil nature, not engendered by vicious training or corrupting books or licentious living, but born within him and innate, in short 'a depravity according to nature' ".

. . . The thing which in eminent instances signalizes so exceptional a nature is this: though the man's even temper and discreet bearing would seem to intimate a mind peculiarly subject to the law of reason, not the less in his heart he would seem to riot in complete exemption from that law, having apparently little to do with reason further than to employ it as an ambidexter implement for effecting the irrational. That is to say: toward the accomplishment of an aim which in wantonness of malignity would seem to partake of the insane, he will direct a cool judgment, sagacious and sound.

These men are true madmen, and of the most dangerous sort, for their lunacy is not continuous but occasional, evoked by some special object; it is probably secretive, which is as much to say it is self-contained, so that when, moreover, most active, it is to the average mind not distinguishable from sanity, and for the reason above suggested that whatever its aims may be, and the aim is never declared, the method and the outward proceeding is always perfectly rational.

Billy's prototype is not to be found in Melville's other writings, unless we stretch the point a bit and call him a younger Jack Chase irregularly ennobled and deprived of the ability to quote *The Lusiad*. Claggart, on the other hand, is obviously enough a better born and educated Jackson, a more dramatic Bland. [Captain the Honorable Edward Fairfax Vere [2] is the author's mouthpiece and perhaps has some few points of external resemblance to him. A reserved and bookish man, his taste is for those "books treating of actual men and events, no matter of what era—history, biography, and unconventional writers, who, free from cant and convention, like Montaigne, honestly, and in the spirit of common sense, philosophize upon realities". He at once understands the amazing natural phenomenon Billy is when the young man is brought before him charged by the master-at-arms with sedition and understands, too, why Claggart has made his charges. Melville speaks in his own person as author in analyzing Claggart's motives, but it is Vere who says that Billy's case is finally one "for psychologic

---

[2] "Passion, and passion in its profoundest, is not a thing demanding a palatial stage whereon to play its part. Down among the groundlings, among the beggars and rakers of the garbage, profound passion is enacted," says Melville. Still all three characters in this drama are in their different fashions "allied to the higher nobility", even though two of them may not come upon the quarterdeck except by invitation.

theologians to discuss" but unfortunately is being tried under the Mutiny Act and "in feature no child can resemble his father more than that Act resembles in spirit the thing from which it derives—War". Melville says of Claggart's hatred:

If askance he eyed the good looks, cheery health, and frank enjoyment of young life in Billy Budd, it was because these went along with a nature that, as Claggart magnetically felt, had in its simplicity never willed malice or experienced the reactionary spite of that serpent. . . . And the insight but intensified his passion, which assuming various secret forms within him, at times assumed that of cynic disdain—disdain of innocence—to be nothing more than innocent! Yet in an aesthetic way he saw the charm of it, the courageous free-and-easy temper of it, and fain would have shared it, but he depaired of it.

With no power to annul the evil element in him, though readily enough he could hide it; apprehending the good, but powerless to be it; a nature like Claggart's, surcharged with energy as such natures almost invariably are, what recourse is left to it but to recoil upon itself and, like the scorpion for which the Creator alone is responsible, act out to the end the part allotted it.

"It is the divine judgment of Ananias!" says Vere when Claggart has fallen dead. "Struck dead by an angel of God. Yet the angel must hang!" He himself carries the news of the sentence to Billy and remains some minutes closeted with the condemned man. Whatever transpires in that interview, "that the condemned one suffered less than he who mainly had effected the condemnation was apparently indicated by the former's exclamation" just before the hanging—"God bless Captain Vere!" The crew repeated Billy's cry and at its sound Captain Vere "stood erectly rigid as a musket in the ship-armorer's rack".]

The hull, deliberately recovering from the periodic roll to leeward, was just regaining an even keel, when the last signal, the preconcerted dumb one, was given. At the same moment it chanced that the vapory fleece hanging low in the East was shot through with a soft glory as of the fleece of the lamb of God seen in mystical vision and simultaneously therewith, watched by the wedged mass of upturned faces, Billy ascended; and, ascending, took the full rose of the dawn.

In the pinioned figure arrived at the yard-end, to the wonder of all, no motion was apparent save that created by the ship's motion, in moderate weather so majestic in a great ship ponderously cannoned.

For the modern reader, trained in a non-moral casuistry for which the declared motive is never the true one, the fact that Claggart looked on "belted Billy rolling along the upper gun-deck . . . with a settled, meditative, and melancholy expression, his eyes strangely suffused with incipient feverish tears" will at once suggest a key to the story's meaning. And when Melville says that "sometimes the melancholy expression would have in it a touch of soft yearning, as if Claggart could even have loved Billy but for fate and ban", it will be plain that the iniquity considered here is the one to which Sodom has given its name. There is no doubt that the story lends itself not at all implausibly to this interpretation: if Claggart entertains a perversion of love for Billy, it is psychologically quite credible that such a love should be further perverted into hate. Actually, this provides no explanation to the mystery of iniquity. Would evil cease to operate in the world if the "ban" were removed or would Billy never have been hanged had Claggart been questioned by a psychiatrist before being mustered into the King's navy?

Quite possibly Melville intended that Claggart's immediate motives—obscure even to Claggart—were to be understood for what is now called ambivalent, but if Melville sought to disguise this matter of the sexually illicit, it was a concealment prompted by politeness, not by the belief that here was a piece of esoteric doctrine, explaining the most obscure mysteries, to be revealed only to the initiate. Each age has things it does not talk about, but they are not necessarily mysterious. Melville constantly addresses himself to the metaphysical implications of Claggart's depravity, and if these are not his chief concern with the matter, we are left with the curious spectacle of a highly intelligent old man devoting the last three years of his life to pondering a simple case of thwarted pederasty.

The frequent references to Billy's beauty we can hardly take as morbid. Anyone a half-century beyond it must feel youth's beauty with an especial poignancy, but the celebration of Billy's good looks is also forced on Melville by his conception of Billy's character. A simple (and perhaps humanly quite impossible) goodness like Billy's submits itself neither to analysis nor to being exposited in action; Billy's goodness simply *is*, and the only way in which the novelist can make it carry any kind of conviction is by insisting on the young man's outer appearance as the token of his inward excellence. Aside from the good will with which he accepts his own death, Billy shows nothing approaching heroic virtue, and had Melville not made plain the larger significance he attached to him, the handsome sailor could not make much more claim on our sympathy than the "dog of generous breed" to which he is at one point compared.

Claggart's evilness, however, does not present the same difficulty; *that* it is always feasible to represent in action precisely because pure evil the mind cannot even conceive. Being negative, evil always has to borrow existence from human vitality, potentially good; the very curse of evil is that, seeking to deny being, it is yet curiously tied to the specific, so that the Devil never reposes in enjoyment of his own identity but must always be busy. Claggart's is not a depravity according to nature but according to what he does: there is no other way of being depraved. Neither the spider, the scorpion, nor the shark, "pale ravener of horrible meat", is evil.

[This assumed polar opposition of Billy and Claggart shows that *Billy Budd* is in the pattern of Melville's other works; its central problem is not only the one that engaged him in *Moby-Dick* and *Pierre* but is also set out in nearly the same terms. The mood is, of course, quite different; the exasperation and the rage are gone and there is a note of what can quite specifically be called hope. That hope is not merely the residual optimism of old age—the feeling that since a long life has not seen the accomplishment of any of the things which once seemed imperative and since a man must eventually lower his conceit of attainable felicity, one's energies are better saved than expended. It seems, indeed, quite close to hope as it has been defined by Gabriel Marcel: the assertion "that there is at the heart of being, beyond all data, beyond all inventories and calculations, a mysterious principle which is in connivance with me, which cannot but will that which I will, if what I will deserves to be willed and is, in fact, willed by the whole of my being".[3]

Mr. Watson has called *Billy Budd* "Melville's testament of acceptance"[4] and Mr. F. Barron Freeman has seen in it "the recognition of necessity". By no intellectual process, since for him there was still a profound dichotomy in human life with two nearly equal forces at conflict there, Melville had arrived at the willingness to allow that whatever is must be. Such an admission of necessity is in some measure optimistic, as even Schopenhauer (whom Melville read attentively in his last years) was forced to admit, for on what grounds will the individual complain

[3] *The Philosophy of Existence* by Gabriel Marcel, translated by Manya Harari (London, 1948: The Harvill Press).

[4] "Melville's Testament of Acceptance" by E. L. Grant Watson, *The New England Quarterly*, June, 1933.

when nothing can be other than it is? Yet, as I have suggested in using M. Marcel's definition of hope, Melville did not feel that he existed in this realm of necessity by chance or sufferance but for a purpose. Caught though all sooner or later were at the point where the conflicting forces of the world met, each man had his moment of freedom, and in this lay the justification of what in other respects was so dark a situation. The freedom there exercised could only be with regard to some final end, and Melville's affirmation of freedom was of its kind religious. The message of *Billy Budd*, to put it at its very simplest, is that the last victory allowed to man cannot be of this world: the nature of the victory and of the world deny each other.

Christian doctrines no doubt helped to form the picture of the world contained in *Billy Budd*, but the reflection of them therein is a monstrous one—both in the sense of a departure from the natural and in the etymological sense of forecasting dire things. Without blasphemous intention, Melville may have designed Billy's death to recall the Crucifixion, but certainly anyone so well acquainted as he with the four Gospels cannot have thought that the Personality revealed there could be represented by the simple sailor of his man-of-war tragedy. Billy's death in its religious significance is quite primitive, figuring forth the recurrent intuition men have that the best amongst them is always sacrificed to the failings of the others. Nor is Billy to be identified with the essential Christian; as the inevitable victim of Claggart's innate depravity, the area of his choice is too limited for that. Though his stutter is equated with original sin, as we have seen, Melville on a later page expresses what he calls "an irruption of heretic thought hard to suppress": "the young sailor's essential innocence". So the stutter is merely the limitation of human capacity, while, in Christian doctrine, our *felix culpa* is our responsibility and our responsibility is the inevitable condition of our freedom. Billy is destroyed by his stutter or human fault, but his impregnable innocence assures his salvation. Nothing in Billy's will contributes either to his fall or his redemption, so far as these terms can be validly applied to him; everything follows from the human circumstance itself, summed up in the persons of Billy and Claggart, who are each other's victims and render judgment on each other.

We may, I believe, say that Billy and Claggart, while yet remaining individuals in a drama of human conflicts, are the embodiments of Light and Darkness. (It is interesting to note that Claggart's pale brow has "silken jet curls partly clustering over it" while Billy's curls are yellow, though it is likely Melville intended no symbolism in these complexions.) A representative of Light, Billy has no defect except in his having been born, but, having been born, he is placed in the human circumstance, in which darkness must touch him somewhere. The very course of history places Billy in the moment most propitious for his undoing by Claggart—the time of the Great Mutiny and the French Directory. The evil that undoes Billy operates as a force entirely exterior to him and, so far as this world goes, he cannot prevail against it, for though Claggart is, quite literally, struck down by Billy's goodness, his plans for Billy's destruction succeed. There is no entire victory either for Light or for Darkness, but the triumph of Light is that it endures, simply as itself, after its thwarting in the temporal sphere.

In the human condition, the divorce between good and evil is not absolute; and we are shown in Captain Vere a good person who is an agent of evil. Once more, the independent power of evil is dramatized here; evil inheres in all those instruments whose use is required by the earthly life of man. Melville says that Vere is required to offer up Billy much as Abraham was required to offer up Isaac, and perhaps he meant to stress the parallel by hinting at the same blood relationship. However, even for Melville's purposes the parallel must not appear to be complete. When Abraham acted "in obedience to the exacting behest", however much he went against his heart's promptings, he observed the commands of a just God, and those commands remained just in any matter they touched upon (and, made from within God's foresight, were not humanly unreasonable—as the ram that appeared in the thicket showed). Captain Vere was well aware that he served no absolute justice in hanging Billy; he did not obey a law whose authority and applicability surpassed his understanding but one whose limitations were quite evident.

The circumstances of the story are so contrived that there is no alternative to Vere's following this lesser law: there are two orders of justice, but only one is achieved in the lives of men—whose allegiance remains double. Melville insists so strongly on making plain the historical details of his story because he wishes to establish beyond any explaining-away the validity of each justice and the inevitable conflict of the two. As in *Pierre* the two orders of time, chronometrical and horological, followed from the ambiguity at the heart of creation, so in *Billy Budd* followed the two orders of justice, earthly and heavenly.

Plainly enough, the problem with which Melville had wrestled through a long lifetime met no intellectual solution here: the contradiction at the heart of things was for the last time affirmed and the intellect's helplessness was implicit in that affirmation. Melville had come by a long, sad, and round-about route, as we have seen M. Simon declares, to the Calvinism from which he had started. He had not, indeed, ever departed very far from the Calvinist attitude, whose incipient Manichaeanism had colored what doctrines he had held as well as his revolt against other doctrines. A large measure of his anguish had been caused by his demand that all those things which he discretely observed and experienced in the universe be correlated in some rationally coherent scheme; but the basic irrationality with which he gave primacy to his own will made that scheme impossible. The deepest experience, his books insisted, showed some inscrutable malice sinewing the universe. How else could be explained the will's defeat in its constant aspiration—inherent in its nature—to realize the ideal? Drowning men do drown, he said; it cannot be denied and it must be accounted for. Accounted for in any neat philosophical equivalent of double-entry bookkeeping it never was, for by his seventieth year Melville was too much the creature of his own thought ever to abide any simply rational demonstration in the heart's province.

In one of those ironies that seem too apt for chance, he found his answer in the living act, the undoubted deed, in that intractable external universe which maintains its created independence against all the human creature's claims of total sovereignty—in the world which Taji had fled, against which Ahab had flung his harpoon, and which Pierre had sought to extinguish by suicide. For Melville, not by choice but by gift, the living act was art, which is an imitation of nature in the profound sense that a work of art achieves a self-subsistence much like that of an object in nature. In the final exercise of his talent for making such a thing, Melville once again came upon what he had long before called "this *Being* of the matter". He directly confronted this being in the intuition of reality that the imaginative writer has in the rare moments when his vision appears with an authority absolute in its own realm and says "This is so!" The talent that had once been the instrument of his rage, then, fittingly enough, had been inadequate for expressing the sense of universal inadequacy which is despair, had at last set before Melville what his discursive efforts could not reach.

We need suppose no sudden or extraordinary illumination here. For a writer the business of writing is as valid an experience as falling in love or being insulted or anything else that happens once or daily in a lifetime; it brings him equally, and very often more deeply, into contact with life. The experience *Billy Budd* brought to Melville could not supply him with a theology and a metaphysics adequate to more than his own long-confirmed habits, but it did bring him, on a level that may have been either above or below reason, to the conviction that even an existence like Billy's was justified. Only the men who say *no*, he had written to Hawthorne, are free, for "they cross the frontiers into Eternity with nothing but a carpet-bag—that is to say, the Ego". On September 28th, 1891, after several months of illness that Elizabeth believed had been brought on by his practice of walking in the "bitter cold air", Herman Melville quietly passed the frontier into eternity. He carried with him only the ego, that being of the matter, and all the bitter years had been designed to teach him that it should say *yes* and was good.

BIBLIOGRAPHY

The following bibliography, which is limited to fairly recent works, does not pretend to be complete nor even to list everything I have consulted. I have merely put down as a token of my obligation those contemporary writers who have in an especial degree informed, stimulated, or annoyed me. An excellent general bibliography, including 19th-century material, will be found in Mr. Thorp's *Herman Melville* (which, in the unprepossessing guise of a selection from Melville's works for college students, presents much valuable material not otherwise available in print). Lewis Leary's *Articles on American Literature Appearing in Current Periodicals, 1920–1945* (Durham, N. C., 1947: Duke University Press) contains a full list of pieces dealing with Melville during the period indicated.

There is no satisfactory single text of all Melville's works. The Constable edition—which was limited to 750 sets and is now beyond most private means—is not always accurately edited, is without notes, and does not include the travel journals or any letters. The best single volumes now available are the following (all of them carefully edited and with worthwhile introductions): Mrs. Metcalf's *Journal of a Visit to London and the Continent*, Mr. Thorp's *Moby-Dick*, Mr. Forsythe's *Pierre* and Dr. Murray's, Mr. Oliver's *Piazza Tales*, Mr. Vincent's *Collected Poems*, and Mr. Freeman's *Billy Budd*. *Typee* and *Omoo* can be had in Everyman's. *Redburn* and *The Confidence-Man* are available only in English editions, following the Constable text and with introductions by Mr. Plomer and Mr. Fuller. The volumes edited by Mr. Oliver, Dr. Murray, and Mr. Vincent are the first three to appear in a "Complete Works" under the general editorship of Mr. Vincent announced by Hendricks House, Farrar Straus of New York. Mr. Birss promises an edition of all Melville's letters and a definitive bibliography.

The original sources I have consulted are the Duyckinck, Gansevoort-Lansing, and Berg collections in the New York Public Library, but I am under the impression that any material which I have taken from them is to be found somewhere in print.

Anderson, Charles Roberts: *Journal of a Cruise in the Pacific Ocean, 1842–1844, in the Frigate United States with Notes on Herman Melville* (Durham, N. C., 1937: Duke University Press).

—— *Melville in the South Seas* (New York, 1939: Columbia University Press).

—— "Melville's English Debut", *American Literature*, March, 1939.

—— "The Genesis of *Billy Budd*", *American Literature*, November, 1940.

Anonymous: "Journal of Melville's Voyage in a Clipper Ship", *The New England Quarterly*, January, 1929.

Belgion, Montgomery: Introduction to *Moby-Dick* (London, 1946: The Cresset Press).

Bezanson, Walter Everett: *Herman Melville's Clarel*, unpublished doctoral dissertation (New Haven, Conn., 1943: Yale University).

Billson, James: "Some Melville Letters", *Nation and Athenaeum*, August 13, 1921.

Birss, John Howard: " 'A Mere Sale to Effect' with Letters of Herman Melville", *The New Colophon*, July, 1948.

—— "Herman Melville and *The Atlantic Monthly*", *Notes & Queries*, September 29, 1934.

—— "Herman Melville Lectures in Yonkers", *The American Book Collector*, February, 1934.

—— "'Travelling': A New Lecture by Herman Melville", *The New England Quarterly*, December, 1934.

Blackmur, R. P.: *The Expense of Greatness* (New York, 1940: Arrow Editions).

Boynton, Percy H.: *More Contemporary Americans* (Chicago, Ill., 1927: Chicago University Press).

Braswell, William: "A Note on 'The Anatomy of Melville's Fame'", *American Literature*, January, 1934.

—— *Melville's Religious Thought* (Durham, N. C., 1943: Duke University Press).

—— "The Satirical Temper of Melville's *Pierre*", *American Literature*, January, 1936.

Brill, A. A.: Introduction to *Leonardo da Vinci: A Study in Psychosexuality* by Sigmund Freud (New York, 1947: Random House).

Brooks, Van Wyck: *Emerson and Others* (New York, 1927: E. P. Dutton & Company).

—— *The Times of Melville and Whitman* (New York, 1947: E. P. Dutton & Company).

Canby, Henry Seidel: *Classic Americans* (New York, 1931: Harcourt, Brace & Company).

Charvat, William: "Melville's Income", *American Literature*, November, 1943.

Chase, Richard: "An Approach to Melville", *Partisan Review*, May-June, 1947.

—— "Dissent on *Billy Budd*", *Partisan Review*, November, 1948.

Curl, Vega: *Pasteboard Masks: Facts as Spiritual Symbols in the Novels of Hawthorne and Melville* (Cambridge, Mass., 1931: Harvard University Press).

Eby, E. H.: "Herman Melville's 'Tartarus of Maids'", *Modern Language Quarterly*, March, 1940.

Eliot, Alexander: "Melville and Bartleby", *Furioso*, Fall, 1947.

Forster, E. M.: *Aspects of the Novel* (New York, 1927: Harcourt, Brace & Company).

Forsythe, Robert S.: *Pierre or The Ambiguities* by Herman Melville (New York, 1930: Alfred A. Knopf).

—— Review of *Journal up the Straits, American Literature,* March, 1936.

Freeman, F. Barron: *Melville's Billy Budd* (Cambridge, Mass., 1948: Harvard University Press).

Freeman, John: *Herman Melville* (New York, 1926: The Macmillan Company).

Fuller, Roy: *The Confidence Man* by Herman Melville (London, 1948: John Lehmann).

Geist, Stanley: *Herman Melville: The Tragic Vision and the Heroic Ideal* (Cambridge, Mass., 1939: Harvard University Press).

Gleim, William S.: *The Meaning of Moby Dick* (New York, 1938: The Brick Row Book Shop).

Hagen, Victor Wolfgang von: *The Encantadas or, Enchanted Isles* (Burlingame, Calif., 1940: William P. Wreden).

Hart, James D.: "Melville and Dana", *American Literature,* March, 1937.

Hayford, Harrison: "Two New Letters of Herman Melville", *ELH,* March, 1944.

Hillway, Tyrus: "Taji's Abdication in Herman Melville's *Mardi*", *American Literature,* November, 1944.

Holt, Achilles Madison: *The Theme of Moby Dick as Developed by Similes,* unpublished M. A. thesis (Stanford University, Calif., 1937).

Homans, George C.: "The Dark Angel: The Tragedy of Herman Melville", *The New England Quarterly,* October, 1932.

Jünger, Ernst: *Gärten und Strassen* (Berlin, 1942: E. S. Mittler & Sohn).

Kummer, George: "Herman Melville and the Ohio Press", *The Ohio State Archaeological and Historical Quarterly,* January, 1936.

Lawrence, D. H.: *Studies in Classical American Literature* (New York, 1922: The Viking Press).

Lloyd, Francis V., Jr.: "Melville's First Lectures", *American Literature*, January, 1942.

Mansfield, Luther Stearns: "Glimpses of Herman Melville's Life in Pittsfield, 1850–1851", *American Literature*, March, 1937.

—— *Herman Melville: Author and New Yorker*, unpublished doctoral dissertation (Chicago, Ill., 1936: University of Chicago).

—— "Melville's Comic Articles on Zachary Taylor", *American Literature*, January, 1938.

Matthiessen, F. O.: *American Renaissance: Art and Expression in the Age of Emerson and Whitman* (New York, 1941: Oxford University Press).

Metcalf, Eleanor Melville: "A Pilgrim by Land and Sea", *Horn Book*, February, 1927.

—— *Journal of a Visit to London and the Continent by Herman Melville, 1849–1850* (Cambridge, Mass., 1948: Harvard University Press).

Minnigerode, Meade: *Some Personal Letters of Herman Melville* (New York, 1922: The Brick Row Book Shop).

Morison, Samuel E.: "Melville's 'Agatha' Letter to Hawthorne", *The New England Quarterly*, April, 1929.

Morris, Lloyd: *The Rebellious Puritan: Portrait of Mr. Hawthorne* (New York, 1927: Harcourt, Brace & Company).

Mumford, Lewis: *Herman Melville* (New York, 1929: Harcourt, Brace & Company).

Murray, Henry: *Pierre; or, The Ambiguities* by Herman Melville (New York, 1949: Hendricks House, Farrar Straus).

—— Review of *Herman Melville* by Lewis Mumford, *The New England Quarterly*, July, 1929.

Oliver, Egbert S.: *Piazza Tales* by Herman Melville (New York, 1948: Hendricks House, Farrar Straus).

Olson, Charles: *Call Me Ishmael* (New York, 1947: Reynal & Hitchcock).

Paltsits, Victor Hugo: *Family Correspondence of Herman Melville, 1830–1904* (New York, 1929: The New York Public Library).

—— "Herman Melville's Background and New Light on the Publication of *Typee*", *Bookman's Holiday* (New York, 1943: The New York Public Library).

Plomer, William: *Redburn* by Herman Melville (London, 1948; Jonathan Cape).

—— *Selected Poems of Herman Melville* (London, 1943: The Hogarth Press).

Riegel, O. W.: "The Anatomy of Melville's Fame", *American Literature*, May, 1931.

Rosenheim, Frederick: "Flight from Home: Some Episodes in the Life of Herman Melville", *American Imago*, December, 1940.

Scudder, Harold H.: "Melville's *Benito Cereno* and Captain Delano's Voyages", *PMLA*, June, 1928.

Sealts, Merton M., Jr.: "Herman Melville's 'I and My Chimney' ", *American Literature*, May, 1941.

—— "Melville's Reading: A Check-List of Books Owned and Borrowed", *Harvard Library Bulletin*, Spring, 1948, Autumn, 1948, Winter, 1949, ff.

Sedgwick, William Ellery: *Herman Melville: The Tragedy of Mind* (Cambridge, Mass., 1944: Harvard University Press).

Simon, Jean: *Herman Melville: Marin, Métaphysicien, et Poète* (Paris, 1939: Boivin & Cie).

Stewart, Randall: *The American Notebooks* by Nathaniel Hawthorne (New Haven, Conn., 1932: Yale University Press).

—— "Hawthorne's Contributions to *The Salem Advertiser*", *American Literature*, January, 1934.

Thorp, Willard: " 'Grace Greenwood' Parodies *Typee*", *American Literature*, January, 1938.

—— *Herman Melville: Representative Selections, with Introduction, Bibliography, and Notes* (New York, 1938: American Book Company).

—— "Herman Melville's Silent Years", *University Review*, Summer, 1937.

—— *Moby-Dick or The Whale* by Herman Melville (New York, 1947: Oxford University Press).

—— "Redburn's Prosy Old Guidebook", *PMLA*, December, 1938.

Tomlinson, H. M.: Preface to *Pierre*, edited with an Introduction by John B. Moore (New York, 1929: E. P. Dutton & Company).

Van Vechten, Carl: *Excavations* (New York, 1926: Alfred A. Knopf).

Vincent, Howard P.: *Collected Poems of Herman Melville* (Chicago, Ill., 1947: Packard & Company).

Watson, E. L. Grant: "Melville's *Pierre*", *The New England Quarterly*, April, 1930.

—— "Melville's Testament of Acceptance", *The New England Quarterly*, June, 1933.

Watters, R. E.: "Melville's Metaphysics of Evil", *The University of Toronto Quarterly*, January, 1940.

Weaver, Raymond M.: *Herman Melville: Journal up the Straits, October 11, 1856–May 5, 1857* (New York, 1935: The Colophon).

—— *Herman Melville: Mariner and Mystic* (New York, 1921: George H. Doran & Company).

—— *The Works of Herman Melville* (Standard Edition, 16 vols.) (London, 1922–1924: Constable & Company).

White, Viola Chittenden: *Symbolism in Herman Melville's Writing*, unpublished doctoral dissertation (Chapel Hill, N. C., 1934: University of North Carolina).

Wilson, Edmund: *The Shock of Recognition* (Garden City, N. Y., 1943: Doubleday & Company).

Winters, Yvor: *Maule's Curse: Seven Studies in the History of American Obscurantism* (Norfolk, Conn., 1938: New Directions).

INDEX

Index

Index

Index

Franklin, Benjamin, 120, 223, 224
France, 19, 193
Freeman, F. Barron, 301 n., 314
Freeman, John, 31, 91, 192
Freudianism, 72, 188
"Fruits of Travel Long Ago", 251
Fuller, Margaret, 74

Galapagos, the, 51, 91, 216
Galena, Ill., 22
Gansevoort, Catherine (Mrs. Abraham Lansing), 20, 54 n., 271, 276, 301
Gansevoort, Guert, 21, 300, 301 n.
Gansevoort, Henry, 227, 249, 250, 261
Gansevoort, Leonard Herman, 21
Gansevoort, Peter (grandfather), 14, 152, 193
Gansevoort, Peter (uncle), 20, 41, 42, 54, 229 n., 249–250, 257, 275, 277
Geist, Stanley, 156
Genesis, 47
Genoa, 252
Gentian, Jack, 43, 246, 247
Germany, 252
Gibraltar, 236
Glasgow, 237
Glasgow, the, 237
Glendinning, Mary, 190, 192, 193, 196, 208
Glendinning, Pierre, 30, 45 n., 147–148, 160, 187 n., 190–198, 202–210, 213 n., 305, 318
Glendinning, Pierre (father), 9, 190–191
Gnosticism, 185
God, 3, 8, 9, 50, 52, 64, 101, 111, 155, 159 n., 161–164, 166, 167, 173, 182, 184, 194, 213, 227, 233, 263, 281, 282, 284, 287, 288, 291, 317
Godwin, William, 1
Good Hope, Cape of, 51, 235 n.
Grace Church, 37
Grandvin, Marquis de, 43
Great Barrington, Mass., 137
Greeley, Horace, 74
Greenbush, N. Y., 42

Greene, Richard Tobias, 58–60, 69 n., 80
Greylock, Mt., 145, 146, 151
Guérin, Maurice de, 223

Hagar, 228
Hagen, Victor Wolfgang von, 216
Halleck, Fitz-Greene, 54
Hamlet, 119, 215
Hannibal, Don, 294
Happars, the, 56 n., 59, 60
Harper & Brothers, 80, 87, 152, 188, 193, 216, 270
Harper's New Monthly Magazine, 118, 214
Hautia, 98, 104
Hawaiian Islands, 51, 64, 66
"Hawthorne and his Mosses", 138–145
Hawthorne, Julian, 142, 154 n., 211
Hawthorne, Nathaniel, 8, 39, 54, 55–56, 65, 76, 77 n., 137–145, 151–159, 161, 162, 183, 187, 211, 212, 227, 238, 252, 280, 319
Hawthorne, Sophia Peabody, 83, 138, 151, 165, 188, 253
Hazlitt, William, 38 n., 121
Hegel, G. W. F., 111
Herbert, Lord of Cherbury, 293
Highlander, the, 20, 24–35, 110
Hillway, Tyrus, 99 n.
Hivohitee, 95
Hoadley, John C., 260, 288
Hobbes, Thomas, 122
Hoffman, Charles Fenno, 213 n.
Holland, 34, 252
Holmes, Oliver Wendell, 11 n., 137, 138, 145, 212, 295
Holy Land, the, 109, 149 n., 157, 243–245, 277, 278
Home, Dougald, 251
Honolulu, 51, 71
Hope, Thomas, 240
Horn, Cape, 51, 235 n., 256
Housatonic River, 177
Howe, Julia Ward, 250
Howells, William Dean, 281

Index

Index

Index

Moore, Thomas, 99
More, Henry, 122
Morewood, Sarah, 152
Mormon, Book of, 277
Morris, Lloyd, 158 n.
Mortmain, 281, 284, 286
Mosblech, Boniface, 58 n.
Mosby, John S., 261
Moses, 186
Moxon, Edward, 114
Mumford, Lewis, 45 n., 68, 69, 84, 189, 203 n., 251, 260, 270, 279, 297
Murray, Henry A., 11 n., 187 n., 203
Murray, John, 50, 55, 114, 115

Nantucket, 168, 180, 211
Naples, 246–247
"Naples in the Time of Bomba", 246
Nathan, 279, 281
Nehemiah, 278–279, 281, 285
Nelson, Horatio, 307
Nesle, the Sire de, 84 n.
Neversink, the, 126–135
New Amsterdam, 16
New Bedford, Mass., 44, 47, 48, 51, 165, 166, 168, 211
New Hampshire, 86
Newton, Isaac, 122
New York City, 8, 12, 13, 16–17, 22, 23, 24, 41, 54 n., 74, 75, 76, 78, 80, 86, 136, 148, 188, 192, 208, 226, 239, 258, 259
New York Evangelist, The, 79 n.
New York Male High School, 18
New York State Bank, 20
Niebuhr, Barthold Georg, 245
Noah, 186
Norris, Frank, 225
Nukaheva, 21, 52, 56–65, 66

O'Brien, Fitz-James, 231–232
O'Brien, James, 220
October Mountain, 146
Olson, Charles, 47, 90, 175, 186, 227
Olympus, Mt., 239

Omoo, 50, 63, 64, 65–73, 78 n., 80, 89, 125
Othello, 119
Oxford, 252

Pacific Ocean, 21, 49, 52, 54, 70, 71, 235, 236
Padua, 248, 251
Palestine (see Holy Land, the)
Paley, William, 282
Paltsits, Victor Hugo, 80
Panama, 110, 257
Papeetee, 70
"Paradise of Bachelors and Tartarus of Maids", 37, 118
Paris, 12, 16, 119–120, 123, 224
Parkman, Francis, 107 n.
Parthenon, the, 246
Patmos, 245, 247
Paul, St., 298
Paulding, J. K., 17
Pausilippo, 247
Pearl Street, No. 6, 8
Pease, Valentine, 48, 56
Peck, George Washington, 78 n.
Penny Magazine, The, 38
Pequod, the, 48, 51, 124, 168–186, 208, 211, 231
Perry, Matthew C., 211
Peru, 51
Peters, Mrs., 153
Philadelphia Centennial Exposition, 296
Piazza Tales, The, 146, 221
Pierce, Franklin, 211
Pierre, 9, 11, 27, 64, 81, 123, 136, 147, 148, 150, 152, 187–210, 212, 213, 215, 227, 231, 233, 280, 314, 317
Pilate, 283
Pip, 178, 183–184
Piraeus, 245
Piranesi, G.-B., 226
Pisa, 250
Pittsfield, Mass., 18, 19, 20, 21, 41, 137, 145–152, 212, 254

333

Index

Index